# THATCHER

# THATCHER

by

## KENNETH HARRIS

LITTLE, BROWN AND COMPANY

BOSTON        TORONTO        LONDON

FIRST U.S. EDITION

*Library of Congress Cataloging-in-Publication Data*

Harris, Kenneth, 1919–
    Thatcher / Kenneth Harris.
      p.  cm.
    Includes index.
    ISBN 0-316-34837-6
    1. Thatcher, Margaret.  2. Prime ministers — Great Britain —
Biography.  3. Great Britain — Politics and government — 1979–
I. Title.
DA591.T47H39 1988
941.085′8′0924 — dc19
[B]                                  88-19179
                                       CIP

10  9  8  7  6  5  4  3  2

MV

*Published simultaneously in Canada
by Little, Brown & Company (Canada) Limited*

PRINTED IN THE UNITED STATES OF AMERICA

# CONTENTS

# ILLUSTRATIONS

# ACKNOWLEDGEMENTS

I owe an outstanding debt of gratitude to Richard Cockett who helped me to find much of the material for this book and advised me how to use it.

Lord Weidenfeld has waited for the manuscript with great patience and has made many suggestions relating to its contents. His editor, Alex MacCormick, has been extremely helpful. I owe thanks also to Paul Duncan for assistance with research on Mrs Thatcher's early life. I am grateful to Sally Griffiths for swift and expert typing and to Keith Pye for computer advice.

My thanks are due to those authors of books and writings about Mrs Thatcher or the period whose names appear in Source Notes or the Bibliography, or are cited in the text, and in particular to Geoffrey Parkhouse, Political Editor of the *Glasgow Herald*.

In the course of preparing this book I had conversations with sixty-five other people, including members of the Cabinet, leading politicians, businessmen, civil servants and people who have known Mrs Thatcher personally. Some would have been happy about information being attributed to them, others not; in consequence I have not listed any of their names.

# 1

# PERSPECTIVE

For most Conservatives, and for many of her critics, Margaret
Thatcher's standing today is higher than that of any Prime
Minister since the Second World War, higher than Harold Macmillan's at his peak after he had led the Conservative Party to its
record-breaking three-in-a-row victory in the general election of 1959.
Leaving out of account the *réclame* of Churchill as leader of the all-
party coalition which won the Second World War, her reputation today
rivals that of Baldwin in his finest hour in the mid 1930s, before his
record had been blotted with the charge of Appeasement. No Prime
Minister's star has been so high in the ascendant for so long since Lloyd
George's during and immediately after the First World War. No Prime
Minister since Lord Liverpool, 1812 to 1827, has held office for so
long without a break. It can be claimed for her that she is the most
outstanding peacetime Prime Minister of the century.

No other British prime minister has inspired or named an 'ism'.
There was no Disraeliism, no Baldwinism, no Churchillism. There was
Socialism, but no Attleeism. Nor has any outstanding political figure
who was not a leader of his party put a name on an ism that was
anything like a coherent body of policies. 'Bevanism' was a convenient
reference for what was a collection not of positive and related ideas but
of negative and disparate attitudes – a ragbag – which a minority within
the Labour Party put together in protest against the policies of the
majority. There was no Mosleyism: Mosley simply embraced Fascism.
But there *is* an ism called Thatcherism, and not only did she name it,

1

not only could it not have come into existence without her, but she has been, and continues to be, the very essence of it.

Two governments tower above all the others in the history of Britain since the end of the Second World War: Attlee's, between 1945 and 1951, and Margaret Thatcher's, from 1979 on. These two administrations stand out from the others – Mrs Thatcher's stands out from them all on account of her being a woman – for three shared reasons: both came to power promising positive controversial and sweeping programmes intended not just to manage but to change society; both kept their promises; the policies of both were based on morals, a sense of what was right and wrong. The Attlee government's Socialism owed more to Christianity than to Marx. The Thatcher government's Thatcherism owes more to Methodism than to Milton Friedman. Attlee has been described as the most ethical prime minister Britain has ever had. Mrs Thatcher is similarly praised by her admirers.

The Labour and Conservative governments between Attlee and Thatcher did not aim to reshape or restructure British society. They were pragmatic in character, and moderate in conduct, and whichever of them was in power Britain was governed on the basis of a consensus, not spoken of at election times, but which operated nearly all of the time in between. This gave birth to the word 'Butskellism', coined in the early years of the first post-war Conservative administration, the neologism being made up of the first part of the surname of R. A. Butler, Chancellor of the Exchequer in the Conservative government 1951–5, and the latter part of the surname of Hugh Gaitskell, who had held the same post in the preceding Labour administration. Whichever party was in power, from 1951 to 1976, Britain was governed by Butskellism, this being possible because the two major parties had arrived at a considerable degree of consensus about what was, and was not, politically acceptable; the pattern which consequently appeared was described as 'consensus politics'.

This continuum of consensus politics makes it difficult in retrospect to make sharp distinctions between successive Conservative and Labour governments in the period of nearly thirty years between Attlee and Margaret Thatcher. From time to time in the course of an administration important new policies were initiated; for example, Harold Macmillan's 'Wind of Change' which accelerated the granting to Britain's former colonies in Africa of self-government and independence; and Ted Heath's successful campaign for Britain's membership of the EEC. Now and again there were great crises, pregnant with change for the future, such as Suez in 1956, which signalled the end of Britain's long reign as an imperial power. Otherwise, even if this be a comment on their visibility rather than their achievement, it is not easy to tell one of the interim governments from another.

The existence of the long period of consensus, almost bi-partisan, politics is the paradoxical link between Attlee and Thatcher, since without Attlee there would have been no consensus and without the consensus there would have been no Thatcher. The post-war consensus between the two major parties emerged partly because they agreed that some features of British political society should be preserved whoever was in power, and partly because they feared they would lose electoral support if they tried to undo everything the other party had done, or openly attacked what the other party stood for. For example, though it was the Attlee government which had introduced the Welfare State, in many subsequent elections the leaders of the Conservative Party promised that it would remain intact. On these and many issues there was genuine common ground. But even on some issues on which they differed profoundly from the Labour Party, the Conservatives refrained from giving battle on the hustings, because they had learned that if they wanted to get elected they must steal some of their opponents' clothes.

By contrast with the consensus leaders, Attlee and Thatcher not only accepted but explicitly stated that the programmes which they intended to put into effect would mean major breaks with the past. This is what makes them and their governments visible to a degree that those who came in between are not. Which of the post-war governments were 'good' and which 'bad' is another matter. 'Managerial' governments on the basis of consensus politics may perhaps turn out to be what Britain needs and wants, for most if not all of the time, but that kind of government does not lead to high visibility.

The high visibility of the Attlee and the Thatcher governments is made more spectacular because it is just those major changes introduced by Attlee between 1945 and 1951 which Thatcher from 1979 to the present day has wanted to un-change. By establishing the Welfare State and introducing the nationalization of basic industries, Attlee, in Mrs Thatcher's opinion, took Britain a long way down the road to becoming a Socialist state. By her policy of denationalization – 'privatization' – and of dismantling much of the apparatus of the Welfare State, Mrs Thatcher is trying to take the state back to the values and ambience of freedom and private enterprise in the pursuit of healthy competition and wider choice. The paradox of the comparison is the contrast; much of what the one did the other intends to undo.

3

What Attlee and Thatcher most have in common is that unlike other prime ministers in the post-war period each of them brought into government their own agendas, and set the pace for British politics for many years to come. For nearly thirty years after the Attlee Government came to an end, the parameters of British politics were mainly those laid down by Attlee. The political agenda today is no longer his: it is Thatcher's. It is always possible that Mrs Thatcher's agenda will not long survive her Government, but few people would subscribe to such a view, and most people probably would agree that much of what she has done – or undone – will be left much as it is now by subsequent governments, whatever their political colour. Attlee and Thatcher have been agenda-setters, and caused their opponents to re-set *their* agendas. The Labour Party currently led by Neil Kinnock is engaged in the search for policies which depart a long way from what it stood for in the past, and accept a good deal of what Mrs Thatcher has achieved in the present. The same can be said of the Liberals and the SDP. If a great prime minister is to be measured not only by the changes he brings about but also by the extent to which his opponents feel forced to accept and perpetuate those changes, Attlee and Thatcher are great prime ministers.

One of the reasons for the standing Mrs Thatcher has acquired today is that whereas successive premiers since Attlee seemed to their electors to renegue on many of the promises they made when they were in opposition, Mrs Thatcher has striven to do what she said she would do, and with very considerable success. Her main three undertakings were: to bring down drastically the rate of inflation, the main complaint of the British people for most of the post-war years whether they voted Labour, Liberal or Conservative; to curb the power of the trade unions, which had become a threat to democratic government and the freedom of the individual; and to denationalize the basic industries, whose losses and inefficiencies had become a burden on the public, which could be removed only by restoring their activities to private enterprise. Mrs Thatcher has carried out these major undertakings. She has kept her promises. Unlike the Conservative Government which preceded hers, she has made no U-turns.

Mrs Thatcher is the only post-war prime minister who came to power with the odds stacked heavily against her. She did not have the confidence of the majority of the Tory leaders: they did not approve of her ideas, her policies, her personality or her methods. She was not their kind of Tory. She was untried. Attlee, on the other hand, became premier with many advantages. Though some of his colleagues thought they would be better at the job, they preferred him to anybody else. They had no objection to his policies, which indeed were theirs. The Party, leaders and rank and file, supported him. He had the advantage of being able to offer the country a kind of New Deal, a programme which bid fair to succeed. The country did not want to experience again the poverty and unemployment of the 1930s, and the Labour Government presented them with a programme which promised to prevent a recrudescence of those evils. It was a programme which, since it had never been tried before, could not be said to have failed. It was buttressed with several specific schemes which had been worked out in detail during the 1930s, and debated and endorsed at a series of Labour Party Conferences. Many of Attlee's political opponents were in sympathy with what his Government proposed to do. The Keynesian thinking which underpinned his economic policy was acceptable to many of the leaders of the Conservative Party, and Keynesianism had permeated the Civil Service. In short Attlee came to power at the head of a more or less united Party and Cabinet, furnished with blue-prints for restructure and reform which had the backing of his Party rank and file, reinforced by considerable good will on the part of the Opposition and by widespread support in the country as a whole.

Mrs Thatcher came to power in very different circumstances. Having been appointed leader of a divided party (most of whose senior figures had been opposed to her election), she took up her responsibilities with a divided Cabinet, most of whom were opposed to her economic policies and to the methods by which she intended to put them into action. These policies, and the social attitudes which they reflected, were not only repugnant to them in themselves, but according to the conventional wisdom the same policies and attitudes had been responsible for the poverty and unemployment of the 1930s, the memory of which had brought about the defeat of the Conservatives in the election of 1945. In contrast to Attlee's New Deal which at any rate had never been tried, she offered in 1979 an Old Deal which in the opinion of many of her senior colleagues had been tried, had failed, and had badly damaged the Party. Attlee had the aftermath of a traumatic war to dynamize his programme. Margaret Thatcher had to launch hers in a sluggish, dispirited time of peace.

How did Mrs Thatcher succeed in overcoming the odds so heavily stacked against her? How many would have thought when she decided to challenge Edward Heath for the party leadership in 1974 that within not much more than a decade she would be Britain's first woman Prime Minister and a world statesman? How did she win the opportunity to make the attempt to do these things? How did she cross the great divide between being merely the statutory woman member of a Conservative Cabinet and being elected leader of the Party? How did she succeed in going on from there to create a record by winning three consecutive general elections? It is at the far side of that great divide that an inquiry into, and record of, the Thatcher phenomenon naturally begins.

# 2

# DOUBTS ABOUT HEATH

I t is sometimes said that Margaret Thatcher became the leader of
the Conservative Party by accident. How true this is can be judged
by considering the sequence of events from the defeat of the
Conservative Government in February 1974 to the leadership election
twelve months later.

The general election of February 1974 was precipitated by the
Government's refusal to grant the pay claim which the miners put
forward in the previous November. There had already been serious
conflict with the miners. In July 1971 the National Union of Mineworkers had demanded a pay rise of up to 47% and, when this was not
met, had in November of that year imposed a ban on overtime and had
called for a national strike the following January. Attempts by Robert
Carr, the Secretary of State for Employment, to reach an agreement
came to nothing, and a state of emergency to maintain essential services
and supplies was declared on 9 February. There were violent scenes on
the picket lines in some parts of the country and, when the Chief
Constable of Birmingham informed the Cabinet that he was closing the
gates of the Saltley cokeworks in Birmingham because he feared the
police might be overrun by the massed pickets, the Cabinet decided
that a compromise with the miners was unavoidable. It consequently
set up an inquiry under the chairmanship of Lord Wilberforce and, as
a result, the miners were offered an increase of 22%. The miners were
in no hurry to accept this and, while their leaders, including Arthur
Scargill, debated the matter, the Cabinet sat waiting in candlelight, a

condition imposed upon them by the power cuts. Taking their own time about it, the miners eventually accepted the 22%. This settlement was widely resented within the Conservative Party: it was felt that Ted Heath had 'surrendered'.

The miners were due to submit their next pay claim in November 1973. By then, Mr Heath's voluntary prices and incomes policy had collapsed, and he had resorted to a statutory system. Having no desire for a confrontation with the miners, he spent much time during the summer trying to find a way of making an award to the NUM which would not breach the Government's pay policy and open the door to wage demands from other unions. As early as July, Mr Heath, accompanied by Sir William Armstrong, the Permanent Head of the Civil Service, but not by any of the Cabinet, had several private talks with Joe Gormley, President of the NUM, and, as a result, came to the conclusion that, when the miners put in their wage claim in November, they would settle for an increase within the limits required by the Government's pay policy if they were also granted a special increase for having to work 'unsocial hours'.

Mr Heath was mistaken. When November came, and their claim was rejected, the miners declared a ban on overtime. They rejected the offer of an increase within the pay policy plus special remuneration for unsocial working hours, and continued to press their claim. In the last week of January they voted to begin an official national strike. On 7 February, Mr Heath announced a general election for 28 February to answer the crucial question: 'Who is to govern Britain: the duly elected Government, with the authority of Parliament, or the mineworkers' union?' Deeply disturbed by the mounting power of the unions, which they saw as the main cause of the rising rate of inflation as well as a threat to democratic government, the Conservative Party welcomed the election and rallied loyally to Mr Heath's call.

Though it was as far as was possible concealed at the time, there were Conservatives who were not enthusiastic about Mr Heath's leadership. He had 'surrendered' to the miners in 1972. He had subsequently introduced a statutory prices and incomes policy, a measure which many Conservatives deplored as a Socialist-type governmental interference between employer and employed, and which, in this case, would have been unnecessary if he had not 'surrendered'. The consequence of his action, in their view, had been to put the miners in a position in which they were able to create this present crisis, which had led to a three-day working week with restrictions on lighting, heating and broadcasting, and other inflictions which now seemed to have been a painful waste of time.

There were other misgivings. It was known that some members of the Cabinet had recommended that the election should be held three weeks earlier, but that Mr Heath had opted for delay, a decision which his colleagues had found difficult to contest since their leader had told the Cabinet very little about his private talks with Sir William Armstrong and Mr Gormley. Consequently, though the Conservatives went into the election officially united behind their leader and ahead of the Opposition in the opinion polls, some of them had doubts about Mr Heath's record as Prime Minister, caused in the main by their perception of his conduct of the Government's relations with the unions. The effect of these forebodings within the Conservative Party was to be seen much more clearly when the election had been lost.

The failure to win the general election came as a great blow to the morale of the Party. Jim Prior wrote in his memoirs: 'Ted was completely shell-shocked.' The Conservatives polled a majority of the votes, but they won only 297 seats to Labour's 301. The Liberals won 14 seats, though they had polled nearly 20% of the votes. In an election held on the issue of who was to govern Britain, Parliament or the unions, Mr Heath had failed to persuade enough voters to keep the Government in power. Many Conservatives, though not in public, put the blame for the defeat on him personally. Some complained that he had called the election too late, after he had given the impression of being indecisive, and others complained that he had called it too soon, before the country had seen that the miners were not just a nuisance but a menace. Others complained that particularly on television Heath had failed to rouse public opinion to the gravity of the situation and had not created the image of a national leader. Dissatisfied Conservatives, at different levels within the Party, in the Cabinet, in Parliament and in the constituencies, complained: 'The right issue but the wrong leader.'

Mr Heath immediately sought to form a coalition with the Liberals. Mr Jeremy Thorpe, the Liberal leader, told Mr Heath that he could not bring his thirteen colleagues into the government unless there was a promise of electoral reform. Heath could only undertake to put the matter to a Speaker's conference, which might then make a recommendation to the House of Commons, which might then reject it. On these terms Mr Thorpe could not get his colleagues to agree to enter a coalition. Facing these facts, Mr Heath tendered his resignation to the Queen, who then asked the Labour leader to form a government, which he promptly did. Behind closed doors, within the Conservative Party there was now further criticism of Mr Heath: having gone into the campaign on a strong issue and with a lead in the polls, he had not only lost, but had failed to bring the Liberals into a coalition and had let Labour into power. But there was no move to unseat him, if only because it was assumed that, since Wilson, the new Premier, had such a small majority, another election would be called shortly and the Conservatives would be able to win it – if in the meantime they did not spoil their chances with an internecine debate about whether there should be a change of leadership.

Harold Wilson called a second election for 10 October. Four weeks before it, the 1922 Committee – the Conservative backbench MPs – met at the Europa Hotel in Grosvenor Square under the chairmanship of Mr (now Sir) Edward Du Cann. Also present were Parliamentary candidates and agents. Mr Heath addressed it, but his speech, though clear and competent, was no trumpet call to battle; it was Edward Du Cann who sounded the clarion, admirably pointing up the appearance of unity and loyalty which on the whole – the exceptions will be dealt with later – the Party had maintained since the February defeat. 'You do not only lead but command our Party,' said Mr Du Cann. 'We are a wholly loyal and united party ... We know we can count abundantly on you, and you equally know that you can rely on us.'

For the second time that year the Conservatives were defeated in a general election. The Labour Party won; its 319 seats, though only providing an overall majority of 4 enabled Wilson to form a Government. The result led to further criticism of Mr Heath, and some of this became public. His friend and colleague, Jim Prior, probably closer to him at the time than any other senior member of the Party, says in his memoirs: 'Our defeat was nothing like as heavy as most of us had feared. But within twenty-four hours I told Ted that his only chance of carrying on as leader was if he submitted himself to an early election through the 1922 Committee ... I was surprised by the number of people who were saying that they disliked him, and by the degree of bitterness and the spiteful determination that he had to go.' Mr Heath's response to Mr Prior's advice throws light on much that was to happen later. 'He replied,' wrote Mr Prior, 'that he didn't intend to submit himself to a leadership election because he was determined to fight the right wing. I told him that if he refused to go, he would probably end up giving them exactly what they wanted.' Mr Prior spoke far more candidly to Mr Heath than any other of his friends did at the time, but even he did not go so far as to disclose that 'I doubted if he could [remain leader] in any circumstances'.

Mr Heath had campaigned prominently on the need for, and promise of, some kind of coalition. Some Conservatives thought that this was a mistake; others that the voters were attracted by it, and that had he delivered his message more effectively he would have won. In any case, after this defeat, the second in a year and the third out of four, the Conservatives were far more ready to put the blame for failure on him personally, not only on his record but on his personality. Candidates and canvassers reported on encounters on the doorstep with voters who had said that they would have voted Conservative had it not been for Mr Heath.

Three days later, the Executive Committee of the 1922 Committee met at the home of Mr Du Cann, and decided that a leadership election should be held. When this decision was put to Mr Heath, he did not accept it, saying that for the time being the Executive had no authority; there would be no Executive Committee with authority until a new Executive was elected or the old one re-elected, when the 1922 Committee met in the new Parliament. In November, he agreed to set up a committee under Sir Alec Home to review the procedure for the election of the leader, a process which everybody knew would take several weeks. The committee's report, which recommended important changes in the rules, was presented on 17 December. By that time many things had become clear, among them: if he wished to remain leader, Mr Heath would not be able to avoid an election; if he stood for re-election, he would probably not succeed; and, if somebody stood who was closely associated with his policies, he too might be defeated, since an opposition was forming within the party, the 'right wing' he had spoken of to Prior soon after the election.

This 'right wing' was not offering a policy that was markedly different from Heath's. The opposition to him was still based, mainly, on a desire to have a new leader who would give the Party a new look. But, though differences of policy were not widely spoken about and did not play an important part in the process by which Mr Heath was removed from the leadership, the differences were there and were to become very important in the future. They were already significant, for had they not existed, Margaret Thatcher would not have been in a position from which she could throw down a gauntlet to Mr Heath's leadership. Their significance would be much greater in the future when they had become the basis of Thatcherism. To understand what these differences in policy were and, equally important, what they were not, it is necessary

11

to look back into the past of the Conservative Party a long way beyond the first electoral defeat of 1974, indeed to the end of the war in 1945.

# 3

# CONSENSUS IS OUT

I n the period 1940–45, while Churchill and Eden concentrated their attention on winning the war, the conduct of day-to-day domestic policy and the preparation of post-war domestic policy was left to a small number of Conservative leaders who worked on good terms with the leaders of the Labour and Liberal Parties. The structure of the post-war Welfare State owed much to Conservative Party thinking before the war and considerably more to what was agreed between the three parties while the war was being fought. The thinking which led to the presentation of the Beveridge Plan in 1942 was to some extent the fruit of work done by the Conservative Government in the late 1930s. The highly progressive Butler Act of 1944, a milestone in British education, was the result of co-operation between all three parties, the legislation being guided through Parliament by the Conservative Minister of Education, R. A. Butler, assisted by the Labour Parliamentary Secretary to the Department of Education, Chuter Ede. Much of the support for such measures came from a large and influential group within the Conservative Party who were resolved to lift the curse on their party of having been seen in the 1930s as 'the Party of unemployment'.

After the war, though the Conservative Opposition fought the Labour Government's nationalization programme tooth and nail, it did not in general attack the Welfare State nor the government's commitment to full employment. Nor did the Conservative Party, as a whole, challenge the economic policy, dominated by the ideas of Keynes, on which the financing of the Welfare State and full employment was based. After the Conservatives won the election of 1951, they made so little change in national economic policy that the term 'Butskellism' was coined to describe it. Much of the Conservative government's disinclination to undo what the post-war Labour Government had done was due to the feeling that a lot of it was good and that an attempt to dismantle it would be electorally dangerous. Churchill's influence was important: his overriding objective was to restore British power to its proper place in the world, on a par with that of the United States and the Soviet Union. He wanted no domestic disaffection or disruption which might embarrass him in his efforts, and instructed his Minister of Labour, Sir Walter Monckton, accordingly. Other colleagues were told to keep their hands off the Welfare State and not antagonize the increasingly strong trade unions, whose leaders, arguably, became more influential in the years of the Churchill Government than they had under Attlee.

The consequence of this state of affairs was the development of a long period of 'consensus' politics, lasting from 1945 to 1970, when there was a brief interruption. Successive Conservative Governments co-operated with the trade unions much as Labour Governments had maintained the Welfare State, pursued the same objective of very high, if not full, employment, and based economic policy on much the same set of Keynesian techniques and assumptions. Conservative Governments were as ready as Labour to intervene to prevent or end strikes (by now the Government of the day, because of nationalization, was by far the nation's biggest employer), to prime the market when recession threatened or to raise the interest rate when inflation looked like getting out of hand, a policy which added the term 'stop-go' to Butskellism and consensus. They subsidized private industry as Labour Governments had, and encouraged the movement of manufacture and labour through the financial interventions of the Board of Trade. Like Labour Governments, they maintained a high level of public expenditure on the social services, particularly education, social security and health. In order to pay for this, like Labour Governments they practised deficit budgeting, tolerated – though they claimed to be trying to reduce it – a mildly rising rate of inflation, and, as their critics put it, 'printed money'. Like Labour leaders, Conservative leaders continued to have great faith in the massive State planning which had been essential in the Second World War.

Over the whole period, government became more managerial and less doctrinaire, and the emphasis was on economic expansion; growth, it was assumed, would continue indefinitely. The Conservatives were not ideological in their approach to political and economic matters, and the

Labour leaders tried to become less so, a process marked by Gaitskell's attempt – unsuccessful – after the 1959 general election to persuade Labour to drop from its constitution the historic Clause IV, which had committed the party to public ownership. Butskellism, consensus, and managerial politics, whether or not good for the country, proved good for the Conservative Party: having come to power in 1951, they increased their number of seats in 1955, and did so again in 1959, becoming the first British Government to win three consecutive general elections, the third victory being associated with Harold Macmillan's famous question, frequently misquoted as a statement, 'Most people have never had it so good. But will it last?'

It would not be fair to the leaders of the Conservative Party between 1951 and 1970 to say that their acceptance of Butskellism and consensus politics was inspired by political opportunism. Macmillan remembered the unemployment and consequent poverty which he had seen as a young MP for Stockton, and to prevent a recrudescence of it was the main object of his domestic policy for the rest of his life. Rab Butler, Iain Macleod, Reginald Maudling, Anthony Barber, all, like Macmillan, Chancellor of the Exchequer in their time, had similar views and were able to put them into effect in years of relatively low inflation and of apparently permanent potential economic growth. In their day, they assumed these conditions would continue. They were wrong, but so were the leaders of the Labour Party, as were most economists.

There were many Conservatives who were in varying degrees unhappy about the readiness of their leaders to tolerate, if not to promote, Butskellite, consensus and managerial politics, and the Keynesianisms on which the conduct of the never-had-it-so-good society was based. Their voices could be heard in the early days of the post-war Attlee government, but the first loud protest, with action as well as words, came in January 1958, a year after Harold Macmillan had succeeded Sir Anthony Eden as Prime Minister, when the Chancellor of the Exchequer, Peter Thorneycroft, accompanied by his two lieutenants at the Treasury, Nigel Birch and Enoch Powell, resigned in protest against the Cabinet's refusal to accept their proposals for cuts in public expenditure. In spite of Mr Macmillan nonchalantly dismissing the event as 'a little local difficulty', there was increased pressure within the Party for 'a return to sound Conservative principles', including demands for more use of monetary control and reduction in public expenditure. But when, in 1962, the Chancellor of the Exchequer, Selwyn Lloyd, tried to conduct a deflationary policy, Mr Macmillan dismissed him.

Sounds of dissent within the Conservative Party were to be heard again after Labour came to power in 1964, but so long as Harold Wilson had a majority of only four, and another election, which the Conservatives reasonably hoped to win, was around the corner, demands for an end to consensus politics were noticeably muted. After the election of 1966, as a result of which Mr Wilson vastly increased his Parliamentary majority, dissatisfaction among the Conservatives began to mount, and for the first time since 1945 it appeared that the leaders of the Party were paying attention to it. A note particularly discordant with those the Party had registered in the past was struck by a speech at the annual Conservative conference in Blackpool in October 1968. It was delivered not to the full conference but in a lecture given under the auspices of the Conservative Political Centre, the Party's think-tank. To be asked to address the CPC at the annual conference is an honour reserved for members of the Cabinet, when the Party is in power, or for members of the Shadow Cabinet, when it is in Opposition. The speech did not receive a floodlight of attention at the time, but in retrospect it shines like a beacon in the history of the Conservative Party.

The title of the lecture was 'What's Wrong with Politics'. The name of the lecturer was Margaret Thatcher. Her main theme was that since the war successive governments had intruded into fields best left to the free market and individual enterprise, an intervention which had been economically debilitating and politically dangerous. What she said was aimed at Labour governments, but applied in great part to Conservative as well, as did her call for a change of direction and for government based on sound Conservative principles.

Though Mrs Thatcher was acknowledged to be an MP with a future – a year previously she had been promoted to the Shadow Cabinet – she was by no means regarded as a pundit or a prophet, or of being a power within the party. Her speech did not make the headlines and her senior colleagues did not lose any sleep that night. This was partly because some of them were also moving away from Butskellism and consensus politics, not so much in response to disaffection within the Party as in the belief that the national interest required a different approach. The rate of inflation was increasing; public expenditure was accelerating; the strength of sterling, even after the Labour Government had devalued the pound in 1967, was in decline; the power of the trade unions had become so damaging to the economy that Labour had tried – unsuccessfully – to introduce legislation to bring it under control; subsidies from public funds to prolong the life of industries which were clearly moribund, paid under pressure from the trade unions to keep men and women employed, were costing the tax-payer money without any benefit to the economy as a whole.

When Wilson called a general election for 18 June 1970, Heath took the Conservative Party into the campaign with a manifesto and with speeches altogether more polemical in tone and content than had been heard for twenty years. Unexpectedly, he won. At the annual Party conference in October, there were denunciations of government policy of the past which, though aimed at Labour, reflected on Conservative administrations as well. Members of the Cabinet promised to reduce the role of the State in all aspects of the life of the nation except law and order, to reduce public expenditure, restore competition, curb the excessive power of the unions, jettison prices and incomes policy, and not to give money to ailing industries. The new Secretary of State for Trade and Industry, John Davies, a distinguished industrialist but a newcomer to politics, told a cheering conference: 'We shall not prop up lame ducks.'

Anybody who listened to what Mr Heath and his senior colleagues said in the campaign, which brought them to power with a working majority, and to what they said at the Party conference, might reasonably have concluded that the principles and practices outlined by Margaret Thatcher at Blackpool two years previously were now to become the flesh and blood of the Conservative Government's policy. This looked to be the case for the next two years. Then came the change. It began with the failure of the Government to deal effectively with the unions. It kept its promise to try to curb their power by law, and succeeded in putting an Act on the statute book – more than the Wilson government had been able to achieve – but that was as far as it got. The powerful Amalgamated Union of Engineering Workers led the way in ignoring the new Act, and from then on it was virtually as though the new law had never existed. The disillusionment of the Conservative Party about its Government's ability to make good its promises was even greater in the case of public funds for chronically ailing industry. In accordance with their pledge not to subsidize lame ducks, the Government had decided to allow the Upper Clyde Shipbuilders to shut down; but, when the Chief Constable of Glasgow reported that if the works were closed he could not promise to be able to maintain public order, the Government rescinded its decision. It decided also that rather than let Rolls-Royce go bankrupt, public money would be invested in it to keep it solvent. In 1972, two years after he came to power, Ted Heath had begun to make his famous U-turns, and had headed back to Butskellism and consensus politics.

Mr Heath now decided on measures which brought about rapid

17

economic expansion. This gave a new impetus to inflation. To deal with this, the following year he introduced a statutory prices and incomes policy. This was objectionable to the unions and anathema to many members of his own party. It was the most significant of his U-turns. By the time the miners declared their second national strike, at the end of 1973, Mr Heath seemed to his critics in the Conservative Party to have sown again the worst seeds of Butskellite and consensus politics, and to have reaped the worst possible harvest. It was against this background that those critics – and many of his faithful supporters – in the Conservative Party saw him belatedly rally the country to an election under the banner of 'Who governs . . .?', ride uncertainly into battle, and lose – and lose again before the year was out.

During the summer between the lost elections there were several developments inside the Conservative Party which, though they did not alarm Mr Heath and his senior colleagues, caused them some concern.

The first was a recommendation by the former Minister for the Social Services, Sir Keith Joseph, that a new party research unit be established, to be known as the Centre for Political Studies. Sir Keith argued that with inflation now the outstanding problem of the times and the most crucial with which the Conservatives would have to grapple if they won the next election, it would be advantageous to study, for instance, the great success of the Germans in managing inflation and promoting economic growth by, as he was to put it later, 'using the engine of a decentralized, profit-seeking competitive economic system more understandingly than we had done'. This, though an implied criticism of previous Conservative Governments in Britain, was not an outright condemnation of them, and chimed with the note Mr Heath had struck between winning the election of 1970 and making his U-turns two years later. Mr Heath was not enthusiastic about creating a new relatively independent organ within the Party which, he suspected, might produce advice different from what was coming from the Conservative Political Centre, which he as leader personally controlled, but he accepted Sir Keith's suggestion. It was agreed that Adam Ridley, formerly of the Government Think-Tank, now of the Conservative Political Centre, and Robert Carr, Heath's former Secretary of State for Employment, should sit on the board of the new organization to represent Mr Heath's interests. Sir Keith funded the new Centre with contributions from businessmen. Alfred (now Sir Alfred) Sherman, an economist and writer, who believed that the Conservative Party had been on the right track when Mr Heath won the election of 1970 but had lost its way when he made his U-turns, became its director. As president of the new organization Sir Keith appointed Margaret Thatcher.

Alfred Sherman believed that, in the interests of human liberty and economic efficiency, the role of the Government in the market should be kept to a minimum and its influence restricted to control of the supply of money. He believed that, far from an extension of public ownership being desirable, much of Britain's existing nationalized industry should be privatized. There should be state monopoly only in special cases; healthy open competition should be restored, subject only to the rule of law, and free and varied choice should be made available to the consumer. Some public expenditure was proper, but currently it was excessive and must be reduced, in some fields eliminated altogether. The much increased power of the unions, politically dangerous, was a kind of monopoly and, being therefore an interference with the freedom of the market and of the individual, it would have to be reduced. The overriding evil, threatening the political and economic life of Britain, was inflation, which must speedily and drastically be reduced to zero. Sherman's ideas are most conveniently – though not accurately – covered by the term 'monetarist'. He believed, as he told Sir Keith early in 1974, that 'Keynes is dead'. By the summer of that year he had converted Sir Keith to that point of view, and Sir Keith had become, if not a monetarist (though that was how his colleagues in the Shadow Cabinet were beginning to see him), a disciple of what he called 'monetary continence'.

Sir Keith was to play three important roles in the political career of Margaret Thatcher. As the first prominent Conservative openly to challenge the policies of Mr Heath, he paved the way for her to contest the leadership – he was a kind of John the Baptist. Secondly, he furnished her with the troops with which she took on Heath and vanquished him; thirdly, he supplied the political philosophy and language with which she could convey her intuitions and homespun experience to a sophisticated audience: he intellectualized her instinctive feelings. In her own words in an interview with the author in 1979: 'We have accomplished the revival of the philosophy and principles of a free society, and the acceptance of it. And that is absolutely the thing I live for. History will accord a very great place to Keith Joseph for that accomplishment. A tremendous place.'

Many influences had gone into forming the mind of the man who had become the pathfinder for the future prime minister. Sir Keith was born into a wealthy and public-spirited family, with many interests in the business world. After a brilliant career at Oxford – he was elected a

Fellow of All Souls College – he joined the family firm of Bovis Ltd, the construction engineers, and soon entered municipal politics, motivated by two deep concerns: how to rescue human beings from poverty, and how to preserve individual freedom. From local government he went into the House of Commons as member for Leeds North-East, then a safe Conservative seat. When Heath came to power in 1970, Joseph became Minister for Health and Social Services.

After the Conservative defeat in February 1974, Sir Keith began to think deeply about the future of Britain. The crucial problem, it seemed to him, was the rapidly rising rate of inflation, a problem which successive Conservative and Labour Governments had failed to solve. It was inflation above all else which threatened the Western democracies with the fate that Germany had suffered in the 1920s. To try and deal with it, as Sir Keith now saw it, the Heath Government after 1972 had pursued a policy of intervention in economic and industrial decisions, in much the same way as previous Labour Governments had done, and, like them, had had no success, their failure dramatically registered by the uncontrollable expansion of 1972–3, by the miners' strike, the electoral defeat of 1974, and an even greater rate of inflation than there had been before. Even allowing for the tremendous impact on prices of the oil crisis of 1973, he began to think, government intervention seemed not to alleviate the problem of inflation but to make it worse. West Germany had found a way to deal with it, it seemed to him, so he turned his attention in that direction. He told the author in 1986:

> I was deeply impressed by Erhard's concept of the Social Market, and by what it had achieved. West Germany now had an economy characterized by free enterprise, decentralized ownership and decision-making, and competition subject to the rule of law. The pursuit of profit without fair competition, in my view, is immoral. There must be safety nets. The poor and sick and the handicapped must be cared for. This is what a humane society should want, and be able to provide. The safety net is perfectly consistent with the Social Market; the Social Market is better able to provide it.

After the defeat of February 1974, the Shadow Cabinet's main concern became inflation. Sir Keith paid more and more attention to Erhard's achievement in Germany. 'Then,' he says, 'Alfred Sherman entered my life.' Sherman convinced him that the inflation which had scourged Britain in the past and now bid to ruin it in the future had been 'unnecessary, avoidable and politically immoral'.

'He told me that I had been a party to the debauching of the currency, that I and my colleagues had meant well, but that to have meant well did not excuse the damage we had done. "You must grasp the fact", he told me, "that Keynes is dead." At first, I couldn't believe this; I had been brought up on Keynes – everybody had. But I began to see that Sherman was right.' Sir Keith also began to talk to Professor Peter Bauer (now Lord Bauer), then Professor of Economics at the London School of Economics, and to Alan (now Sir Alan) Walters then Cassel Professor at the same institution.

In September 1974 Sir Keith made a speech at Preston. It was not an ordinary speech, but a powerful treatise which today some of Mrs Thatcher's supporters might consider to rank among the great statements in Conservative Party history along with Sir Robert Peel's Tamworth manifesto and Disraeli's address to the electors of Beaconsfield. It was written by Sherman. The subject was inflation. Its tone and import is conveyed by the opening words of the foreword Sir Keith wrote for a collection of speeches, including the Preston speech, which he published some time later:

> About twenty years ago I joined the Conservative Party, and later was adopted as Conservative candidate for the then safe seat of Leeds North-East. In 1959 I was given my first ministerial post. But it was only in April 1974 that I was converted to Conservatism. (I had thought that I was a Conservative but I now see that I was not really one at all.) The series of speeches which follows records my strengthening awareness as I became surer of my ground.

Successive Conservative Governments, said Sir Keith at Preston, had made a great mistake, and he blamed himself as a member of some of them. The inflation from which Britain so dangerously suffered was a self-inflicted wound. It should never have happened, and was the result of successive Governments creating too much money. Why had they done this wrong thing? They had assumed that the inflation which they created would only be mild; that it could be stopped; and, above all that mild inflation seemed a painless way of maintaining full employment, encouraging growth and expanding the social services – all highly desired objectives. 'We see now that inflation has turned out to be a mortal threat to all three.' Sir Keith went on to advocate the abandonment of many of the policies which successive Governments had introduced to deal with the problem of inflation: a voluntary incomes policy, a statutory incomes policy, and so on. These and other expedients would not only fail but make things worse if the main influence on the economy was not the control of the supply of money.

Whatever else might be deduced from Sir Keith's speech, the conclusion that Governments, whether Labour or Conservative, must break with the past and make a fresh start was inescapable. While many who heard it or read it may not have understood much of his views about the importance of controlling the money supply, they would have grasped the fact that Sir Keith was saying that previous Conservative administrations had been leading the country into highly dangerous territory because they had been using the wrong map.

Mr Heath and his colleagues had heard in advance that Sir Keith was going to make a major speech on inflation, and that, in the words of Jim Prior, it would be 'his most outspoken attack yet on our policy in Government'. They were worried: they believed that there would be an election in October, and they feared the effect which Sir Keith's advocacy of anti-inflationary measures leading to increased unemployment would have on their campaign. Several members of the Shadow Cabinet tried to persuade him not to make the speech. Jim Prior records: 'I even had a word with Margaret Thatcher, who by then seemed to have become one of Keith's followers. "You know this is a disastrous speech – can't you stop him giving it?" Margaret replied that it was the work of Alfred Sherman: she felt that Keith did not always understand the political impact of arguments, but that she did not have much influence over him.'

The speech contained some of the fundamentals of what was to become known as Thatcherism. 'Inflation is threatening to destroy our society. It is threatening not just the relative prosperity to which most of us have become accustomed, but the savings and plans of each person and family and the working capital of each business and organization. The distress and unemployment that will follow unless the trend is stopped will be catastrophic. There is a risk, moreover, that political parties which preside with well-intentioned ineffectiveness over such a universal frustration will pave the way for those who will offer solutions at the cost of freedom. It has happened elsewhere. It could happen here.' A misunderstanding of what Keynes had said had led successive Governments who had feared the return of high unemployment like that of the 1930s to try and spend their way out of threatened recession by deficit budgeting and public expenditures financed not by real savings but by Bank of England operations, that is to say by artificially increasing the supply of money. 'The effect of over-reacting to temporary recessions has been to push up inflation to ever higher levels, not to help the unemployed, but to increase their numbers.'

Governments should realize the error of their ways, said Sir Keith. 'My point is that (by logic of hindsight) on each occasion Governments should weigh the short-lived – I repeat, short-lived – benefits they may bring to a quarter of a million or even 300,000 to 400,000 men and their families against the permanent – and I repeat, permanent – repercussions of such deficit financing on the whole population of fifty-five million people. All these fifty-five million people have, on each such occasion since the war, seen inflation increasingly stimulated and savings increasingly eroded.' He agreed that in the short term some jobs would be threatened. But, he said, 'We cannot talk about fighting inflation as the overriding priority and then in the same or another speech say that we can take no monetary action which might threaten some jobs.'

Governments must no longer print money to keep people in work. This did not mean that nothing would be done to help the unemployed or to create alternative employment, and did not mean that a certain level of unemployment was essential to prevent inflation. On the contrary, there would be a great effort to bring those out of work to further employment. 'What we have to do is to set a level of domestic demand sufficient for that level of full employment, which cannot be sustained without inflationary pressures, and then to work within it to deal with specific employment problems, while helping to soften the potentially harsh process of change by generous short-term unemployment, resettlement and retraining grants, and particularly help to individual areas.'

If the common-sense views about economic policy which he was expressing were labelled as monetarism, Sir Keith said, he would 'gladly accept the label'. But he would not accept the false interpretation of monetarism which was frequently purveyed. 'The monetarist thesis has been caricatured as implying that, if we get the flow of money-spending right, everything will be right. This is not – repeat, *not* – my belief. What I believe is that if we get the money supply wrong – too high or too low – nothing will come right. Monetary control is a pre-essential for everything else we need and want to do; an opportunity to tackle the real problems – labour shortage in one place, unemployed in another. . . .'

He made other observations. Some of them disturbed his senior colleagues more than his central thesis, with much of which some of them agreed. What he was advocating, he said, was not a comfortable course. 'This prescription will not be easy nor enjoyable.' It would not give remedies overnight. 'If I had to give a personal guess about the total time horizon of a successful anti-inflation policy, I would say three or four years.'

At the start of his speech he had said, 'I begin by accepting my full share of the collective responsibility' for what had gone wrong, implying that the Cabinet in which he had sat *had* gone wrong. At the end of the speech he had again indicted the Conservative Party: 'Electioneering breeds inflationeering. We, the Conservatives, are not without blemish, I freely admit . . .' and he finished the sentence, the last but three of his speech with these words: '. . . but how much of this [blemish] derives from bi-partisanship, from middle-of-the-road policies, from confusing a distinctive Conservative approach with dogmatism.' There was no mark of interrogation at the end of that sentence; Sir Keith was not asking a question, but making a declaration.

Though this speech was to have considerable consequences later and has outstanding historical importance seen in retrospect, it did not create a sensation at the time. Inflation was indeed the outstanding problem of the day, and the Labour Government was having no success in coping with it – its energies were concentrated on how to increase its majority at the coming general election. Sir Keith's speech was regarded by many not as an indictment of past Conservative policies but as an attack on those which the Labour Government of the day was pursuing, and even that Government was responding publicly to the need to control inflation and was declaring that past policies would have to be revised. Had Sir Keith's party been in government, such a speech would have made an altogether greater impact, but he was in opposition, and in opposition Party champions are expected to indulge in declarations and diatribes which would not be permitted in government. If the wider public was not overwhelmed by the speech at Preston, however, a smaller but more influential audience gave it considerable attention. It was printed in full by *The Times*, and was given a great deal of space in other newspapers. Commentators on economic and political affairs discussed it, including Samuel Brittan, the economic columnist of the *Financial Times*, and Peter Jay, then economic editor of *The Times*, both of whom had contributed to Sir Keith's ideas.

# 4

# THE LEADERSHIP CONTEST

H ad anybody known at the time of the Preston speech in September that the Conservatives would lose the general election in October, and in December would hold a leadership contest, he might have assumed that, if Ted Heath were to be opposed, it would be by Sir Keith Joseph and that there would be considerable support for him. Three or four other names might have occurred to such a speculator, but it is unlikely that they would have included that of Margaret Thatcher. Things turned out differently.

On 19 October, ten days after the election, when it was not even certain that a leadership election would be called, Sir Keith made another speech, this time in Edgbaston on social policy. This too was written for him by Sherman, but on this occasion Sir Keith insisted on adding material of his own, which Sherman had urged him to leave out. This included an observation about the deterioration of society's 'human stock' due to mothers in economic classes 4 and 5, as a result of poverty and inferior intelligence, having more babies than other mothers did, a problem which should be dealt with by encouraging them to practise more contraception. This provoked a storm. Four weeks later, when it had become clear that a leadership election must be held, Sir Keith went to see Margaret Thatcher privately and told her that he would not be a candidate. She would not have stood against him, but once she knew that he was not available, she decided to oppose Mr Heath and informed the leader the following day.

At that point the person thought most likely to succeed against Ted

Heath was Edward Du Cann. For several years he had been the chairman of the 1922 Committee. From 1965 to 1967 he had been chairman of the Party. With great experience in the city his expertise in the House was in financial and economic affairs: he had served as Economic Secretary to the Treasury and as Minister of State at the Board of Trade. He was not regarded as a rebel against the Heath establishment, nor as a member of that 'right wing' of which Heath had spoken to Jim Prior about twenty-four hours after the election: several weeks after Sir Keith had made his speech at Preston, Du Cann was publicly calling on the Party to rally round the leader and win the October election.

Though acceptable to many of the Heathite majority within the party, du Cann was also acceptable to many of those who had resolved that Heath must go. In the first place, he had not taken a post in the Heath Government. Secondly, when he was chairman of the Party, Heath had fired him. Thirdly he was known to dislike Heath personally. These qualifications particularly appealed to a backbench MP called Airey Neave, a remarkable man, endowed with great courage, determination and patience, and with the gift of management. Neave had made a brave and resourceful escape from Colditz during the war, and after his return to Britain organized the escape and repatriation of many other prisoners of war. He too disliked Heath, and thought his leadership of the Party had been disastrous. Neave was not particularly antagonistic to existing Party policy; so long as Heath were removed, he would have been ready to support a bid from Whitelaw, Heath's faithful lieutenant, who would have been his first choice. But Whitelaw having made it known that he would not run against his leader, Neave began to organize support for Du Cann.

Sir Alec Home's committee produced its report a few days before Christmas. This made it clear that an election was unavoidable. The committee recommended that the leadership should no longer be a freehold in perpetuity – as Heath had represented it as being to Jim Prior a few weeks previously – but that the leader should offer himself for re-election at the beginning of the session of Parliament which followed a general election, and at the beginning of annual sessions. From now on, in order to win, a candidate must secure a majority of 15% of those who were eligible to vote, not, as had previously been the case, a majority of 15% of those who had actually voted.

This second change in the rules was ominous: most Conservative MPs, including many of Heath's loyal supporters, believed that though on the first ballot he might get a majority of 15% of those who had voted, since many who did not want him as leader but could not bring themselves to vote against him would abstain, he would not get 15% of the *eligible* vote in which the abstainers would count against him. They believed that the change might prevent him from being elected on the first ballot and might cause him to lose on the second. Their only comfort was that the rules permitted new candidates to offer themselves for the second ballot: if Heath was defeated on the first, a Heath nominee, who could not bring himself to oppose the leader on the first ballot, could offer himself on the second, and win. This at the time was an important consideration, since the contest was seen in the main not as about Party policy, but, as it had been in 1965, when Heath was elected to replace Sir Alec Home, about who should be the leader.

When Conservative MPs went home for Christmas, most of them thought that on the first ballot Heath would be opposed by Du Cann, would win, but might fail to gain the necessary 15% margin. In that case there would be a second ballot: Heath would not stand, and Du Cann would be opposed by Willie Whitelaw, who, most of them thought, would probably win. Such calculations had rapidly to be revised, for on 15 January 1975, Edward Du Cann made it known that he had withdrawn from the contest.

When Du Cann had emerged as the principal contender, Mrs Thatcher gave him the same undertaking she had volunteered to Sir Keith: she would not run against him. Now that Du Cann had taken himself out of it, however, she decided that she would run. Airey Neave, having built up a strong anti-Heath contingent in the Party but having lost his two potential candidates, confirmed that Whitelaw would not oppose Heath on the first ballot, and then turned to Margaret Thatcher, and offered her his help. She accepted it, and he became her campaign manager. It is an indication of how unideological was the thinking within the Party at this time that Mrs Thatcher was Neave's third choice and that his first would have been Whitelaw.

In the three weeks before the first ballot on 4 February, the only outstanding aspect of the campaign to remove Heath so far as the country as a whole was concerned was that its beneficiary was a woman. For Conservative MPs and for those who followed politics closely, however, there was more to the contest than one leader being substituted for another. Mrs Thatcher, while she did not advocate new policies, immediately began to echo some of what Keith Joseph had been saying. On the day on which the nominations closed an article by her appeared in the *Daily Telegraph* which contained such observations as 'We' (meaning the previous Heath Government) had 'failed the people'. Though she avoided specifics, she indicated generally that the Conservative Party had failed to deliver what their traditional supporters required: 'Successful governments win elections. So do parties with broadly acceptable policies. We lost.' She said that Conservative Government policy should be based on an understanding of the needs of 'ordinary people', but at the same time she extolled the values of the middle class. To the public at large and to many Conservative MPs she may not have appeared right wing or divisive, but in the view of most of her colleagues in the Shadow Cabinet her advocacy of middle-class values in the *Daily Telegraph* cut across their projection of the Conservatives as the party of One Nation.

On 18 January, addressing her constituents at Finchley, Mrs Thatcher explained why a leadership election was being held and why she was a candidate. Nobody should be surprised, she said, that there was widespread demand for a procedure enabling Mr Heath to submit himself for re-election: the Conservative Party had lost three out of four elections in ten years. Mr Heath might be confirmed in the leadership, but at any rate his colleagues would have been given the chance to support an alternative candidate. Many MPs felt that they should be given the chance formally to express their views, not simply about an individual as leader, but about the whole nature and style of the Party's leadership since 1965 and the general character of its policies.

Mrs Thatcher then went on to talk about her own role in the situation. 'It is not an easy time for me,' she said. 'Some people, in the press and outside it, have not hesitated to impugn my motives, to attribute to me political views which I have never expressed and do not hold, and suggest that the idea of a woman aspiring to lead a great party is absurd; a strangely old-fashioned view, I should have thought. You can forget all the nonsense about "defence of privilege" – I had precious little "privilege" in my early years – and the suggestion that all my supporters are reactionary right-wingers. It seems to me that those who propagate this idea do Mr Heath a poor service by implying that his support lies only on the "left wing" of the party. This is not a confrontation between left and right. I am trying to represent the deep feelings of those many thousands of rank and file Tories in the country – and potential Conservative voters too – who feel let down by our Party and find themselves unrepresented in a political vacuum.'

Mrs Thatcher went on to say that she accepted her full share of collective responsibility for the shortcomings of the Conservative leadership in government and in opposition, but hoped that she had learned something from their failures and mistakes, and could help to plan constructively for the future. 'In the desperate situation of Britain today,' she said, 'our party needs the support of all who value the traditional ideals of Toryism ... There is a widespread feeling in the country that the Conservative Party has not defended these ideals explicitly and toughly enough, so that Britain is set on a course towards inevitable Socialist mediocrity. That course must not only be halted, it must be reversed. The action of the Tory Party to carry out that reversal must begin now while we are in opposition and have time to look at our policies afresh before the next election. That will be a priority task, whatever the outcome of the leadership ballot.'

Within the Party, behind closed doors, there was much criticism of Mrs Thatcher. If she had felt this way, asked Mr Heath's supporters, why had she remained in the Cabinet for the whole four years of the Heath Government and never complained about being 'let down by our Party'? Since the defeat of February 1974, twelve months previously, she had been the party's spokesman on financial affairs and public expenditure; if she had thought the Conservative voter was being 'let down' by the Heath Shadow Cabinet, why had she so enthusiastically expounded its policies? Such criticism was not made publicly; the party leaders had no wish for the leadership contest to appear as a struggle for power between the left and right of the party, or between those who were loyal to Heath and those who were not.

It could not have been said that either Sir Keith Joseph or Edward Du Cann were famous public figures, even less that they were popular ones. The same was even more true of Margaret Thatcher. She was best known for her decision as Minister of Education to abolish the supply of free milk to schools, an action which had earned her the nickname of 'Milk-snatcher'. She had also received much publicity when she withdrew the previous Labour Government's instruction to local authorities to submit plans for the conversion of their State secondary schools into comprehensives. When she addressed the annual conference of the National Union of Teachers consequently, about a hundred of her audience walked out, and a national newspaper printed an article about her under the headline 'The Most Unpopular Woman in Britain'. More of these matters later. With Sir Keith – then Minister for the Social Services – Mrs Thatcher had been among the Government's biggest spenders in the Heath Cabinet, but this had not become widely known.

To the public, knowing her mainly through her appearances on television, she might look bourgeoise and sound stilted. Attractive, articulate, beautifully groomed, she did not appear to have charisma. Her voice, even in conversation, had an artificial quality, a lack of spontaneous light and shade, as though some of her words had been rehearsed. To her fellow MPs, on the other hand, she was a formidable figure, whether in government or in opposition, one of the oustanding debaters in the House, always well equipped with facts, able to handle complicated presentations without notes, and, when occasion required, ready to defend herself and counterattack in the best dialectic traditions of the House. After the defeat of 1974 she had been appointed by Heath to speak for the Shadow Cabinet on economic and financial affairs, second only to Robert Carr, the Shadow Chancellor. She distinguished herself consistently throughout the summer, and as a performer in the House and on television was more effective than her senior colleagues. When MPs began to discuss the possibility that Joseph might replace Heath as leader, many of them spoke of her as the next Shadow Chancellor and, therefore, as potentially the first woman Chancellor. Only a few days after she had made known her decision to stand for the leadership, she had made a devastating attack in the Commons on the Government's economic policies, more than holding her own against the Chancellor, Denis Healey, the most powerful and aggressive debater in the Labour Party. It was widely said at the time that neither Heath nor Whitelaw – nor Carr – would have matched the expertise and rhetoric of her assault. Many Conservative MPs, if they had not believed it before, would now have agreed that she might one day fulfil what was understood to be her only ambition – to be Chancellor of the Exchequer.

The result of the first ballot, held on 4 February was:

| | |
|---|---|
| Thatcher | 130 |
| Heath | 119 |
| Hugh Fraser | 16 |

Heath was out of the contest.

It is still said by some that, if the campaign for Heath had been conducted differently and if he had been able to play a more sympathetic part in it, he might have won; but by then the die had been cast, and he had no hope of winning. A widely held view is that, if he had decided not to stand himself and had backed Willie Whitelaw, Whitelaw would have won on the first ballot and Margaret Thatcher would have been defeated. The great majority of Conservative MPs were surprised at the result. Few expected Heath to win an outright victory, but few thought that Margaret Thatcher would do so well. Heath and his friends were shocked: more than half the MPs had voted against their leader. This was the third hammer blow to the leader's authority in less than a year. Mr Heath now announced his resignation of the leadership of the Party.

A second ballot was held seven days later, Tuesday 11 February. By then, those loyal to Ted Heath were in disarray, depressed not only by the defeat of their leader on the first ballot and the size of the vote for Mrs Thatcher, but also by the realization that if Whitelaw had stood in the first round instead of Heath, he might have won. After some discussion, Whitelaw decided that in the second round he would be a candidate. 'I can only hope,' he said, 'that I might be able to do something to unite our Party.' Jim Prior also decided to take his chance. There were two other candidates, neither of whom could be considered Heathites: Geoffrey Howe and John Peyton.

In the three weeks before the next ballot, newspapers reported that there was much criticism of Mrs Thatcher within the Party. One of her supporters claimed that she was being smeared. Several newspapers, for instance, referred to her 'milk-snatcher' tag. There was mention of an article she had written in which she had advised pensioners to stock tinned food as a protection against inflation, as she was doing herself. Some of her colleagues were quoted, though not by name, as saying that it ill became her to complain about high public spending by the Heath Government when she and Keith Joseph were the highest of the spenders. Questions were raised about the desirability of the Party being led by a Grantham grocer's daughter with a second-class degree in Chemistry, only able to be in politics because she had a rich husband, and totally ignorant of foreign affairs.

There were many who thought that, having struck a telling blow against Heath, a significant number of the rebels would then turn back to support Whitelaw. This did not prove to be the case. Whether Whitelaw was too closely identified with Heath, whether the Thatcher bandwagon was now rolling too fast, whether Whitelaw seemed too old-fashioned a Tory for modern times, or whether he had cut a poor figure on television, the result of the second ballot was decisive:

| | |
|---|---|
| Thatcher | 146 |
| Whitelaw | 79 |
| Howe | 19 |
| Prior | 19 |
| Peyton | 11 |

Though Conservative MPs and Conservative voters up and down the country had been talking about a new look and a new leader for several months, little had been heard in the leadership campaign of Sir Keith Joseph's speech at Preston or of what is now known as Thatcherism. The forces which swept Mrs Thatcher to the leadership of the Party came from the feeling that Ted Heath was a loser, and that a new leader whose image was not associated with him and his defeated policies was essential. The vote for Mrs Thatcher was not so much a vote for her as a vote against consensus, Butskellism, and Heath personally.

It is easy to understand why it is frequently said that Margaret Thatcher became leader as the result of a series of accidents. If Keith Joseph had not made his ill-fated speech at Edgbaston on the merits of contraception for the lower classes, it is probable that he and not she would have run against Heath in February. If Edward Du Cann had not withdrawn, Airey Neave would have organized his campaign and she would have remained in the wings. If Ted Heath had decided after his defeat in the October election to submit himself at once for re-election, he might have regained the leadership. If Whitelaw had stood in the first ballot, when his campaign would have probably been managed by Neave, he might well have won.

Though Mr Heath's supporters were shocked by Mrs Thatcher's victory, and the Party as a whole taken aback, this was not the first time that the leadership had been taken over by a candidate who at a comparatively late stage in the contest was considered an outsider. Few people would have predicted that Baldwin would become leader in 1922, and most would have thought of him only as a potentially able Speaker. Butler was the favourite to succeed Eden in 1957, though Macmillan was regarded as the main alternative, and a month before Macmillan suddenly announced his resignation in 1963 few would have predicted that Alec Home would be chosen as his successor. But, even allowing for these precedents, the election of Margaret Thatcher to the mantle of Peel, Disraeli and Churchill was a great surprise. Her supporters could hardly believe it and her critics within the Party reacted by speaking of her as a stop-gap or a temporary abberation which in due course would be corrected. That the Party had chosen such a dissident and outsider was phenomenon enough. But this dissident outsider was a woman.

A distinction should be made between the reaction of the senior members of the Party and the younger ones. Many young MPs saw it coming and, indeed, a few veterans were neither astonished nor displeased. Among the latter was Lord Margadale, better known as

Major Morrison, often described as the wisest chairman the 1922 Committee ever had. In 1972, in conversation with his son Peter, now Minister of State for Energy and Deputy Chairman of the Conservative Party, Margadale said: 'Mark my words – Margaret Thatcher will be the next leader of the Party.' His son was surprised by his father's prediction and his easy acceptance of the idea of the Party being led by a woman. Two years later, aged twenty-nine, Peter Morrison became MP for Chester. After his first long conversation with Mrs Thatcher, he said to himself, 'Pa was right.' He voted for her in the leadership election.

# 5

# MRS THATCHER TAKES CHARGE

Once Mrs Thatcher became leader, there was, as usual in such circumstances, a call for party unity. The difference now was that there came, simultaneously, the formation of two camps within the Parliamentary Party and two schools within the Shadow Cabinet: the Thatcherites and the Heathites.

After the result had been announced there was an exchange of telephone calls between Mr Heath's office and Mrs Thatcher's, as a result of which Mr Heath made it clear that he would not join the Shadow Cabinet but would go to the back benches, where he would be free to express his personal views. By this time Mr Whitelaw had indicated to Mrs Thatcher that it did not seem a good idea to invite Mr Heath to join the Shadow Cabinet; even had he been willing to accept, to include him would not make sense. Mrs Thatcher saw this, but wanted to do what she could to preserve the spirit and appearance of Party unity. So, on the morning after the result had been declared, 'bearing the olive branch', as one of her friends put it, she went round to Mr Heath's house in Wilton Street. The front door was heavily besieged by newspaper reporters and television cameras.

Only Mrs Thatcher and Mr Heath know what was said at their meeting. There are various versions, some of them very dramatic, but in assessing their veracity it should be remembered that the die had been cast before she entered Mr Heath's study, and each of them knew it and knew that the other knew it. The dialogue was over within seconds; there was nothing new to say; Mrs Thatcher left the room.

Timothy Kitson, Heath's Parliamentary Private Secretary, suggested that before she left she have a cup of coffee; he wanted to conceal the fact that the exchange had been so short; he knew that interpretations might be put upon it which would damage the image of Party unity. About fifteen minutes thus went by before Mrs Thatcher left the house. Years later, speaking with hindsight, one very wise Conservative, sympathetic to both of them, said: 'Margaret should not have gone to see him so soon. She should have waited for him to get over the immediate shock.'

Since this rift between leader and former leader has been a feature of the Conservative Party's history for more than thirteen years, a rift that created serious difficulties for Mrs Thatcher in her first administration and could just conceivably do so again, its history might as well be updated to the present day (early 1988). In early days Mrs Thatcher went out of her way to try and bridge it. A few weeks after the contest, they sat side by side on the platform at the meeting which launched the Conservative Party campaign to keep Britain in Europe. When her turn to speak came, in a warm and deferential tone she addressed Heath directly thus: 'Naturally it is with some temerity that the pupil speaks before the master, because you know more about the Common Market than anybody.' Mr Heath did not indicate that he had heard. Later, in the House of Commons, she spoke of his outstanding efforts in the European cause, and again Mr Heath remained impassive. After she won the election in 1979, she invited him to become British Ambassador in Washington. To this day she has continued to treat her former leader in a manner which he has never reciprocated. Recently, walking with a colleague along a corridor in the House of Commons, observing Mr Heath walking towards her, she greeted him with 'Hullo, Ted. . . .' He said nothing and walked on.

Few people have made the mistake of thinking that, however much Mr Heath shows his disapproval of Mrs Thatcher in a personal way, he is motivated by personal pique. True, personal feelings have been involved; he resented the manner in which after sitting in his Cabinet for four years, not only accepting collective responsibility but never complaining about what was being done, she publicly condemned his administration for betraying the 1970 Party manifesto and for failing to carry out an authentic Conservative policy. He has found it hard to accept the fact that her policies had succeeded in 1979–81 when he had felt compelled to abandon similar ones in 1972 and went on to suffer defeat in two consecutive elections; that she had had the benefit of a change in circumstances in the early eighties which had been denied to him in the early seventies. It must have been galling to hear Conservatives say that the reason why she had succeeded and he had failed was that she had will and vision and he had not.

Such personal feelings have not been on the same level of importance, however, as his unchanged view that much of what she has done, and not done, is dangerous for Britain and the world. He has said many times that reliance on monetary policy to solve the country's economic policies is a perilous error which continues to incur unacceptably high unemployment and to diminish Britain's essential manufacturing base. He has never changed his view that an incomes policy is essential, whereas Mrs Thatcher from her first days as leader was resolved never to have one, and has not. Mr Heath wanted Britain's main ally to be the EEC, not the United States; she has the opposite view. He wanted Britain to be firm within the EEC, but to be enthusiastic and co-operative, and gradually win the leadership of the Community. Mrs Thatcher does not want the leadership of Europe: she wants Britain to get a fair deal from the EEC, and to get it she is prepared by blunt talk and even bullying to forfeit any chance of Britain becoming Europe's leader. He believes her to be taking Britain down the wrong road. He believes that he cannot hold such fundamentally differing views, and express them publicly, and at the same time smile and say nice things about her.

For some time Mr Heath's behaviour may have been conditioned by his feeling that Mrs Thatcher would not last long as leader, and would be replaced by a Heathite. Then, after she became Prime Minister, he may have entertained the idea that the Conservative Government would collapse and that a Government of National Unity, of the kind he spoke about in 1974, would have to be formed, with himself at its head. In both cases it made sense for him to keep his distance from her and to re-state from time to time the fundamental differences between his views on policy and hers.

Much was said and written between 1975 and 1981 about the rift between Heath and Margaret Thatcher. There was not so much discussion of the rift between Heath and the Heathites. The Heathites had an ambivalent attitude to their former leader's public behaviour. In part they deplored it because it marred the necessary reflection of Party unity, but in part they welcomed it because they benefited from it: that he was at large, free to speak his mind – very similar to theirs – and every time he did so received wide publicity, justified the opposition to the Prime Minister which they were putting forward in the Cabinet. Mr Heath's behaviour buttressed their position, as theirs did his, until as a consequence of her sweeping victory in the general election of 1983 Mrs Thatcher established an unchallenged ascendancy of both Cabinet and Party, and stamped modern Toryism in her own image. In a sense the long-lived disaffection of the diminishing band of Heathites has been part of the basis of her domination: she has been seen to succeed in spite of it. Their opposition has sunk, not without trace, but with few indications of why there is any possibility of them challenging her again.

Soon after Mrs Thatcher's visit to Mr Heath, it was announced that Michael Wolff would no longer be the Director-General at the Conservative Central Office, a post completely in the Party leader's gift. Michael Wolff had written Ted Heath's speeches for several years, and was as close to him, if not closer, as any of his Cabinet and Shadow Cabinet colleagues. The removal of Michael Wolff was a portent.

The first appointment Mrs Thatcher made was that of Airey Neave, the organizer of her campaign for the leadership, to be head of her private office; later she made him Opposition spokesman on Northern Ireland. On 18 February she announced the names of her Shadow Cabinet. Willie Whitelaw was appointed deputy leader. Sir Keith Joseph was given a post specially created for him: Overall Responsibility for Policy and Research. He would rank next to Whitelaw. Next to that, the most important appointment was that of Sir Geoffrey Howe to succeed Robert Carr as Shadow Chancellor of the Exchequer. It was not so much the elevation of Howe, who now spoke of himself as having been converted to monetarist policies, as the removal of Carr which caught the eye. 'Apart from Robert Carr,' Jim Prior wrote in his memoirs, '... scarcely anyone in the Party understood industrial relations or knew industrialists, let alone any trade unionists.' Now, Carr was out. 'I know you recognize as much as I do', Mrs Thatcher wrote to him, 'that if we are to be a vigorous and effective opposition and later a government of experience as well as talent, it is essential that opportunities should be provided for the coming generation of leaders and this can only be done by those who have given long service making way for them.' Carr was not then sixty. He was given a peerage later in the year.

Even more significant was her decision not to invite Peter Walker to join the Shadow Cabinet. Walker had been Secretary of State for Trade and Industry in the Heath Government, and thus had been deeply involved in economic policy. He had also managed Mr Heath's campaign in the leadership election. On the day the new leader announced the changes Mr Walker issued a statement which included the following passages: 'In excluding me from the Shadow Cabinet Margaret Thatcher has chosen what I believe to be the only wholly honest solution and one which I accept and welcome.' He went on to promise her his loyal support, but added: 'I have for the past few months, however, voiced in a series of speeches my grave doubts about the extreme monetarist policies currently fashionable within parts of the Conservative Party ... I believe and hope that the Conservative Party led by Margaret, whose power of intellect I hold in deep respect, will over the next few months and years be persuaded not to accept the deceptive temptation of a rigid monetarist policy.'

All but one of the economic policy jobs in the new Shadow Cabinet were occupied by those who thought along the same lines as Keith Joseph. The stage was set for work to begin in Conservative Party headquarters on changing the image of the Party and its policy. This could not be too drastically or incontinently done. The appearance of unity had to be preserved. The ideas which Mrs Thatcher and Sir Keith favoured – curbing the power of the trade unions, abandoning a prices and incomes policy, cuts in public expenditure – were agreeable to most Conservative voters but not, necessarily, to a majority in the country, and therefore should be presented with caution and right timing. There was to be no sudden launching of a rewritten Conservative manifesto. In any case the first priority, given the need for the preservation of the appearance of unity, was to make the new leader widely known and cause her to be seen in the most attractive political light.

The key men in the new Shadow Cabinet were the economic policy makers, Joseph, Howe, Howell and Biffen. Nominally headed by Sir Keith, their real leader was Geoffrey Howe, who was the only one of them who had had a seat in the Heath Cabinet which had involved him in economic policy. As Solicitor-General he had drafted the Heath Government's legislation on the trade unions, and got it onto the statute book as the Industrial Relations Act of 1971. As Minister for Trade and Consumer Affairs at the Department of Trade and Industry he had played his part in the fight against inflation. He now became Opposition spokesman on Treasury and Economic Affairs – Shadow Chancellor.

Sir Geoffrey had the benefit of the expertise of Nigel Lawson. A student at Oxford under Keynes's protégé and biographer, Roy Harrod (who once said Lawson was his cleverest pupil), Lawson came into Parliament in February 1974. From 1956 on he had been one of the most lively and influential financial commentators in Britain, and after a spell as special assistant to Sir Alec Home when he was Prime Minister had been editor of the *Spectator* for four years. The year before he entered Parliament he was a special policy adviser at Conservative Party headquarters.

Lawson's forte was economic policy. For nearly twenty years as a journalist he had interviewed Labour and Conservative Prime Ministers and Chancellors on their conduct of affairs and had written trenchantly about their successes and failures. He had known and argued with top politicians, trade union leaders, businessmen and international statesmen, and had moved from being a disillusioned Keynesian to becoming a sophisticated though not simplistic monetarist. Highly articulate, combative and not afraid to speak his mind, he was able to put at Howe's disposal experience and access which Howe, a lawyer, did not have. In time Howe became Mrs Thatcher's first Chancellor of the Exchequer, Lawson her second.

The new Shadow Cabinet took its business very seriously. If it was to get economic policy wrong when it got to Government, the fault would not be want of intensive preparation beforehand. Its members, under the eagle eye of the Shadow Prime Minister, went to the greatest pains to prepare itself for the day when it would come to power, not only by study, consultation, brain-picking and the creation of policy, but by session after session behind closed doors modelled on real life Cabinets. At these gatherings Shadow Ministers put forward Shadow Department proposals with advisers playing the role of civil servants. Their submissions were dissected, rejected, and sometimes torn to pieces with such a degree of verisimilitude that tempers frequently ran high, so that on one occasion Shadow Education Secretary St John-Stevas, in protest at Shadow cuts made in his Shadow budget, heatedly submitted his Shadow resignation and stalked out of the Shadow Cabinet room.

# 6

# ALFRED ROBERTS'S DAUGHTER

Over the next ten months, up to and including the Party conference to be held that year at Blackpool, the country learned a great deal about Margaret Thatcher, about her background, her education, the influences on her early life, her philosophy, the origins and the nature of her Conservative faith, the reason why she had challenged Heath's leadership, what she wanted the Conservative Party to stand for and achieve in government, and, above all, her vision of Britain's future.

There rapidly emerged the image of a simple, lower-middle-class, self-made person, who by hard work, application and determination had made it to the top, and wanted to create a society in which everybody would have the same chance. Margaret Thatcher believed in equality, but only in the sense of an equal chance. The State had certain duties, but its powers should be confined to creating a framework within which the individual was free to do the best he could for himself. The moral and political basis of society should be the Victorian virtues: thrift, effort, honesty, self-help, and a sense of responsibility for the less fortunate. Socialism, corporatism, and centralization were morally wrong and politically dangerous. The Free Market was a marvellous mechanism which should as far as possible be left to work on its own. The national economy should be run as a prudent person would run the home economy. No section of society should be allowed to exploit another, whether it were a monopolistic business or a powerful trade union. Resemblances were noted between the views of Mrs Thatcher and those expressed by Hayek and Friedman, but it soon became clear that her ideas – her brand of nineteenth-century economic liberalism – owed less to political theorists than to her upbringing in her father's grocery shop.

Margaret Thatcher was born in 1925. The main influence on her has been, and remains, that of her father. 'He was a severe man, but we were not frightened of him, and he was tremendously ambitious for us. To know Margaret you have to know him.' Thus her elder sister, now Mrs Muriel Cullen, several years later.[1] She thought the world of him, and for him she was not only a daughter, but pupil, protégée and potential *alter ego*, the offspring who could and would achieve the greater, wider life which circumstances and the accident of birth had denied him. Their relationship became even closer and more communicative after, when Margaret was only thirteen, her elder sister, five years older, left home to train as a physiotherapist.

Alfred Roberts was born in Ringstead, Northamptonshire, one of the seven children of a shoemaker. He left school at the age of twelve and, because his eyesight was poor, did not follow his father's trade, but was apprenticed to a grocer. In his late teens, he moved to Grantham, a market town with some industry, in Lincolnshire, to become manager of a small store. He was a devoted Methodist, and in the local church met Beatrice Stephenson, a seamstress and daughter of a railway cloakroom attendant. They married and, pooling their savings, bought a small grocery shop with a sub-post office attached on the outskirts of the town. They lived above the shop, and both Margaret and Muriel were born there. There was no bathroom or indoor lavatory, and when they wanted hot water they heated it themselves. There was no garden. Her parents still lived there when Margaret went to Oxford.

Alfred Roberts was an impressive man, six feet three inches with curly blond hair which had turned white when he was still young. His bright blue eyes looked out through thick-lensed spectacles which heightened the effect of a piercing gaze. Uneducated but extremely well self-taught – every weekend Margaret went to the public library to bring back histories and biographies for him – he talked fluently and informedly about the past and present of public affairs. He had presence. His wife, quiet, unassuming, admiring, remained in the background. They shared the same Victorian values and virtues, running the whole range from Godliness to Cleanliness, the first considered to be as practical as the last; the former not so much a matter of spiritual experience as of treating one's neighbour as one would like to be treated oneself; the latter of being, in Margaret Thatcher's words, 'neat, tidy, always

41

as well dressed as they could afford, the kind of people who even if they had only one shirt or blouse would get up a few minutes earlier in the morning to put an iron over it.'

Asked by the author what first came into her mind when she looked back on her father she answered: 'His simple conviction that some things are right, and some are wrong. His belief that life is ultimately about character, that character comes from what you make of yourself. You must work hard to earn money to support yourself, but hard work was even more important in the formation of character. You must learn to stand on your own feet. There was great emphasis on learning to stand on your own feet. There are many things which ought never to be done for money – marriage, for instance. Money was only a means to an end. Ends never justified means.' When one listens to Mrs Thatcher talking about her father it is easy to understand why she says: 'One of my favourite quotations is: "That which thy father bequeathed thee, earn it anew, if thou wouldst possess it".' This mildly puritanical atmosphere and regime of the home – no games or books on Sundays and three visits to church, a walk of a mile each way – was strengthened by the presence for several years of Beatrice's mother, a woman of vigorous moral convictions expressed in sayings such as, 'If a thing is worth doing, it's worth doing well.'

Alfred Roberts was a lay preacher, in great demand in the neighbouring villages. When his wife baked bread and cakes, which she did twice a week, she always made more than the family needed so that the two girls could take some to neighbours who were sick or needy. After school, and in the holidays – the girls had a week at the seaside, Skegness, with their mother while Alfred minded the store – Margaret and Muriel helped in the shop, selling sweets or biscuits, or weighed butter and tea. Apart from homework and family chat when the shop had been closed for the day, the cultural life of the family centred on the Finkin Street Methodist church: musical evenings, youth club, talks, and, on Sunday nights after the three sessions at church, supper in their home for a few Methodist or Chamber of Trade friends.

Many years later, in 1975, soon after she had become leader of the Conservative Party, the author asked her about the impression she created on television of seeming to be a cool, collected, very controlled type of person, and therefore lacking in feeling, in compassion, rather a cold person. She replied, 'I can understand why some people might think that. I try to be controlled. I was brought up to be. My parents, who were the main influence in my life, and on my attitude to life, including politics, taught us – my sister and me – to *be* controlled. I was brought up to believe that you *never* lost your temper, at least not in public. That you didn't complain. You counted your blessings. You never spoke of your failures – of course, you had failures and disappointments, but you didn't talk about them; you just got on with the job. This doesn't mean that you aren't compassionate in the face of *other people's* failures and disappointments: it means you don't indulge in self-pity, and that you don't encourage anybody else to. If I feel let down, if I am hurt by what is said or written about me, and I sometimes am, I don't think it right to bemoan my fate in public. Or to brood over it in private. It's harder to feel this way when other people are hurt on one's account, one's family or one's friends. But tomorrow is a new day, and how one deals with that is what really counts.'

Did she think that a person might display so much self-control that he or she might put people off, seem to be a cold fish, which would be a shortcoming in a political leader? She answered: 'I don't think it would be the self-control that would put people off. I think people recognize the difference between a person who is self-controlled and a person who is a cold fish. Cold fish people put one off, and a cold fish would not be effective in politics, because politics – what *I* mean by politics – is about helping people to live a better life.'

To be born in a shop is to some degree to enter public life. Alfred was not only a lay preacher, a pillar of the Finkin Street Methodist Church, and a school governor; he was also a Borough Councillor, later an alderman and mayor of Grantham. He thrived on talk about public affairs. It was his true vocation. His shop became a meeting place for kindred spirits. Small businessmen active in the town's Chamber of Trade came in to discuss the problems of the day, Grantham's and the nation's. Margaret was thus brought up in an ambience of family life, work, and the discussion of public affairs.

Though Alfred Roberts was not by nature a political partisan, things being as they were in Grantham he had to take sides. In his day, the parties on the local council were on the one hand the members nominated by the Chamber of Trade and, on the other, those put forward by the local Co-operative movement. The latter was supported by the Labour Party. The former for the most part were Conservatives, but included Liberals and Independents. Alfred stood as an Independent, although it is said that in those days he was at heart a sympathizer with what would now be described as the right wing of the Labour Party. In the year she became leader Mrs Thatcher spoke of him as having been in early life a Liberal of the vintage that believed in free enterprise, social conscience and individual liberty. 'He had been brought up in a Liberal family, and he may have been a Liberal himself at one time, but that was before I can remember. He came to some of my early election meetings to speak, before I, as candidate, arrived. On one occasion he said that his family had been Liberal, but that in his own day the Conservatives stood for what the Liberals had stood for in his father's time.'

Margaret was a precocious political activist. In the general election of 1935, when she was ten, she carried lists of those who had voted from the interviewers standing outside the polling booth to the Party committee room so that those who had not yet voted could be rounded up and persuaded to turn out. She took notes from her father to colleagues on the council. In local elections, when her mother was working in the Conservative Party committee rooms, she ran messages. When her father was unable to get to political meetings, Conservative, Labour or Liberal, especially if they were to be addressed by important visiting speakers, Margaret would be sent to bring back a report. It became second nature to her to be involved in political life, addressing and stamping envelopes, delivering leaflets, getting people out of their houses and into the polling booth. Everyday life, family relationships, earning a livelihood, the Methodist Church, local and national politics and the goings and comings in the great world outside Grantham, were all parts of a – with a few exceptions – thoroughly acceptable world over which her admired father presided.

Grantham did not suffer from the high unemployment of the early 1930s, but many of the workers at the local manufacturers of steam engines, Ruston and Hornsby, lost their jobs, and on the way to school in the mornings Margaret saw queues of jobless outside the Labour Exchange, as it was then called. She knew of the mounting list of customers to whom her father was giving extended credit – 'He never refused'. In time, the queues dwindled, and her father was repaid most of his debts. By the time Margaret was into her teens, the problem of unemployment was diminishing. It had not scarred the social life of what was largely a prosperous market town, but it had given people like the Roberts family a sense of the wounds inflicted on other parts of Britain. 'We had some personal friends who were unemployed and I remember the joy we all felt when one of them found a job. We talked about the need for a wider range of industry in Grantham.'

But, as she recalls, 'At that time I was becoming aware of politics, the big issues were international – peace and war, the rise of Fascism and the threat to democracy.' She cannot remember Hitler reoccupying the Rhineland in March 1936, but she remembers vividly the invasion of Austria in March 1938 – 'We listened to every news bulletin on the radio.' There was a personal element in their anxiety. Muriel had a pen friend in Vienna, a Jewish girl called Edith. The girl's parents wrote to Alfred Roberts, and asked if he could help her to make a temporary home in Britain. Edith came to Grantham and lived in his house. Edith's account of the Nazi regime, and of the persecution of the Austrian Jews, made a deep impression on the thirteen-year-old Margaret, in which horror of repression and compassion for the Jews combined to produce in her a precocious awareness of the struggle for democracy in a world threatened by brutal dictatorship and aggressive anti-Semitism.

It was in this ambience that Margaret became a dedicated Conservative. 'I remember the difference in attitudes to rearmament. Winston Churchill was warning us that war was coming, and that we needed to rearm. The Labour Party had been voting against the rearmament programme and even voted against conscription after Hitler had marched into Czechoslovakia. Whatever the many shortcomings of the Conservative Party in the 1930s, they were way ahead of the Labour Party in their practical effort to prepare the country to resist the tyranny of Hitler and defend the democratic way of life.'

The war broke out the following year. She was fourteen when it began, and she began a routine of going around the neighbouring villages giving recitals of poetry, mostly out of Palgrave's *Golden Treasury*, but her favourite was Kipling. The war left her with a profound sense of the strength of patriotism and of the need for courage and self-sacrifice as expressed by Winston Churchill. Churchill became her hero, not only because of his leadership while the war was on, but because of the courage and vision he had displayed before it, his denunciation of appeasement and his stand for principle. There came a moment when compromise must give way to commitment, when diplomacy must cease and action must begin: Churchill had called on the democracies to confront the dictators before it was too late. He had been prepared to go it alone.

The lessons she learned from the war remained with her, and when her time came she would apply them without flinching, as during the Falklands crisis of 1982. The war left her too with an abiding compassion for Jews and a resolve to protect them: no British Prime Minister since Churchill has been so sympathetic to the problems of Israel.

Asked once about what she learned from her father that had influenced her most, Mrs Thatcher replied: 'Example rather than precept, I think. Nothing very specific. It was the atmosphere that was created in the home. There was a great sense of effort, of always doing something, not necessarily work – talk, discussion, playing the piano – but always something. You worked hard not because work was every-thing, but because work was necessary to give you what you wanted. There was also the feeling that idleness was a waste. You worked hard at school, not only to improve your mind, but to enable you to get a job that was interesting and demanding. It was very important to use your life to some purpose. The more you put into your life, the more you would get out. To pursue pleasure for its own sake was wrong.'

Her parents being always busy, and her sister being much older than she was, might she have been a lonely child? 'No. Our family was stable and affectionate, and there was always something going on. People were in and out of the shop by day – customers, commercial travellers, callers who came to see my father about some problem. It may not have suited all girls, but it suited me.'

She does not seem to have had close friends at school, and she does not seem to have been much of a mixer. Home, not school, was the centre of her life. At school she was respected, grudgingly by some, rather than liked. Some of her contemporaries, aware of her ambitions, thought her 'snobby'; some of the older girls resented the self-confident way in which as a junior she put sophisticated questions to visiting lecturers – 'showing off' – and others were jealous of her success. What irked them most was what they called her priggishness. A contem-porary, Mrs John Foster, records: 'Margaret was always well groomed and well behaved. She always seemed grown-up. Mothers would say to their daughters: "Why can't you be more like Margaret Roberts?"'[2]

Though not given to prescriptive advice, Margaret's father told her two things which remained in the front of her mind ever after. One was: 'You must make your own decisions. You don't do something because your friends are doing it. You do it because you think it's the best thing to do.' The second was: 'Don't follow the crowd; don't be afraid of being different. You decide what you ought to do, and if necessary you lead the crowd. But you never just follow.'

She applied this advice to the problem of gaining admission to Oxford University. Though rarely out of the top two or three in her form at a high-quality grammar school, and a good speaker and debater, Margaret was not brilliant academically. When therefore, she announced that she wanted to go to Oxford University, her headmistress, Miss Dorothy Gillies, did not encourage her, pointing out that she knew no Latin, that for admission to Oxford Latin was essential, and that the school could not pay the fee for the entrance examination. Margaret should think again, said Miss Gillies: there were other places of higher education which were more accessible. Undeterred, and supported by her father, Margaret told her headmistress that her father would pay for the entrance examination and for private lessons in Latin.

'She was a very determined single-minded young woman,' said Mrs Gillies several years later. 'She decided it could be done. I took her for private lessons in my room, and arranged for a master at the boys' school to help her too. She passed the Latin exam in one year from scratch.'[3] She found time for extra homework by giving up the piano – with great regret, since she was getting good at it – and crammed a four year Latin course into twelve months.

About this time Miss Gillies asked her what kind of career she hoped to pursue. 'She was incredibly self-possessed. She replied that she was thinking about something like the Indian Civil Service.' Kipling's influence, possibly. 'I pointed out', Miss Gillies said, 'that this would be putting her very much into competition with men. Do you know what she said? "Wouldn't that make it all the more creditable?"'[4]

Margaret decided that when she got to Oxford she would read Chemistry, partly because it would mean less competition than there was to read, for example, History or Classics, and partly because she thought a degree in Chemistry would give her a decent living. But well before she went up to Oxford, she had made up her mind to acquire later a second qualification, in Law. Her interest in Law began when she was sixteen. That year her father was elected mayor of Grantham and became a J P. Margaret frequently accompanied him to the magistrates' court, and consequently made the acquaintance of the Recorder of Grantham, Norman Winning. On one occasion she talked with him about Law as a career. 'I told him that I had a very good Chemistry teacher,' she recorded later,[5] 'and it seemed that if I could get a place at university, I would be doing science. I also told him that the visits to the court had awakened my interest in the Law, but it seemed too late to change to that subject. He told me not to worry about it. He had taken a Physics degree at Cambridge and then gone into the Law and there was no reason why I should not do the same. This of course is what I went on to do. That talk with Mr Winning was really crucial to my life.'

From then on she kept in mind the possibility of later on reading for the Bar, which in due course might help to facilitate her entry into public life. For by the time she went up to Oxford, she was orientated towards, if not a political career, at least one in which political activity would play a primary part. She had not gone up to Oxford with an explicit ambition to become a Member of Parliament, but she had not ruled it out; indeed, according to some of her contemporaries, she had definitely ruled it in – but only as a desirable possibility. In her own words to the author: 'I knew that I had to get my qualifications, then a job, and that political activity would have to come second to that. So I saw politics in terms of voluntary part-time activity on a local level. Looking at it from a strictly financial point of view at the time we are speaking of, MPs were paid £9 a week. I couldn't have done a proper job as an MP on £9 a week to cover secretarial help and living in London as well as a constituency. I had no private income or trade union to back me. I just didn't think of being a Member of Parliament.'

In October 1943 she went into residence at Somerville College, Oxford, and immediately joined the University Conservative Association. It was an extension of life in Grantham. 'I spent a good deal of my spare time talking and discussing political matters, as I had done at home.' She soon became known as an earnest, open, articulate, though not charismatic exponent of sound traditional Conservative principles, who, though not aggressive or intolerant, was more interested in the affirmation of attitudes and principles than in arguments which might lead to fresh conclusions. Nobody expected to convert her, nor did anybody expect to be converted by her; but she was honest, consistent, good-natured, and when there was any hard work to be done she could be relied upon to get it done.

At Oxford, most conscientious students work at their books or attend lectures for the whole of the morning, and work again between tea and dinner, and some evenings after dinner; afternoons are meant for recreation, walks or games. For students of the sciences the timetable is fuller because of the hours spent in the laboratories. 'I worked all day ... a lot of laboratory work in the daytime, and lectures in the early evening.' But Oxford was not all hard work: it opened the door to pleasures she had not enjoyed before.

She had been well suited by the affectionate parental regime culturally centred on the Finkin Street Methodist Church, but as she said, looking back, 'I would have liked some things to have been different. For instance, on Saturday nights some of the girls at my school would go to dances or parties. It sounded very nice. But my sister and I didn't go dancing.' At Oxford things were different. She took lessons in ballroom dancing, and she went to and gave many parties. She was a very good hostess: whatever drinks or food she provided, there was enough to go round, and she saw that everybody met everybody else. 'You might think she was a bit bossy,' one of her contemporaries said, 'but on the other hand you didn't see anybody standing around without anybody to talk to, which you did see at many other people's parties.' Not in fundamentals, but in secondary matters, Oxford for her was, as she said of it herself, 'a period of transition'.

What did she see as the problems of the day when the war ended in 1945? 'On international affairs? The main problem was the re-establishment of a world peace, without the fatal flaws in the treaties made after the First World War. I think the main thing that young people today don't understand is the value of peace. They take peace for granted. In that immediate post-war period we knew what it felt like to be free of the threat of war, and we knew that the peace had to be rebuilt. We knew that the mistakes of the old League of Nations had to be avoided. On the domestic front, the main problem was how to stop a whole way of life being swept away by the Labour Government's policies of nationalization and controls. It looked as if they would nationalize everything and control everything. They seemed to like controls for their own sake, and several new ones were introduced after the war was over. What worried us most was that some young people were growing up who had known no other kind of society.'

What did she think about the Welfare State? Was she opposed to it? 'No. The Beveridge Report and the other measures which became the basis of the Welfare State were planned by Churchill's wartime coalition government, and supported by Conservatives, who were in a very great majority in that Government. Even in the depths of the war we had great faith in the future of Britain. I remember going for a walk with my father during the war when the news was at its most frightening. Neither of us had the slightest doubt that we were going to win. We were typical. We all had faith in the future, in our ability to rise again. Churchill was constantly thinking about the problems of reconstruction. The White Paper on Employment, on which so much post-war policy was built, was published in 1944. It still makes good reading. Churchill's concept of the Welfare State was that society needed a ladder and a safety net – a ladder by which people could improve their lot by effort, and a safety net below which nobody could fall. Post-war Labour Governments produced the safety net, but cut down the ladder.'

In 1946, as President of the Oxford University Conservative Association, Margaret Thatcher attended the annual conference of the Party at Blackpool. Her contemporaries saw her at that time as a middle-of-the-road Conservative who deplored the Labour Party's nationalization programme but not the establishment of the Welfare State. 'There were some highly vocal right-wing young conservatives in those days,' says one of her fellow undergraduates, 'but I thought of Margaret as a humane and moderate supporter of Rab Butler and his Industrial Charter.' By now those fellow undergraduates who knew her at all well took it for granted that she would take an active interest in politics from the moment she went down from the University, and that her objective was the House of Commons. She would not have argued with them.

But first a job. Among other firms, British Xylonite were recruiting bright young people from Oxford. Margaret was taken on as a research chemist, and sent to their plant in Manningtree, Essex. She took digs in Colchester ten miles or so away, travelling to work in the firm's bus. She lost no time in joining the local Conservative Association. From the beginning she devoted herself to the cause; whatever activity the association laid on, Margaret was there to help. She discussed politics in the canteen; she tried to proselytize her fellow employees whilst travelling to and from work in the company bus. She was regarded with a mixture of amusement and respect. Some of her colleagues thought her 'a bit boring at times' but nobody disliked her, and most of them took to her 'because she was friendly and nice'. The worst thing said about her, it seems, was, though she had not had a sheltered life, 'she had a lot to learn about the real world outside'.

Meanwhile, she kept up her connection with Oxford. In 1948 she was asked to go to the Party conference at Llandudno on behalf of the Oxford University Graduates' Association. In the course of the conference she sat down next to an old Oxford friend, on whose other side was the chairman of the Dartford Conservative Association. It transpired that Dartford was without a Conservative candidate for the next election – not surprising since Dartford was a Labour stronghold, held by a particularly popular and respected Member, Norman Dodds. Later in the week, Margaret met some of the Dartford delegates, and when she got back to Colchester, she sent in her request to be considered for the seat. Early in 1949 she was interviewed, and then shortlisted, the youngest candidate and the only woman. Impressed by her ability to deal with complicated matters in clear and simple language, the selection committee recommended her to the Association, which duly adopted her. She was twenty-four years old.

The next general election was confidently predicted for not later than 1950. Dartford was too far from Manningtree to permit her to work for British Xylonite by day and nurse her constituency by night. She decided to move to the other side of the Thames and got a job in Hammersmith in the research department of J. Lyons and Co. She took digs in Dartford, and commuted every day. She had let herself in for a strenuous life, and had shown great determination and initiative. It was at this point that Margaret Roberts met Denis Thatcher. They were introduced at a friend's house in Dartford just after she had been adopted as Conservative candidate. Denis was managing director of his family's paint and chemicals business in Erith. He was thirty-six, had served with the Royal Artillery during the war, and had been mentioned in despatches for bravery at Anzio. A brief early marriage had not survived the war; he had been on his own for several years, and his wife had remarried. On the occasion of their first meeting, Denis drove Margaret to Liverpool Street Station so that she could catch her train to Hammersmith. Later they began to see more of each other and found they had things in common. He was interested in politics and had once stood, unsuccessfully, for Kent County Council. She was a chemist and knew something about his products; Denis was on the financial side of the business, and she was interested in economics. He was very active in the local Conservative Association. They both enjoyed music. They found they both liked simple holidays, such as touring in a car, moving on each day. Denis was strongminded, forthright and direct, not at all introspective; he was good-natured, good-humoured and uncomplicated – the kind of person who appealed to her. In some ways he was like her father: a strong character and very much his own man.

In the general election of January 1950, young Margaret, against a majority of nearly 20,000 in one of the safest Labour seats in the country, put up a spirited fight. Her attacks on the Labour Party were in the mode of Churchill rather than Butler: the election was between the party of freedom and the party of serfdom. Everybody, including the Labour candidate, Norman Dodds, considered she had acquitted herself well, and she reduced the majority by 1,000. In the House of Commons, Labour's majority had fallen from nearly 150 to 5. This meant that another election could not be more than a year or two away, and that the Conservatives were likely to win it. Eighteen months were enough to force Attlee's hand, and in October 1951 Margaret stood for Dartford again, taking another 1,000 off Norman Dodd's majority. She was twenty-six.

In December she and Denis were married at the Wesleyan chapel in City Road, East London. After a honeymoon in Madeira, they began their married life in a flat in Swan Court, off Flood Street, Chelsea. For the next eight years, her life, though not so visible to the wider world as it had been, became extremely busy: being a wife and mother; seeking a parliamentary constituency; and reading for the Bar. After

51

consultation with her friends, particularly with a view to how it might help her political career, she decided to specialize in taxation law, and she was called to the Bar in 1954. A tax barrister is not required in court very much, most of his time being spent in conference with clients and colleagues. One of his most important qualifications is to be able to assimilate and deploy his briefs, and to do so with speed. Margaret Thatcher showed, according to her colleagues, a natural gift for this, which, accompanied by tenacity, a quick grasp of the essence of the case and the ability to express herself succinctly and clearly, would have taken her a long way in that profession had she cared to pursue it. Though she planned to capitalize on her legal knowledge and was to benefit immensely from her legal training, her sights were set now on a political career and on getting back into the mainstream of politics as soon as the twins, Carol and Mark, born in 1953, were old enough to make that possible.

Finding a constituency was not easy. Because of her family commitments and Denis's work, she wanted a safe seat in or near London. There were some disappointments, but in her characteristic way she pressed on without changing tack. In 1957 she was adopted by Finchley, a safe Conservative seat, whose centre was within ten miles as the crow flies from her home and the Houses of Parliament, with a majority at the 1955 election of 12,825. The next general election came two years later, in October 1959. She was elected with a majority of over 16,000.

The fact that she became the MP for Finchley has had a considerable influence on her. A large part of the population of Finchley is Jewish, and some of the most stalwart Conservative supporters come from that sector. Mrs Thatcher has made many friendships among them, learned much from them, and it is partly out of this experience that she is regarded by them as the most pro-Zionist Prime Minister of the century.

In the new House of Commons she got off to a good start, having a remarkable piece of good luck of which she took even more remarkable advantage when, immediately after taking her seat, she drew second place in the ballot for Private Members' bills. Such is the volume of public business in the House that Government business has precedence at all sittings except a very small number, known as Private Members' days, and since the number of Members who would like to introduce bills far exceeds the time available to them, to be drawn high on the ballot is an outstanding opportunity. Mrs Thatcher thus had the chance to present a bill, and, if the Government decided to back it, the likelihood of getting it on the statute book – an auspicious début for a 34-year-old newcomer, and a woman.

After discussion with Ministers concerned and the Party Whips, she agreed to introduce a bill for the reform of that section of the Local Government Act of 1933 which dealt with the admission of the press to meetings of local councils. Some councils had recently, from various motives, been excluding newspapermen from their meetings, and the Government wanted to limit their freedom to do this. Mrs Thatcher introduced her bill in her maiden speech. Whereas nearly all maiden speeches are made long after the new Member first enters the House, and are conventional and non-controversial in character, often related to some matter of concern only to his constituency, Margaret Thatcher's was a high-powered speech delivered to obtain the enactment of a most important piece of national legislation.

The Public Bodies (Admission of the Press to Meetings) Bill was naturally of great interest to newspapers all over the country, and the press gallery was packed. The person who introduced the bill, therefore, even if his or her performance were not particularly distinguished, would be in the limelight. Again, Mrs Thatcher made good use of her chance. Putting forward a clear, constructive, well-reasoned case with great skill and confidence, she had the ear of the House from start to finish. Members and reporters observed that in the course of a twenty-seven-minute speech she did not once refer to a note. For a seasoned Parliamentarian it would have been an outstanding performance; for a novice it was a *tour de force*. Henry Brooke, then Minister of Housing and Local Government, was full of praise for her. The following day, the *Daily Telegraph* pronounced it to be 'of Front Bench quality'. On the opposite side of the House, Barbara Castle praised it. On her own Front Bench, Sir Keith Joseph, Brooke's Parliamentary Secretary, rose to commend 'her cogent, charming, lucid and competent manner'. Her bill became law. All in all it was an auspicious beginning.

The 1959 Parliament lasted five years. During this time, she built steadily and visibly on the success of her début. The features of her interventions were their factual content, her debating skill, the toughness with she would from time to time berate the Opposition, and her readiness on occasion to be critical of the Government, all coming from a very attractive young woman, who invariably spoke in a cool and steady tone. The senior members of her Party soon saw that she had promise. As months went by, her expertise and interest in financial and economic matters became more evident, and in October 1961 she was given her first ministerial job as Joint Parliamentary Secretary to the Ministry of Pensions and National Insurance. The job gave her experience of the problems of people living on social security. MPs of all parties, going to her with their constituents' complaints, found her well informed, conscientious and helpful. She was always available. Her concern for the pensioners did not temper her attitude to her political opponents. In her first speech as a minister the following March, she subjected the House to a blast of facts and figures defending the Government's refusal to increase pensions.

The Conservatives having lost the 1964 general election, Mrs Thatcher continued to deal with pensions, but as Shadow. A year later, when Ted Heath succeeded Sir Alec Home as leader, he gave her Housing and Land. She discharged this wider brief well, and when the party was beaten again in 1966, she was given substantial promotion, being appointed Number Two spokesman on Treasury matters under the Shadow Chancellor, Iain Macleod. He was impressed by her performances in the House, and also by the grasp of financial affairs she displayed in private conversation. She was no mere statutory woman, he told some of his colleagues, but a future Cabinet Minister. A year and a half later, Peter Walker, who had succeeded her as candidate for Dartford and had got to know her quite well, suggested to Ted Heath that he should take her into the Shadow Cabinet: she had, Walker told Heath, high intelligence, debating skill, a formidable character, and a high reputation as a constituency representative, as he knew from talk of her in Dartford. Heath invited her to become Shadow Minister for Fuel and Power. Next she became Shadow Minister for Transport. That she was on her way to high office in the next Conservative Government was publicly marked by the invitation in 1968 to deliver the Conservative Political Centre annual speech at the annual party conference. The following year Heath made her Shadow Minister of Education. When the general election came in 1970, in her six years in opposition she had shadowed five Government departments.

Ted Heath, having won the election, appointed her Minister of Education. She would have a difficult row to hoe. In the last Conservative Party annual conference before the 1970 election, Sir Edward Boyle, Shadow Minister for Education, had aroused the ire of the Party by in their view supporting the programme for the conversion of secondary into comprehensive schools introduced by previous Labour Governments. What in fact he had been doing was to point out that to reverse the process would require considerable legislation and take a good deal of time. The reward for his advice was such a flood of abuse that he decided to withdraw from politics and accept the invitation to become Vice-chancellor of Leeds University. The new Minister for Education was expected to do what Sir Edward had not been able to promise. She must reverse the tide that threatened to make all secondary schools comprehensive.

No Education Minister could have at a stroke reversed the effects of the 1950s legislation. But something could be done at once to halt the process and Mrs Thatcher's first act was to do it. Under the previous Labour Government, the Ministry of Education had issued two 'circulars', 10/65 and 10/66, the effect of which was to require local authorities to make their existing secondary schools and those they proposed to build into comprehensives. On becoming Minister for Education Mrs Thatcher immediately issued a new circular, 10/70, which withdrew 10/65 and 10/66. Henceforth there would be no pressure on local governments to go comprehensive. Since this measure did nothing about comprehensives which already existed, and did not prevent them being built by those local authorities which wanted to build them, it did not satisfy all members of the Conservative Party. What it did was to anger all who favoured comprehensive schools, and to infuriate the Labour Opposition. In the last stages of the Labour Government, Mr Ted Short, then the Labour Government's Minister of Education, had introduced a bill virtually to make comprehensivization compulsory, but it had been aborted by the coming of the general election. Now, the new Minister of Education had halted the process which the bill had been intended to accelerate. Mrs Thatcher was bitterly attacked in the House of Commons, and for these attacks, secondary education being of wide parental interest, there was unstinted media coverage.

There was another problem for her. In the years preceding his victory in 1970, Mr Heath had promised to cut public expenditure and eliminate waste. Education was a good target; Mrs Thatcher would be expected to economize. Yet she was expected as Minister to satisfy the demands and aspirations of the nation as a whole, and especially the parents, students and teachers. Education, by the time Mrs Thatcher took responsibility for it, had become a very hot political issue, not only between the two major parties but also within the Conservative Party; as was evident in the 1969 annual conference, the party faithful thought their leaders were spending to much and being too permissive.·

Apart from the political pressures she came under in this period, she had difficulties in dealing with the Civil Service; with the Service rather than the Servants, since there was nothing personal about her problems, and by the time she had left the Ministry she had made many friends. Her difficulty was with the style and practice of the Service. It was uncongenial to her, especially that of the Ministry of Education which was traditionally inward-looking and academically-minded. She was quick to judge, quick to decide and quick to act. A brisk argument, which she would begin and after which she might change her mind, was perfectly acceptable to her. But when after a decision had been taken she was presented with more argument and more delay in getting something done, she became impatient and did not conceal it. Her civil servants, on the other hand, were not used to dealing with a woman minister, and found her self-confident and sometimes abrasive approach disconcerting and confusing. The view she formed of the Civil Service might have been different if her Permanent Secretary at the Ministry had made a better impression on her. 'He was a most able man', said one of his colleagues, 'but more suited to the High Table of an Oxford college than to the board of a successful business.'

Though the Ministry of Education under Mrs Thatcher suffered fewer cuts in expenditure than any other department except the Social Services (when the Treasury demanded the first round of cuts she fought them more fiercely than anybody else in the Cabinet), the impression grew outside the Government that Education was being victimized. Difficult decisions had to be taken, and these caused tensions within the Ministry. When she announced that schools would no longer supply free milk for seven- to eleven-year-olds there was a public outcry. Her civil servants and some of her colleagues in the Cabinet were disturbed. In an article headed 'The Most Unpopular Woman in Britain' the *Sun* said: 'At a time when Mr Heath's Government is desperately seeking an image of compassion and concern Mrs Thatcher is fast emerging as a liability.' She incurred further adverse publicity when she proposed that the funds of student unions should be controlled by the academic authorities so that union executives could not finance activities not directly related to student welfare, such as political activities outside Britain. Students demonstrated and several academics, including some vice-chancellors, objected, and there were protests from many local authorities. The proposal was withdrawn, temporarily it was said by the Ministry, but was never heard of again.

Mrs Thatcher did not deserve to be an unpopular Minister of Education. She got funds for rebuilding primary schools; she sought to raise the age for leaving school; she would not consider a demand for the abolition of the Open University. In December 1972 her department brought out a White Paper entitled 'Framework for Expansion', a plan for development over the next ten years. While she was Minister, national spending on education exceeded spending on defence for the first time. But such facts were not given as much publicity as her 'milk-snatching'. She was not seen as one of Heath's Butskellite inner cabinet, men like Reginald Maudling, Peter Carrington, Iain Macleod (who died exactly one month after Heath took office), James Prior, Robert Carr, Anthony Barber and Peter Walker. Nor was she seen as what later would be called a Thatcherite – Peter Walker would not have recommended her membership of the Shadow Cabinet if he had thought that she was. It was simply because she was regarded as too junior to be considered one of them; her portfolio did not put her into the group within the Cabinet which discussed and formed the Government's economic policy.

Margaret Thatcher could not have been hailed as a popular success at the Ministry of Education. She had done things which had upset widespread sections of public opinion, many Conservative MPs, and some of her Cabinet colleagues. She had not been able to philosophize or preach a gospel either in Parliament or in the country which might have caught the general imagination. She had been seen to do things that seemed to many to be mean, hard or uncaring, and what she had done that was expansionist, though well received by the press and by educationists, had not been of the kind that would make an impact on the wider public. Education is not usually an exciting or a glamorous political subject, and her views about it were not such as to be able to alter this. Within the Cabinet her views on what mattered altogether more to Mr Heath and his lieutenants, economic policy, were not sought. It was noted that she had been allotted a seat at the Cabinet table well outside the Prime Minister's range of vision. When the Heath Government came to an end in 1974, her stock did not seem to have risen significantly. If at the beginning of her stint as Minister for Education most people would not have thought of her as a future Prime Minister, by the end of it they would have seen nothing to cause them to change their minds.

At the same time, she had answered positively and impressively some important questions which had been asked about her when she was given her first Cabinet post. She had shown at the despatch box that she could make long, detailed speeches on complex and controversial issues. What she said was always relevant, lucid and precise. No orator, no great Parliamentarian, no favourite of the House, she was however a first-class performer, always cool, consistent, steady and strong. She could handle interruptions, ribald jests and barracking as well as any man. She displayed an imperturbability and determination to get her way, a readiness to fight for it, which made her a tough colleague and a formidable opponent. Not many would claim that they could make her out, or say what they thought it was that made her tick. But many

57

might echo a remark that Iain Macleod had made about her in a House of Commons smoking-room discussion about women MPs: 'This one is different.'

She had also shown to those close to her, and to herself, that she could stand up to militant criticism. The worst time for her was the first six months as Minister, as a result of the uproars over the ending of milk for schools and the issue of circular 10/70. She had had to face hostility in Parliament, attacks in the press, and demonstrations in public places which required the intervention of mounted policemen. Heath supported her uncompromisingly in public, but in private some members of the Cabinet expressed doubts about her wisdom and staying-power. By the Christmas holiday of 1970 there was gossip in high circles that she might resign. On Christmas Eve, when Denis could see that she was under stress, and not in the mood to enjoy the holiday, he put it to her that it might be best to 'chuck it all in'. After all, what had she got to prove? She rejected the idea: 'I've got a lot of things to *do*.'

# 7

# UPHILL STRUGGLE

T he four years between the Conservative Party leadership election
in 1975 and the general election in 1979 was a testing time for
Margaret Thatcher as the new and inexperienced leader of the
Conservative Party. At the time she was elected, the Party was in low
heart, depressed by the two defeats of 1974, worried about the state of
its finances, and wondering how it could make a better claim than the
Labour Government to be able to deal with inflation and the power of
the trade unions. Conservative MPs carried the extra psychological
burden of knowing that there were divisions within their Party: perhaps
as many as two thirds of them would have preferred to be led by
somebody other than Margaret Thatcher, and the Shadow Cabinet were
divided about her in something like the same ratio.

On the surface it seemed that the new leader was disturbed neither
by the mood of the Party nor by the feelings of the Shadow Cabinet.
Like matron presiding over a small boys' tea-party, she handed round
the cups and smiled and bossed impartially, generally behaving as
though all was well. In fact, she was aware of the difficulties of her
situation and knew that her position was not secure. Leaving aside the
fact that she was a woman, she had not formerly been a senior member
of the Shadow Cabinet, still less a member of the ruling group, had had
experience of running only one Government department, and under her
predecessor had never been invited to educate herself in the overridingly
important issues of the economy and foreign affairs.

However, she had some advantages which might have been denied her. First, Ted Heath had declined to join the Shadow Cabinet and, though this was to some degree unfortunate since it protracted and advertised the divisions within the Party, on balance it was better for him to be on the back-benches than sitting in the Shadow Cabinet pontificating or sulking. That Whitelaw was the titular head of the Heathite majority was another advantage; though he was shrewd and perceptive, he was not a good speaker or debater in Cabinet, and his good-natured and easygoing personality was not of the kind that would best focus disaffection directed against her. Her greatest advantage was that she was a woman. Just as left-handed boxers have an edge because they fight more right-handed boxers than left-handed ones, women politicians have more experience of dealing with men politicians than the men have of dealing with women. It was not only that the new leader was a woman, but also that she was the kind of woman she was. Her companions in the Shadow Cabinet were used to dealing with women from the aristocracy, upper and middle classes, who had been to a boarding school, and possibly to a finishing school – some of their own wives came from this background – but they had not had so much experience of dealing with the daughter of an upwardly mobile, overtly confident small-town grocer. They were not used to being in a sub-ordinate relationship with a self-made woman used to saying what she thought without being asked, who liked to begin a discussion by putting forward her own views, would interrupt the subsequent speaker as soon as he said something with which she did not agree, and appeared to have the conviction, which she did not trouble to conceal, that the opinion she held was almost certain to be right. This was the impression she created on many of her colleagues in her early months as leader. It may have been heightened by her inner feeling of insecurity. She felt she had to assert herself and make herself strong before her opponent had the chance to embattle himself against her.

However, as was often to be the case in years to come, though she spoke boldly, she acted with caution. One of the features of her regime in its early days was the number of Heathites she had retained in the Shadow Cabinet, which, as the author put it to her, still looked very much like the Cabinet which had lost the previous general election. 'However good tempered the election of a new leader is,' she replied, 'it is bound for a time to cause divisions in the Party. There's nothing unnatural about that. If divisions didn't exist, there would have been no need for an election in the first place. But when the election is over, the new leader must do what is possible to restore the underlying unity and heal the wounds. In 1957, after the Suez crisis, Harold Macmillan succeeded Anthony Eden at a time when the Conservative Party had been much divided. Sir Edward Boyle had resigned from the Eden Government as a protest against the action that Eden had taken over Suez. Soon after he became Prime Minister, Macmillan, though he had supported Eden, asked Boyle to come back. He acted to reunite the party, and he succeeded.'

Outside Parliament and the Shadow Cabinet, her first big test, in so far as one could be predicted, would be the Party conference in October. How she performed there and how she was received could well be a measure of what she had achieved. In those first eight months it could not be said that she had achieved very much. Apart from the removal of Mr Heath and the substitution of Mrs Thatcher, little seemed to have changed. There was no talk of Thatcherism, nor a great deal outside the Shadow Cabinet of monetarism, and her speeches did not express a new Conservative orthodoxy. But in hindsight it is clear that she was making changes out of which Thatcherism would grow, and on the eve of the conference she began to make statements which, looking back, make this strikingly clear. 'Tory ideals', she said just before the conference opened, 'have not been upheld and defended explicitly enough. We all have to share the blame for that. In the next election we shall be fighting with a clear philosophy which asserts and protects the rights of the citizen and his family against ever increasing power and direction by governments . . . There must be more personal savings, more personal control of one's own life. Too much is now controlled by the State. At the moment, the State spends what it considers suitable, and leaves the remainder in the hands of the taxpayer. Currently this is about 46%. In the next election the Conservative Party will go to the country asserting the need to leave more of what is earned in the hands of the taxpayer to spend for himself.'

She spoke of the need for the Conservatives to practise 'the politics of persuasion', as opposed to what she called the 'technocratic politics' which even Conservative Governments had practised in the past, 'by which I mean trying to get political solutions by implementing a set of economic and industrial policies which may have been theoretically correct, but which were not necessarily acceptable'. The emphasis, she said, should be on persuasion. 'There's a limit to what you can arrange; more is achieved by people doing things for themselves.' Then she said something which was to become an important part of 'Thatcherism', conveying her vision of an approach to government different from that of her predecessor: 'You can present people with ideas they may come to believe in, and as a result of them they will act, if they have the opportunities. Presenting people with opportunities is part of what politics is about.'

It was also becoming clear that at any rate with the Conservative rank and file she had developed a considerable rapport, and that this was extending beyond the Conservative Party. The phrases she chose, the ideas she expressed, the tone of her remarks, the level of her appeals on the one hand and denunciations on the other, were much more related to the man and woman in the street than those delivered by most of her less adventurous colleagues in the course of the previous twenty years. Particularly when she spoke about immigration, the trade unions, and Government spending, she could strike chords in the mind of the common man as none of her senior colleagues in the Shadow Cabinet could. In the House of Commons she frequently delivered facts and figures like a professor, and argued on a highly sophisticated level. But she could also lay about her on the level of everyday argument, deliver personal attacks in the language of the market place, and more than hold her own if a shouting match began. Her voice was refined, her appearance was elegant, her manner cool and calm, but the com-monsense and basic values she expressed came from the grocer's daughter. Among the other qualities she now displayed was that of being the nearest thing to a demagogue the leaders of the Conservative Party had ever produced. She bid fair to become the first Conservative Populist.

The main criticism of her by the time the conference came round was her lack of experience of foreign affairs. In September, a few weeks beforehand, she made a visit to the United States which was given a good deal of favourable publicity. After she got back, she said, 'A grasp of the basic problems of foreign policy is what is most necessary today, rather than detailed diplomatic knowledge. This is acquired through meeting foreign statesmen here, and meeting them abroad in their own countries, and at conferences, and by discussing matters with our own experts.' That more than satisfied the Conservative Party for the time being.

In the weeks before the conference in October, there had been many reports of tensions within the Shadow Cabinet, of misgivings within the Parliamentary Party, and of a feeling among Conservatives up and down the country that the Parliamentarians had been disloyal to Mr Heath and had made a mistake in electing a woman to succeed him. There was a growing feeling, according to these reports, that Mrs Thatcher, tolerable as a stop-gap leader, would not stay the distance and could not lead the Party into the next general election. These reports gave rise to speculation: would such sentiments be expressed at the conference, in open or in coded language? Would there be a rift?

Nobody was more aware of what might happen than Mrs Thatcher, and when she arrived in Blackpool there were some disagreeable experiences for her. Ted Heath walked to his seat on the conference platform directly, without pausing to greet her. In the next few days, though they were frequently seen in public at the same time and place, he did not acknowledge her, and gave the impression that he was trying to avoid her. Some of the senior members of the Shadow Cabinet, while observing the proprieties and keeping up appearances – at the minimum – were clearly not at ease with her. At one point during the conference, it was whispered, Willie Whitelaw was to have had a private meeting with her at the end of the day, but failed to turn up; after a two-hour wait, one of her aides telephoned Mr Whitelaw, who said that he had been very busy and it was now too late for the meeting to take place.

The big and, in her case, critical moment of the Conservative annual conference is the delivery of the leader's winding-up speech on the last day. She drove down to make it, accompanied by her husband. He could see that she was apprehensive. He put his hand on hers. Some time later, looking back, he told a friend, 'She was a little nervous, but I was more frightened than any time in the war.' Nevertheless, the speech was well received. Even allowing for the manifestation of loyalty, confidence and devotion which the Conservative Party habitually accords the leader, the ovation given to her was much more than she could have hoped for and certainly more than some of the Shadow Cabinet felt she had deserved.

In the three and a half years which passed between that conference and the general election of May 1979, the political situation changed considerably. The problem of inflation, which had been chronic, now became acute. The cost of living, mainly as a result of the dramatic rise in oil prices after the Yom Kippur war of October 1973, a factor which pervaded the whole of the economy, rose to an unprecedented level at an unprecedented speed. The prices and incomes policy introduced by the Labour Government could not cope with it. The Retail Price Index had gone up 75% in 1975. At the end of 1975 inflation was at 26%. The Labour Government, by strenuous efforts which later were to take their toll, succeeded in reducing that, but even so prices more than doubled between the beginning of 1974 and the end of 1978.

The economic crisis came to a head in the summer of 1976. Labour had inherited a deteriorating economic position from the Conservatives in 1974 and the unprecedented inflation rate of 26% was at least partly a direct result of Heath's 'dash for growth' policy of 1972–4 when his Chancellor, Anthony Barber, had presided over a series of expansionary budgets. By 1976, the economic situation was no longer tenable and Government was forced to start borrowing huge quantities of money to finance the burgeoning Public Sector Borrowing Requirement, while sterling continued on its precipitous downward spiral.

The worsening situation focused attention on the money supply; a factor in the economy as a whole that had attracted only scant interest before 1974, but which quickly came to dominate economic thinking in Whitehall. The money supply was now generally acknowledged to be going out of control because of Barber's expansionary budgets and fuelling inflation. The Labour Government, however, proved to be understandably reluctant to get to grips with the crisis – principally because the Treasury solutions of public expenditure cuts and statutory wage controls would naturally be politically offensive to the Government's own supporters in the trade union movement who would stand to lose most under such policies.

There was, none the less, a realization in Whitehall that Keynesian economics were simply no longer working; the main enemy was now runaway inflation, and there was nothing in Keynes which seemed to tell one how to deal with that. Even before the International Monetary Fund (IMF) imposed monetary targets on the Government in 1976 as a condition of its loan, these monetary targets had already become a primary focus of attention in the Treasury. The attention on the money supply allowed the Government to see that money growth was running well above the Treasury's confidential 12% target and, as Bernard Donoughue has written, this meant that 'Monetarism already secretly ruled and we were failing the basic monetarist test.'

This heralded a fundamental change in Government economic policy. All post-war governments up to 1976 had made it their principal task to maintain full employment – the historic task of Keynesianism and the Butskellite consensus. During 1976 what Callaghan called the 'overriding priority' shifted from maintaining full employment to beating inflation. These two aims were now perceived to be mutually exclusive – the choice was between high employment and hyper-inflation or low and stable inflation accompanied by high unemployment. The monetarist argument claimed that the first alternative now also courted the risk of a collapse of the currency and thus ultimate financial ruin. As William

Keegan has explained, the main thrust of the monetarist argument was 'inflationary financial policies were being pursued in the name of full employment, and they contained the seeds of their own destruction'. The Labour Government of 1976 decided to break with the past and pursue the second course.

Bernard Donoughue watched the switch in policy from his desk in Downing Street as head of the Prime Minister's Policy Unit, as Callaghan proceeded to adopt 'a tighter monetary policy, with big expenditure cuts and higher unemployment being an inescapable force of that policy'. The Labour Government had to force through public expenditure cuts of £1 billion in July 1976, and in order to obtain financial backing from the IMF agreed to institute a further £2.5 billion programme of cuts in October of that year. It was thus Jim Callaghan who had reluctantly to preside over the first dose of 'Thatcherite' remedies to be administered to the British economy in a prescription that was accompanied by a rise in unemployment to $1\frac{1}{2}$ million. The writing was on the wall for those who cared to read.

There was bitter opposition to these measures within the Labour Party, most of it political rather than economic. Comparisons were made with Ramsay MacDonald's behaviour in 1931 when, according to the Labour Party faithful, he had thrown the Party's programme overboard – and with it their electoral prospects – to get a loan from the New York bankers. Attlee had described MacDonald's conduct as 'the biggest political betrayal in the history of this country'. At the general election a few weeks later the Party was nearly ruined. Atavistic fears were roused in 1976; once again, in the eyes of the faithful, a Labour Government was putting an axe through its Ark and Covenant. One junior Minister resigned, protesting that 'The Labour Party is the party of public expenditure'. Monetarism might have been ruling the roost in the Treasury and the IMF, but it was still very much a minority view outside.

None the less, powerful opinion formers were at work in the press to publicize the monetarist doctrines and to apply them to the particulars of the British situation. Foremost among them were two financial journalists, Peter Jay on *The Times* and Samuel Brittan (brother of the one-time Tory Cabinet Minister Leon) of the *Financial Times*. It is indicative of the gathering monetarist consensus that was now crystallizing amongst those acquainted with the country's desperate economic plight in 1976 that it was to one of these journalists, Peter Jay, that Callaghan should have looked for help in describing the severity of Britain's economic disease and the harsh nature of the required medicine to what would be his most hostile audience, the Labour Party Conference. Jay, Callaghan's son-in-law, 'prepared' those passages of Callaghan's speech on 28 September 1976 that mark the public breach with the Keynesian consensus which Callaghan was reluctantly to introduce and which Mrs Thatcher was positively to embrace:

> For too long, perhaps ever since the war, we postponed facing up to fundamental choices and fundamental changes in our society and in our economy. That is what I mean when I say we have been living on borrowed time. For too long this country – all of us, yes, this conference too – has been ready to settle for borrowing money abroad to maintain our standards of life, instead of grappling with the fundamental problem of British industry.... The cosy world we were told would go on for ever, where full employment would be guaranteed at a stroke of the Chancellor's pen, cutting taxes, deficit spending – that cosy world is gone.... We used to think that you could just spend your way out of a recession to increase employment by cutting taxes and boosting Government spending. I tell you in all candour that that option no longer exists and that insofar as it ever did exist it worked by injecting inflation into the economy.

The speech marks a watershed in post-war British politics: the tide was now running for Thatcher. The political and economic climate at the time was one in which Heath might have defeated the miners and have been re-elected in 1974. The continuation of winds and temperatures favoured the germination of Thatcherism. It was Callaghan who in 1976 pronounced the death of the cosy world of Keynes and ushered in the harsh winds of Thatcherism. This, up to a point, was her good luck. Characteristically, she spotted it and made the most of it.

So much did she make of it that several of her most senior colleagues did their best to rein her in. It was not what she said about monetarism that worried them as what she said about the trade unions. On monetary policy Mrs Thatcher did not say a great deal, though she said enough to make it clear that she was entirely with those in her Shadow Cabinet who advocated monetarist policies. These members were diplomatic in talking about monetarism in public, and were restrained and sensible in talking about it in private. A great deal of the credit for this goes to Geoffrey Howe. He persuaded Mrs Thatcher to allow him to try and work out an economic policy acceptable to – as would be said now – both 'Wets' and 'Drys', and to this end got her to agree to the setting up of a committee to be called the Economic Reconstruction Group, which he would chair as Shadow Chancellor. With great judgement, Howe appointed Adam Ridley to be secretary to the group. It was an imaginative move: Ridley had previously been one of Heath's key economic advisers and a former member of the Think-Tank. He had a great knowledge of Conservative economic policy, had come to see where the teachings of Keynes could no longer be applied, and had an excellent mind and an agreeable personality. Howe and Ridley laboured long, hard and patiently to find as much common ground as possible between the leading monetarists on the committee, Keith Joseph and David Howell, and the leading Heathite, Jim Prior. Their efforts were to be rewarded. When, in October 1977, the Group produced a fifty-four-page booklet entitled *The Right Approach to the Economy* as the basis of Conservative economic policy for the next election, the monetarists were happy to accept it and the Heathites could claim that it was much like the economic policy with which Heath had gone into the election of 1970.

If there was one section of the booklet which more than any other was a tribute to Howe's diplomacy and Ridley's ingenuity, it was a paragraph relating to incomes policy. Many of Mrs Thatcher's colleagues, notably Prior, who had had the responsibility of dealing with the unions and knew that he would have to shoulder it again, were worried by her hostility to the idea of an incomes policy. She thought not that it was useless, but that it was a dangerous interference with economic and political freedom, and inconsistent with Conservative Party principles. Prior, on the other hand, was convinced that no government of either party could manage the economy without an incomes policy and that, though a statutory policy could be avoided, a voluntary policy was essential to deal with those who worked in the public sector of industry and in the civil services, vast groups whose pay increases had a distortionary effect on the economy as a whole. Prior reminded his colleagues in the Economic Reconstruction Group that in opposition the Conservatives had denounced all incomes policies, but after coming to power had seen no option but to adopt one. Everybody else would remember that, he said, and to denounce all incomes policies now might well cost the Party votes in the next election, while if it won that election and again found no choice but to resort to an incomes policy, its authority in administering it would be gravely weakened. In *The Right Approach to the Economy*, therefore, the following words appeared: 'In framing its monetary and other policies the Government must come to *some* conclusions about the likely scope for pay increases if excess public expenditure or large-scale unemployment is to be avoided; and this estimate cannot be concealed from the representatives of employers and unions whom it is consulting.'

The inclusion of this passage was not welcomed by Mrs Thatcher.

She resisted it until the very last moment, and all the persuasive powers of Sir Geoffrey had to be deployed before she finally gave way. In his memoirs Mr Prior records: 'Margaret absolutely refused to allow the document to be published as a Shadow Cabinet Paper. So we were warned, or perhaps it was fairer to say, put on notice.' Looking back, this is not surprising, for the statement was not in line with the direction in which Mrs Thatcher's mind was moving. She was giving much thought to inflation, wage demands, and the unions. In 1977, introduced by Sir Keith Joseph, a new man had entered the circle of Thatcherite thinkers, John (later Sir John) Hoskyns. An extremely able man, who had made a fortune as a computer consultant, he was soon asked to write a paper on Britain's problems for the attention of Mrs Thatcher and Sir Geoffrey Howe. This he did with the assistance of another of Sir Keith's acquaintances, Norman Strauss, then employed by Unilever. In their paper, Hoskyns and Strauss strongly contended that the view that governments must humour the unions was altogether out of date. On the contrary, they argued, public opinion now was that it was high time the unions were put in their place: the promise of a tough line with them was a potential vote-winner. Though this conclusion was not in line with the views which Prior and others had been urging on Mrs Thatcher, it was much in line with her own. For some time to come comparatively little of Hoskyns's input showed in Mrs Thatcher's speeches, and those of her colleagues who deplored his influence did not draw attention to it. Official Conservative Party policy on the trade unions continued to be that of *The Right Approach to the Economy*.

In July 1978 there was a debate of the highest importance in the Commons on the Government's White Paper on pay policy. Mr Callaghan put forward a well-argued defence of his pay policy, and then took Mrs Thatcher to task. Her contribution to discussion of the country's economic problems, he said, was negative; the country still did not know what her party really stood for. He castigated her for her 'one-sentence' panaceas. She responded with a full-blooded critique of Government policy, in which she gave full rein to her conviction that incomes policies, statutory or voluntary, were a waste of time. She said the things and reverted to the tone against which she had been warned by Prior and Thorneycroft, the Conservative Party chairman. Many on her own side of the House listened in silence. From the Government benches came angry and derisory shouting. The following day she received a bad press, with some of the usually pro-Conservative newspapers critical of her.

Some of the Shadow Cabinet chose to regard the performance as an outburst, an aberration, a temporary swerving from the way they thought they had persuaded her to tread. They were wrong. The speech was a manifestation of the fact that Mrs Thatcher was moving away from the middle ground which the Conservatives had tried to occupy ever since the war, and was taking up another position. Sir Keith was now making speeches in which he said that the post-war strategy of trying to occupy this middle ground had been proved bad for the Conservative Party and might be fatal for the country. Sir Keith's argument went as follows: the further to the left the legislation of Socialist governments took the country, the further to the left the Conservatives had to move in order to keep on middle ground. The result was that over a period of years the Conservative leadership had committed the Party to policies which were against the Party's principles – policies of huge, rising public expenditures; the maintenance and, in order to maintain them, the subsidizing of nationalized industries; the preservation of controls and regulations of the proper activities of trade unions and employers which the unions and employers should be left to manage for themselves; regulation of the free markets; a general expansion of the public sector of the national economy, and reduction of the private. In short, Sir Keith declared, with a wealth of well-cited fact and opinion, the Labour Party had been taking Britain down the road to becoming a Socialist state, and in their pursuit of the middle ground the Conservatives had been virtually helping them. The Conservative Party had been an accessory after the fact.

Mrs Thatcher shared Keith Joseph's views: the search for the increasingly dangerous middle road must be abandoned. In his memoirs Jim Prior cites a conversation he had with her which is interesting in this context. 'Fairly typical of the mood around this time', he records, 'was an argument I had with Margaret which did become more ferocious than usual. In the end I had to say that I was sorry but I had to leave. To add a little salt to the wound, I added that the reason I had to leave was to attend the relaunch of Harold Macmillan's book *The Middle Way*. She looked at me and said: "Standing in the middle of the road is very dangerous, you get knocked down by the traffic from both sides." '

In talking like this to Prior, Mrs Thatcher was already articulating the divisions that were besetting the Labour Cabinet at the same time. Whilst Mrs Thatcher had only the courage of her own convictions to argue for the demise of the much cherished but economically untenable middle way, the Labour Cabinet was forced to similar conclusions in their discussions over the terms of the IMF loan in October 1976. These discussions revealed that the Cabinet now split three ways into those who supported the Treasury Ministers' calls for close monetary control and massive spending cuts to secure the loan; those who supported the left's 'Alternative Strategy' of import controls and a siege economy; and finally the group who supported the leading Labour theorist in the Cabinet, Anthony Crosland – it was the Croslandites who supported the 'Middle Way' approach and who were appalled by the two alternatives on offer. The 'Alternative Strategy' of the left was expounded for the benefit of the Cabinet by Tony Benn; but his theories were ruthlessly exposed by the Treasury Ministers, who tore his arguments to shreds. When the Tribunite MP Brian Sedgmore met Healey in private to try and convert him to the 'Alternative Strategy', 'Healey just fell about laughing.'[1]

What was thus really significant about this Cabinet debate on the IMF terms, for both the Labour and Conservative parties, was the position of those occupying the middle ground – the Croslandites in the Labour Cabinet and the Butskellites in the Conservative Party. It was these two positions that now totally collapsed in the face of the economic reality. With the 'Alternative Strategy' of the Bennites rejected, it was left to the numerically more numerous Croslandites to argue a case against the IMF cuts; and it was when *their* arguments in Cabinet collapsed under the dead weight of Treasury statistics that one can say that the policies of post-war consensus Keynesianism were proved to be no longer viable. One Labourite observed the phenomenon from close quarters: 'That was the day Croslandism died. He said to me: "This is nonsense, but we must do it." He knew it meant the abandonment of his position as a revisionist theorist. He knew he was going up a cul-de-sac. It was a tormenting time for him. I watched him torturing himself.'[2]

In the face of the full horror of Britain's dire economic plight, the political centre had ignominiously collapsed. Croslandism, middle of the road politics and Butskellism were no longer viable economic alternatives; politics had to become more polarized and it was Mrs Thatcher who embraced the cause of the Treasury and spelt out the need for a radical policy change.

Just as Callaghan had announced the theoretical death of Butskellism in his conference speech, so he supported Healey round the Cabinet table in giving practical effect to his speech by accepting the IMF medicine which entailed cutting public expenditure and following published monetary targets. Labour were reluctant converts to the new economic thinking, but none the less, the first monetarist government was a Labour government – albeit, as one observer has written, 'with a deep reservation that it moved into this posture less out of a deep conviction than because of "force majeure".'[3]

These reservations were clearly demonstrated by Healey's last budget in March 1978 which tried to back the trend by reflating the economy to the tune of £2.56 billion. This, however, only served to build up a head of inflationary pressure which Mrs Thatcher inherited in 1979; but it probably also contributed to the 'winter of discontent' by inflating wage demands. Healey's last Keynesian fling, calculated to appeal to the electorate in what everyone assumed was election year, thus merely underlined the point that these policies were no longer good enough.

What Mrs Thatcher did was to make a virtue of these very economic policies that the Labour Government so reluctantly implemented and which Healey tried to wriggle out of in 1978. She would argue in the 1979 election that such policies were indeed necessary and that they would cause much short-term misery in terms of unemployment and economic dislocation; a prospect that had so alarmed her own Cabinet Wets when her own government had to get down to making the same unpalatable decisions. But she went further, and argued that such unappetizing medicine would also yield excellent long-term benefits in terms of *new* jobs created and *new* industrial enterprises to replace the archaic and unproductive industries that monetarism would do away with. But by arguing for monetarism and public expenditure cuts in 1979 she was suggesting nothing novel; she was merely making a virtue of what was already economic necessity.

The summer of 1978 gave promise of some economic recovery. By early September it was widely and confidently assumed that Mr Callaghan would call an election for October and when he announced that he would make a special appearance on television on 7 September there was a general expectation that he would reveal the date. To almost universal surprise, he declared that there would be no election that year. Some of his closest associates felt that he had deceived them. Most of the trade union leaders felt let down. Their sense of grievance was to matter greatly the following year.

That month it was clear that the Government's pay policy was in disarray, but the Conservatives, it was also clear, were having trouble in convincing the public that they had a better way of dealing with inflationary wage demands. The divisions of opinion within the Shadow Cabinet which *The Right Approach to the Economy* had sought to reconcile or conceal became evident again. On 11 October, at the annual party conference, Mr Heath made a speech in which he said, 'If the Government's pay policy has broken down, there is nothing here for gloating . . . There is a part to play for incomes policy in the economy.' On television the same day he said, 'Free collective bargaining produces massive inflation.' This was the opposite of what Sir Keith Joseph, Shadow Minister for Industry, and Sir Geoffrey Howe, Shadow Chancellor, were telling the massed cohorts of the conference with the full authority of the leader. Mrs Thatcher did not shrink from underlining the difference between the official party view and that of Mr Heath: in her winding-up speech on the last day she made an unqualified promise to restore free collective bargaining when the Conservative Party returned to power. There was tremendous applause. It was clear that she, not Mr Heath, was representing the views of the Party faithful.

The rift between herself and Mr Heath was not something to point up at a time when a general election was in the offing, an election in which economic policy and the relationship between the Government and the unions would almost certainly be the central issue. The polls suggested that Labour was improving its position. Gallup, on 26 October, gave Labour a lead of $5\frac{1}{2}$ points over the Conservatives. The results of two by-elections added credence to this report.

Some of the Conservative leaders attributed this disturbing showing to public concern about the difference of views on economic policy between the present and former leader. When Parliament reassembled two weeks later, Mrs Thatcher elected to minimize the differences between her and Mr Heath on the one hand and between her and the Government on the other. In the debate on the Queen's Speech – which, so far as Mr Callaghan and Mrs Thatcher were concerned, became virtually a debate on the Government's incomes policy – she said: 'Of course in this matter we share the same ends as the Government . . . I had the impression from a number of things the Prime Minister said that we also agreed on a large number of means as well.' She predicted that the phased pay policy was at the end of its tether; but it would have to be accepted that 'most settlements will have to be within single figures'. She went on to say that in the Opposition's view the target figure for settlements should be an *average*, and become a *norm* only under emergency conditions. Two days later on television she represented the difference between her views and those of Mr Heath as no more than the difference between average and norm. Some of the things she said were not completely comprehensible to all members of the public, but the cracks which had appeared in policy now seemed to have gone, to the relief of party planners with an eye on the coming election.

Though the Heathite majority within the Shadow Cabinet might well have thought at this time that Mrs Thatcher had been brought into line with their view of economic policy, they were to find that this was not the case and that public opinion was moving more in her direction than in theirs. This was partly due to the rise in her personal standing, and partly to events.

The winter of 1978–9 brought a series of strikes for higher pay which resulted in industrial output falling to the level of the three-day working week of 1974. The stoppage which hit the country hardest was that of the lorry drivers, compounded by separate action by the tanker drivers. The road transport workers' strike, launched in support of a pay rise demand of 25%, was a massive attack on the Government's official policy of holding all wage increases down to 5%. The strikes caused damage to the economy, disruption of services and discomfort to the citizen. Picketing, especially secondary picketing to prevent the delivery of goods to and from factories by transport not directly involved in the dispute, resulted in angry scenes and considerable violence. Other workers, including many in public services, also went on strike, including ambulance staff, water and sewerage workers, gravediggers and roadmen. The dustmen's strike left piles of uncollected garbage on city streets. In Liverpool unburied bodies were stored in disused premises. A strike of school caretakers caused half a million children to be kept at home. Four public service unions announced they would join in a programme of selective industrial action to be continued indefinitely until their claims were met. All this coincided with extremely severe weather. The combination of strikes, deprivations, physical discomfort and violence on the picket lines angered and alarmed the public.

The television cameras had a field day. Such sights as a NUPE official on picket line duty outside a hospital refusing to let in any sick people was bad enough; but when an interviewer then enticed the official into admitting that 'if people died, so be it', it caused a widespread revulsion throughout the country. The public service sector unions were revealed in a stark new light.

It happened that at the height of this stressful visitation, Mr Callaghan was away at an international summit in sunny Guadeloupe. When he returned to London on 10 January tanned and relaxed, he was met at the airport by a large number of reporters, one of whom asked him a question about the 'mounting chaos' he had come home to. Mr Callaghan replied: 'I don't think that other people in the world would share the view that there is mounting chaos.' He was reported in some papers to have asked: 'Crisis? What crisis?'

The words attributed to Mr Callaghan merely exacerbated the temper of a public already sorely tried. The situation in January gave Mrs Thatcher an unprecedented opportunity to popularize her views on the need to curb the powers of the trade unions. She took full advantage of it. Interviewed by Brian Walden in a much advertised and extensively reported television programme on 14 January, she called on the Prime Minister 'to re-establish the authority of the Government under the law'. She demanded an all-Party agreement to introduce legislation to control secondary picketing, secure Government-financed secret ballots on strike action, to contract with the unions to ensure peaceful picketing, and negotiate a deal with workers in essential services by which they would undertake never to strike in pursuit of pay claims. Surveying the disruptions and disputes, the anger and the violence, she went on: 'The case is now overwhelming. There will be no solution to our difficulties which does not include some restriction on the power of the unions.' In a speech a few days later she said: 'The essence of democracy is that no group in the nation should be more powerful than Parliament ... It is painfully obvious that Mr Callaghan will not do a single thing, because the unions will not let him.'

The zest with which their leader took advantage of her opportunity alarmed some of her colleagues: would she overdo it? Jim Prior, the Shadow Minister for Employment, who would have to deal with the unions when the Conservatives came to power, recorded in his memoirs: 'She wanted to take tougher measures than I was prepared to support, and in fact tougher than anything we have since done in Government. I was telling her all the time that we should take things steadily, and not believe that we could solve all the problems by draconian legislation.' He urged her to moderate her language and her tone. He had some success. 'Her party political broadcast at this time [17 January] was remarkably restrained, given her real feelings.' But he concedes candidly in hindsight that the winter of discontent put her 'much more in tune with the people'. The proposals for trade union reform which she had outlined in the television interview – with some of them she had again gone beyond official Party policy – had been well received by the public. She had registered an important success. She had not only exploited the state of the nation to obtain support for her policy of curbing union power: she had gone a long way to converting the trade union issue from one related to inflation to the deeper and more emotive issue of law and order. Jim Prior's approach to the problem was not so much overtaken as made to look out of date.

Quite apart from the law and order issue, and what capital Mrs Thatcher might make of it, the Government now had a formidable problem on its hands: its pay policy, to which it had rightly attached so much importance, had collapsed under the mass assault made on it by wage demands from so many workers in the public sector. The Government was forced to give way. Many public service workers were soon being awarded increases of 10%. The pay limit increase of 5%, to which the Government's reputation had become attached, was a thing of the past. More workers were given increases in February, more again in early March. The Prime Minister admitted publicly that he had not anticipated such resistance to the Government's guidelines.

In March the Government announced that a new standing commission on pay comparability would be set up with Professor Hugh Clegg as chairman. As we shall see later, during the election campaign Mrs Thatcher announced that the Conservatives would accept and implement the commission's recommendations when they came to power. That undertaking undoubtedly won friends for her, but it was not in line with her previously declared economic policy, and the Clegg recommendations, when they were published, were to be an embarrassment in her early days in Downing Street. It was ironic, therefore, that the setting up of the commission, while out of line with her policy, was so much in line with the views of Mr Heath. During the winter of discontent, he had said, in effect, that the country's industrial troubles were due not to protest against wage restraint, which he continued to advocate as the basis of Government policy as it had been under him, but to the dissatisfaction of workers with their relative standing in society as signified by their remuneration.

After intensive and hasty negotiations with the trade union leaders, on 23 February, the Government arrived at a concordat with them, and the TUC agreed to produce a voluntary code of behaviour to deal with picketing, the closed shop, strike ballots and strikes. For the few weeks that the Government was destined to remain in power, a kind of peace replaced industrial anarchy. But the message was clear: the Government could no longer control the unions. The co-operation between unions and government, which had led to real economic progress in the previous three years, had come to an end. The union leaders could no longer control their rank and file, much less the militants. This was partly the result of animosity towards Callaghan. Many union leaders felt that he had deceived them about the date of the general election. They had, they said, been led to expect it in October and they had not bargained on having to hold wages down for several months beyond that. So the Government's claim that only Labour could handle the unions was severely dented. Labour's trump electoral card had become their Achilles heel.

As many people in the Labour movement recognized at the time, here lay the ultimate and crushing irony of the situation. For it was those very public sector unions who would stand to lose most under Mrs Thatcher's widely publicized programme of public expenditure cuts that had done most to destroy the only Government that could protect them from those cuts! After three years of pay restraint, the unions seemed to wilfully drag the Callaghan Government towards electoral disaster. In effect, the public sector unions elected Mrs Thatcher to power in 1979 – a point that was not lost on Bernard Donoughue in Downing Street, who was to write afterwards of the TUC General Council that if it had 'been constituted of personal representatives of Mrs Thatcher it could not have acted more effectively in the Conservative leader's interest'.

After May 1977 Labour's majority would not have secured it in power had it not been able to make a formal pact with the Liberal Party, who hoped the arrangement would lead to the granting of proportional representation. The pact was buttressed by support from those Scottish and Welsh MPs who hoped that in return Mr Callaghan would introduce legislation for devolution. It was not long before the Liberals came to the conclusion that a general election, in which it would suit them to assert their independence *vis-à-vis* both major parties, was much more likely to hasten proportional representation than was the pact. In May 1978, therefore, they gave notice that the pact would terminate at the end of the Parliamentary session. They kept their word. After this, the Government had to rely for its majority on the Welsh and Scots, who agreed to support it on condition that it kept its word to submit the devolution issue to a Welsh and Scottish referendum. On 1 March the referendum was held. In Wales, devolution was decisively rejected. It was also rejected in Scotland, but the Scots claimed that the majority required was unjust and unrealistic, and that, if the figure had been a reasonable one, devolution would have been accepted. The Welsh and Scottish MPs followed the example of the Liberals. The Government's days seemed numbered.

Seizing her chance, Mrs Thatcher tabled a motion of no confidence in the Government. The Liberals and the Scottish Nationalists, and eight

Ulster Unionists, voted with the Conservatives and the Government was defeated. 'Now that the House has declared itself,' said Mr Callaghan, 'we shall take our case to the country.' He called a general election for 3 May.

Despite the winter of discontent, and the humiliating circumstances in which the Government had been defeated, it looked by no means certain that Labour would not be returned to power. Though polls in January had shown that public opinion was swinging towards the Conservatives and that the Labour Party was losing support on account of its association with the trade unions, in late February and in March, after the worst of the winter of discontent was over, the polls began to show a swing back to Labour.

Such was the state of British politics that the campaign was dominated by the duel between the leaders of the two major parties. Mr Callaghan projected himself as an experienced, urbane, amiable elder statesman who assumed reasonably that in view of what he and his Party had done for the country it was common sense that he be re-elected. Mrs Thatcher presented an image that was entirely different from his, and different from that of previous Conservative leaders – aggressive, challenging and radical. She was prepared to disavow, however mildly, but unmistakably, the policies of past Conservative Governments. She was ready to make statements about Party policy which had not been cleared with the Shadow Cabinet or with her policy advisers. She was ready to say how she would run not only the country but also her Party.

A few weeks before the election was announced she gave an interview to the author, published in *The Observer*, 25 February, 1979, in which she made a number of remarks which even some of her supporters thought did more good to her reputation for outspokenness than to her chances of taking a united party into the election. Asked why she had offered herself for election to the leadership four years previously, she showed that age had not withered her candour: 'There *had* to be an election. The 1922 Committee was insisting on an election. . . . We had had four general elections and we had lost three of them . . . The time had come for rethinking. . . .' Had she felt that she was standing for something that was different from what Mr Heath had stood for? 'I felt, and the Conservatives who elected me presumably felt, that the next leader of the Party must clearly stand up against the direction in which the country had been moving under both previous Governments. We had moved too much towards a society controlled by Government. . . . My aim was, and is, not the extension but the limitation of Government. . . . At the time of the leadership contest which began in November 1974, we were coming to a stage when there really wasn't a party which was clearly standing for the limitation of Government.'

Asked about the extent to which the Party as a whole had come round to her view, she said, 'I think the Conservative Party is now very much to my way of thinking. Why? Because what I have said to you strikes a chord in so many people's hearts, and not only people in the Conservative Party. I think it strikes a chord in the hearts and minds of all of those who joined the Labour Party for idealistic reasons, believing that it was basically an underdog party, and wanted to do better for people who weren't well done by. Karl Marx and Disraeli were contemporaries. They had something in common. They both wanted to do better for ordinary folk. But there the similarity ended. The methods they used were totally different. The Marxist methods have failed. The Disraeli methods have been shown to succeed – in America, for example, and in post-war Germany. The free enterprise societies are very much better off materially. They must be kept better off morally. Moral responsibility must be kept going. Moral responsibility will not keep going if Government steps in and takes all the decisions for you, decisions which you ought to make for yourself. And it is because so many people believe this that my kind of Conservatism is striking a chord, way, way, way beyond my own Party.'

She made it clear that, as well as standing for different policies within the Conservative Party, she stood for a different kind of politics. 'People were beginning to feel guilty about their political beliefs. They were coming to believe that politicians had caused democracy to come to mean a kind of competition in materialistic promises. At election times, each Party seemed to be competing with the other in promising "What we can do for you". *I'm* not participating in that kind of competition. If somebody comes to me and asks: "What are you going to do for us small businessmen?" I say, "The only thing I'm going to do for you is make you freer to do things for yourselves." '

Asked if it had been necessary for her to reconstitute the leadership group within the Party to get her kind of Conservatism accepted, she replied: 'You've got to take everyone along with you. Obviously Keith Joseph, Geoffrey Howe, John Biffen and myself are very much in tune with this whole approach. You can only get other people in tune with you by being a little evangelical about it. But I would think we have a more united Shadow Cabinet today than we've ever had in Opposition. I haven't really had a "leadership group" – there are people to whom I talk – you've got to keep the philosophy going.' The term 'evangelical' was frequently to be quoted by friend and critic alike. She went on to use other terms which were to become part of the nation's political vocabulary: 'I'm not a consensus politician or a pragmatic politician: I'm a conviction politician. And I believe in the politics of persuasion: it's my job to put forward what I believe and try to get people to agree with me.'

By this time she was said to be conducting the meetings of the Shadow Cabinet in a style very different from that displayed by previous leaders. When she was asked about how she would run her Cabinet when she became Prime Minister, she replied: 'If you're going to do the things you want to do – and I'm only in politics to *do* things – you've got to have a togetherness and a unity in your Cabinet. There are two ways of making a Cabinet. One way is to have in it people who represent all the different viewpoints within the Party, within the broad philosophy. The other way is to have in it only the people who want to go in the direction in which every instinct tells me we have to go. Clearly, steadily, firmly, with resolution. We've got to go in an agreed and clear direction.' She paused for a moment, and then made her famous and prophetic remark: 'As Prime Minister I couldn't waste time having any internal arguments.'

She then said some things about the Shadow Cabinet. They were more piquant than what she had said about how she would run the Cabinet, since the question of how she would run her Cabinet was hypothetical, whereas how she ran her Shadow Cabinet was an actual one, and her answer to it was especially interesting since a general election was imminent. It was an answer which, whether she intended it or not, was construed as being a warning to its members, a piece of advice delivered in public with which they intentionally or unintentionally complied from then on until a Conservative Government was elected. Her words were:

> It's the same with the Shadow Cabinet. We've got to be together as a team. A football manager wouldn't put anyone, however brilliant, in his team if he believed that player couldn't work together with the rest. I've got to have togetherness. There must be dedication to a purpose, agreement about direction. As leader I have a duty to try to inspire that. If you choose a team in which you encounter a basic disagreement, you will not be able to carry out a programme, you won't be able to govern. I think that's probably what is wrong with the present Labour Cabinet: there are two basic parties in it, two basic philosophies. We, on the other hand, have a Shadow Cabinet with a unity of purpose. When the time comes to form a real Cabinet, I do think I've got to have a Cabinet with equal unity of purpose and a sense of

dedication to it. It must be a Cabinet that works on something much more than pragmatism or consensus. It must be a *conviction* Cabinet.

If Mrs Thatcher had thoughts about Cabinet and Shadow Cabinet as she entered the election campaign, her Shadow Cabinet certainly had thoughts about her. The majority of them hoped that particularly on the subjects of trade union reform and incomes policy she would not utter diatribes or make promises which would disaffect the less tough-minded members of the Conservative Party and the so-called floating voters. What they particularly feared was that she would indulge an occasional tendency to, as one of them put it, 'shoot from the hip', announcing as though it were Party policy a measure which had not been agreed, perhaps not even discussed, beforehand by the Shadow Cabinet.

There had been an egregious case of this only a few weeks before the campaign had begun. In the widely publicized television interview with Brian Walden, she had said that she would like governments to withold social security benefits from strikers if they had struck without first holding a secret ballot. Even some of her supporters in the Shadow Cabinet were disturbed. Much earlier in her career as leader, she had made a speech on East-West relations to which the then Shadow Foreign Secretary, Reginald Maudling, took exception, partly because he had not been consulted, partly because what she had said was not Party policy, and partly because in his view what she had said was irresponsible. This was in January 1976 at Kensington Town Hall and it was the speech which gave her the sobriquet 'The Iron Lady'. Maudling was shown the draft two days in advance and at once told her that some of its contents were not Party policy and, to boot, were ill advised. Nevertheless, Mrs Thatcher delivered the speech, and some time later Maudling was removed from his position in the Shadow Cabinet and returned to the back benches.

Some of her critics alleged that as well as 'making policy on the box', Mrs Thatcher frequently spoke out in terms which some of her colleagues found unrepresentative of Shadow Cabinet attitudes, sometimes having to withdraw or modify such observations. In another television interview, in which she had been questioned about immigration, she had said that she understood why 'people are really rather afraid that this country might be rather swamped by people with a different culture'. Later, the author suggested to her that she had subsequently 'modified' that statement. She replied with vigour: 'I *never* modified it! I stood by it one hundred per cent. Some people have felt swamped by immigrants.

They've seen the whole character of their neighbourhood change. I stood by that statement one hundred per cent. And continue to stand by it. Of *course* people can feel that they are being swamped. Small minorities can be absorbed – they can be assets to the majority community – but, when a minority in a neighbourhood gets very large, people *do* feel swamped. They feel their whole way of life has been changed.'

Some of her critics within the Shadow Cabinet claimed that her habit of 'announcing' policies in public was due to her knowledge that she would not be able to get them through the Shadow Cabinet in private. This was put to her by the author. 'Is that what they say?' she countered – she did not dispute that they said it, but merely queried it. 'How extraordinary.' She was unrepentant. 'There is a great deal of policy being thought out in the Party,' she went on. 'I have to keep tabs on all of it, because as leader that's my job. You won't, though, find that every member of the Shadow Cabinet with a departmental portfolio knows all of it. I have to see *all* policy papers, because part of my job as leader is to look after and expound the forward future policy.'

As an example of what sometimes happened, she cited the television interview in which she had said that social security benefits should be withheld from strikers if they had acted without holding a secret ballot. The interview, she said, 'came at the end of the Christmas recess, at the end of the holiday period, when I hadn't seen some of my colleagues for several days. What had happened was that I had been seeing work that the several study groups had been doing and I was up to date with it, whereas some of my colleagues might not have been. . . . That proposal was already being discussed in the Party papers I had read – my papers, as leader of the Party. If that's the only criticism my critics had of me, boy, oh boy! we're doing well.'

She said two other things on this occasion which were remembered for some time to come. Her attention was drawn to a poll taken at the time of the Party conference the previous October, when Mr Heath had spoken out in favour of an incomes policy, Mrs Thatcher having ruled it out. The poll indicated that, if Heath were leading the Party, it would have a much better chance of winning the general election than it would if it were being led by Mrs Thatcher. The question of whether it was better to have a man than a woman leading the Party also came up. When asked if she had seen the poll, she replied: 'Yes . . . I noticed that the questions asked were related very much to the circumstances of the time. Other polls reported that people were absolutely behind an incomes policy. Absolutely behind. The reason they were behind it was because they thought it was a way of overcoming the power of the unions. And I was saying even then that the incomes policy would crack and therefore there was no point in fighting it. The real question wasn't this or that incomes policy, but trade union power. And that's the question we'll have to deal with when we come to power.'

She then added: 'I wasn't too concerned about the poll you mentioned first, because the polls before the 1974 election showed public opinion totally behind an incomes policy. Yet we lost the election. Also, if I might point it out, the critical question about a man leader or a woman leader is what they *do* at elections. And the fact is that, whatever the polls say in between elections, we lost three out of four. I'll only be given the chance to lose *one*. If we win, I'll have the chance of another.'

The Conservative Party manifesto of 1979 outlined its programme under five headings: the control of inflation and trade union power; the restoration of incentives; upholding Parliament and the rule of law; support of family life by helping people to become home owners, and providing better education and health services; and the strengthening of Britain's defences. Its contents resembled those of the manifesto which had been drawn up the year before, when it was thought that an election would be held in the coming October, but, because the winter of discontent had intervened, the 1979 manifesto was updated to include new proposals on picketing and the taxing of strikers' benefits. These proposals were given special prominence. There were also promises of three changes 'which must be made at once': the law must be changed to limit the right of secondary picketing; compensation must be provided for workers who lost their jobs through the establishment of a closed shop; public funds must be provided for postal ballots for union elections and 'other important issues'. On the subject of strikes, the manifesto said: 'We shall ensure that unions bear their fair share of the cost of supporting those of their members who are on strike.' The words 'incomes policy' did not appear; in the private sector 'pay bargaining . . . should be left to the companies and workers concerned'. The manifesto conceded that 'different considerations apply to some extent to the public sector', where settlements 'should be such as could be reconciled with the cash limits used to control public spending'.

As the campaign unfolded, it seemed that Mr Callaghan was personally more popular with the electors than Mrs Thatcher, but that the reverse was true of the Parties' policies. Mr Callaghan was seven points ahead of her at the beginning of the campaign and nineteen at the end; Gallup showed that her rating had fallen from 33% to 25%. She lost ground, according to the commentators, because she was seen as less experienced, less 'an ordinary human being', and because she was a woman – it seemed that many people, including Conservatives, had reservations about her on that score alone.

Mr Callaghan presented himself in a bland elder-statesman 'leave-it-to-me' tone, referring frequently to his long record at the head of affairs, and particularly to his experience of international relations. His opponents as well as his supporters considered that it would be in his interest to try and make the election into a choice between the leaders. His supporters emphasized his veteran skills and authority, contrasting these with Mrs Thatcher's inexperience and insecurity. That the campaign was not a bitter one may have been due to the conduct of the two protagonists: Mr Callaghan, who did not want to be seen as a man attacking a woman, rarely referred to her by name, but usually spoke of 'the leader of the Conservative Party'. Mrs Thatcher, on the other hand, did not wish to be perceived as a hectoring female. Neither Party wanted to be associated with extremism: little was heard of Tony Benn or Sir Keith Joseph. The message of Callaghan's campaign was 'steady as we go', of Mrs Thatcher's, the urgent need for change. She stood for alterations in the role, rights and powers of the trade unions, and for a drastic reduction of the Government's role in the economy. This made her, and not the Labour leader, the radical. 'The issue is Thatcher', *The Economist* said on 31 March, and in saying so may be thought to have been the first to identify Thatcherism.

The Director of Publicity for the Conservative Party was Gordon (now Sir Gordon) Reece. A former television producer as well as a journalist, he projected – 'packaged', some said – Mrs Thatcher mainly on television. He was able, and she was willing. He arranged matters so that she was frequently seen shopping or doing her housework. He brought her out as a simple, caring, womanly woman. He tried to keep her out of hard-hitting radio and television interviews, not because she could not hit hard herself, but because she could hit too hard and seem strident and aggressive. What was even more embarrassing to many of her Party was that Mrs Thatcher, in this respect the opposite of her predecessor, appeared on the screen to relish an exchange of hostilities; an impression she had reinforced by saying in public, 'This animal, if attacked, defends itself, so when I come up against somebody who is obviously out to do a very belligerent interview, I say to myself, "By God, anything you can do I can do better", and I'm belligerent back!' Gordon Reece, in pursuit of a more engaging image for her, tried to get her on relaxed programmes like radio's *Jimmy Young Show*.

Reece coached her. She lowered the tone of her voice and sounded more sympathetic. Her hair-style was softened. She spoke more slowly, so that she seemed less combative. She smiled more, and seemed more friendly. Reece did a good job, and she responded. She learned a lot from him. How much his expertise contributed to the result of the election it is difficult to say, but he was thought to have helped her greatly.

Mrs Thatcher did not take all the advice proffered by her staff. In the last days of the campaign, when the Conservative lead in the polls had gone down from an average of 11% to an average of 5%, she rejected suggestions that she should not be too critical of trade union leadership in case she created the impression that she was calling for a crusade against them. She also refused to invite Mr Heath to accompany her to any of her press conferences.

In the result the Conservatives won 339 seats, a net gain of 55, to give them an overall majority in the House of 43. The Labour Party had, nevertheless, secured a larger share of the popular vote than the Conservatives: 39.1% to 35.7%. The outcome could not have been described as a landslide, nor as a monumental triumph for Mrs Thatcher personally. Surveying the campaign in retrospect, *The Economist*, which had supported her throughout, concluded: 'She has emerged as a leader uncertain under pressure and she has yet to demonstrate an ability to inspire great confidence and affection among the uncommitted voters, let alone among those who voted against her.' These words were not reassuring to a leader who was in a minority within her own Shadow Cabinet, nor did they inspire those who were going to share the burdens of Government with her at their head.

The result of the election could not have been interpreted as a vote for what later was to be called Thatcherism. The 1979 manifesto was not greatly different from the one with which Ted Heath had won in 1970; the changes, broadly, were the response to the challenges and opportunities created by the winter of discontent. Many of the remarks made by Mrs Thatcher on television and around the country were not such as Ted Heath or Jim Prior would have made; but campaign rhetoric is not the same thing as party policy, and the fall in her personal ratings during the campaign does not suggest that her idiosyncratic doctrinal digressions made a demonstrable contribution to the victory.

She had, however, won the election, and she had won it very much in her own style and in her own way. Many of her critics had hoped and many of her friends had feared that her stamina or her voice might not stand the strain of the campaign. She had no problem with either.

Further, on 30 March, the day after the election had been announced, Airey Neave, the friend and colleague on whom she had come most to rely, was killed by a bomb put under his car by the Irish National Liberation Army. If ever there was a need for her to display the self-control she claimed her parents had taught her in her childhood, it was then. She met the challenge.

# PRIME MINISTER

In an interview with the author previously cited, Mrs Thatcher described quite clearly the nature of the Cabinet she would choose in the event of her becoming Prime Minister: 'When the time comes to form a real Cabinet, I do think I've got to have a Cabinet with equal unity of purpose and a sense of dedication to it. It must be a Cabinet that works on something much more than pragmatism or consensus. It must be a 'conviction' Government.... We've got to go in an agreed and clear direction. As Prime Minister I couldn't waste time having any internal arguments.'

Some members of her Shadow Cabinet had declared these words to be rhetoric, and wrote them off: if she became Prime Minister, Mrs Thatcher would have to form a Cabinet which included the most influential men on the Party whether they were conviction men or not. Some commentators had taken them seriously, or had affected to, and when the names were announced expressed surprise. Others pointed out that prime ministers, particularly in early days after their first victory at the polls, must not appear to be turning their backs on the erstwhile pillars of their party.

The Cabinet which Mrs Thatcher described to me was in fact the one she intended to have in due course, not one which she expected to have immediately the election was over. She was quite determined to obtain her kind of Cabinet, either as a result of some of the original members accepting her ideas and policies, or of them leaving the Government to be replaced by people who did or would.

In the short term the demands of conviction politics and a Cabinet 'with equal unity of purpose' would prove impossible to resolve. The majority of the Conservative leadership were not conviction politicians – far from it. Most of them were, to varying degrees, still wedded to the basic assumptions of the Butskellite consensus from which Mrs Thatcher was trying to break. And yet for reasons of political prudence she had to pick a Cabinet reflecting all shades of opinion within the Party as well as reflecting the political prestige and seniority of men such as Jim Prior, Lord Carrington and Willie Whitelaw. The fact that she had to do this was both a sign of her own weakness in the Party hierarchy and of her cautious political sense. This latter quality, always there, became apparent only gradually; the make up of her first Cabinet was the first sign of it. The consensus politicians whom she so denigrated were surprised by the character of her Cabinet, and Jim Prior later wrote that, for his wing of the Party, its final composition was better than anything 'I had dreamt possible'.

There were good grounds for Prior's elation. The consensus politicians not only had numerical superiority in the new Cabinet, but seemed also to occupy the most important posts. Willie Whitelaw became Home Secretary, Lord Carrington became Foreign Secretary, Jim Prior was Employment Secretary and Francis Pym went to the Ministry of Defence. As well as these appointments to the more senior Departmental posts, Ian Gilmour became Lord Privy Seal and Norman St John-Stevas was made Chancellor of the Duchy of Lancaster. Mrs Thatcher even went so far as to recall Peter Walker from the political wilderness to become Minister of Agriculture. The consensus politicians thus constituted by far the more experienced and senior group in the Cabinet, as well as being in the majority.

Those whom Mrs Thatcher would have called the conviction politicians may have been in a minority round the Cabinet table, but they occupied the key economic posts. Sir Geoffrey Howe became Chancellor of the Exchequer, with John Biffen as Chief Secretary to the Treasury, his deputy. Sir Keith Joseph was appointed Industry Secretary, John Nott became Trade Secretary and David Howell Energy Secretary. At Junior Ministerial level, the Thatcherite wing of the Party was much better represented: Tom King, Nicholas Ridley, Leon Brittan, Norman Tebbit, Norman Fowler, Nigel Lawson, Cecil Parkinson and Peter Rees all got their first taste of Government. Despite the wealth of talent at this lower level, Mrs Thatcher could never, from the start, hope to have a majority in Cabinet in favour of the bracing conviction politics that she wanted to pursue. Other members, such as Michael Heseltine and

Mark Carlisle, had no defined stance but could certainly not be counted amongst the monetarists.

Owing to the practical political constraints which she had to face in the short term, therefore, Mrs Thatcher had to form a Cabinet seriously divided on ideological grounds, especially on the most important issues of the economy and the unions. In fact, over the course of the next two years it became apparent that her first Cabinet was probably the most divided in twentieth-century British government. That this was not always obvious to the outside world was due to the surprising degree of discipline and loyalty shown for so long in public by her Cabinet detractors; two qualities that had always been highly valued by the Party, and which had always been noticeably absent from the deliberations of their political opponents.

In retrospect, some Conservatives have held her first Cabinet to be her greatest political mistake, arguing that she should have provided herself from the start with a much more cohesive Cabinet, sympathetic to her views. Ted Heath certainly picked his Cabinets with this in mind. There is no doubt that such a course of action, although involving some initial risk, would have spared a lot of the wrangling and blood-letting of the next two years. The fact that the Cabinet was actually balanced against her conviction politics also meant that to get her policies through, she would have to remove the most vital aspects of policy-making from Cabinet discussion.

This is exactly what happened. She had been unable to pick the Cabinet with 'equal unity of purpose' that she had desired, and thus she was in danger, as she had expressed it, of wasting time 'having ... internal arguments'. To obviate the problem, this determined and shrewd politician decided to bypass the Cabinet as a forum for policy discussion and formulation and chose to run her Government through a small group of committees which she could staff with those she came to define as 'one of us.' The most controversial and important of these Cabinet Committees was the E Committee, which met to discuss economic policy and was dominated by her few Cabinet supporters, most notably Howe, Joseph and Biffen. It would develop the core of the Government's economic policy within the ideological parameters of economic liberalism and then present their conclusions to the Cabinet as a set of *faits accomplis*. This was the process which produced Howe's first three budgets. It was the existence of the Committees, above all the E Committee, which was to lead to Mrs Thatcher being accused of neglecting to govern through the Cabinet and resorting to 'Presidential politics.'

To the undiscerning eye the new Government was going to be run by a Cabinet in which a wide spectrum of views could be expressed. In fact, as soon became clear, it would be run by a small group of E Committee Thatcherites whose control of economic policy, the key to everything Mrs Thatcher wanted to change in British society, gave them control of the Cabinet. Her little group of economic policy-makers were the shock troops of the Thatcherite revolution. When she became leader in 1975 it was frequently said that she had hijacked the Conservative Party. When she became Prime Minister in 1979 it could be said she hijacked the Cabinet.

Many of the 'consensus' members of the Cabinet, soon to be labelled 'Wets' by the Prime Minister, assumed that because of their strength in the Government they would be able to cause Mrs Thatcher and her fellow monetarists to moderate their radicalism. Many Conservatives attributed Heath's failure to his headstrong rush to implement the manifesto policies during his first two years of Government. 'I assumed she would take things gradually,' Jim Prior has written, 'bearing in mind the experience of Ted's Government some five years before.' Others presumed that once the excitement of the election was over, what looked to be the more controversial policies in the manifesto might, in time-honoured fashion, be discreetly dropped, the Government returning to the saner and well trodden path of managerial politics.

They were quickly disillusioned. Only three weeks after Mrs Thatcher arrived in Downing Street, Prior, as her Secretary of Employment, sent her a paper suggesting the outlines for a suitable wages and incomes policy – the staple diet of consensus, managerial politics. Within hours it arrived back on Prior's desk with a statement of the Prime Minister's views on the subject. The message, as Prior read it, was, in short, that the new Government was not going to have a wages and incomes policy. If the Prime Minister required a paper on the subject of wages and incomes it would come to her from the Treasury. No more was heard of Prior's paper. It did not get to Cabinet or even to a Cabinet committee. The event conveyed two things to Prior. First, though a wages policy had been hinted at in *The Right Approach to the Economy*, it was now to be ruled out. Secondly, the new Premier was going to get her policy suggestions from where she wanted to get them, and not from where they used to come.

More evidence of the new approach was provided by the method of formulation and the content of the Government's first budget, introduced within a few weeks of coming to power. The substance was decided between Mrs Thatcher and Sir Geoffrey Howe: the Cabinet was never consulted, even on the broad issues. The radical nature of the budget thus came as an 'enormous' shock to Ministers such as Prior, who for the first time realized that they had 'grossly underestimated' her determination to push through the new right-wing policies. There was no secret about the nature of the policies the monetarists wanted to pursue. What surprised and dismayed the consensus politicians was how vigorously and dogmatically they wanted to pursue those policies and the speed with which they intended to put them into effect.

The Government's overriding economic aim was the conquest of inflation, given priority over everything, even trade union reform and control of public expenditure, by Mrs Thatcher in opposition from 1975 to 1979 – to be achieved by, according to *The Right Approach to the Economy*, the 'strict control ... of the rate of growth of the money supply' and 'firm management of Government expenditure'. If this can be described as the more general economic strategy or macro-economic strategy, there was also a micro-economic strategy which was to create the 'enterprise culture' that alone would create the wealth and prosperity that the nationalized industrial concerns had failed to deliver. In the words of Nigel Lawson: 'It is the creation of conditions conducive to growth and employment ... which is ... the objective of micro-economic policy.' This involved mainly negative policies – tax reductions, eliminating Government controls, breaking up monopolies and restrictive practices and freeing the labour market. It was to these two economic objectives that Mrs Thatcher had devoted herself, and for which she had prepared herself as leader of the Opposition.

The June 1979 budget was a bold embodiment of these economic policies and set the pattern for all Howe's subsequent budgets. The most eye-catching measures were the tax reductions. These were regarded as essential to restore incentive and to create a greater sense of individual financial freedom and personal responsibility. The standard rate of income tax was accordingly cut from 33% to 30% and the top rate was cut from 83% to 60%. A total of 1.3 million people were taken out of tax by raising thresholds. The cuts were worth a total of £4,500 million in a full year. To balance this, indirect taxation was increased. This was to become another long-term aim of the Government, to shift the burden of taxation away from direct to indirect taxation, thus allowing greater freedom to choose how to spend one's money. As a result VAT was now increased from 8% to 15%; petrol tax by 10p per gallon, and prescription charges were increased. Furthermore, on the macro-economic level, Howe introduced tighter monetary targets, which would be achieved by a reduction in the Public Sector Borrowing Requirement (PSBR – the amount of money the Government borrows to bridge the difference between what it earns and spends each year), and an increase in the Bank of England minimum lending rate by 2% (in the belief that higher interest rates would restrict borrowing and thus reduce the volume of money in circulation). To achieve the reduction in the PSBR, Howe introduced a range of public expenditure cuts amounting to £1,500 million.

The whole budget was a concise exposition of the new economic policies that were now to prevail: Sir Geoffrey Howe concluded his speech, 'I intend to continue along this path in years ahead.' To those critics who immediately accused the budget of being extreme and severe, John Biffen answered that he did 'not deny for one moment that this is a severe package. The severity is made necessary by the situation we inherited.'[1] To those who really believed in Mrs Thatcher's reforming vision of society, the budget confirmed their hopes that here at last was a leader who meant what she said. To those who had little desire to break out of the cosy world of consensus politics, it came as a rude awakening. It was then that Jim Prior realized that 'Margaret, Geoffrey and Keith really had got the bit between their teeth and were not going to pay attention to the rest of us at all if they could possibly help it.'

The difference in standpoint between the Thatcherites and the consensus politicians largely stemmed from their understanding of the contemporary situation. To the consensus politicians, the prevailing unhealthy economic situation was the consequence of poor economic management – which they wanted to improve – of a mixed Butskellite economy which in essence they wanted to keep. Perhaps the balance within that consensus had gone slightly awry, but this could be remedied by a little managerial adjustment. To the Thatcherites, the consensus was fundamentally wrong. The Wets were always to underestimate Mrs Thatcher's belief that what was needed was wholesale change, not piecemeal tinkering. In her view, as she revealed to the author in 1987, '... [by 1979] we were very near to having what I would call a permanent socialist society where freedom was constantly being diminished'.

The Thatcherites were not merely interested in improving the economy within the existing political framework, they were seeking nothing less than a revolution. Their task, their duty, their mission, was to *save* Britain from what they saw as the all-pervading deadening hand of Socialist planning. There were marked similarities between the policies that Ted Heath tried to pursue between 1970 and 1972 and the policies that Mrs Thatcher began to pursue in 1979, but there was a vital difference that few, if any, of the wets (who had all been supporters of Heath) understood at the time: for Heath the doctrines of *laissez-faire* and the Social Market were merely means to greater productivity; for Mrs Thatcher they were ends in themselves. When using these means landed him in trouble he ceased to go on using them. Seeing them not as means but as ends, she did not.

For her, the Social Market, the free economy, were not economic devices but moral systems which must replace the Socialist society and set the people free. In a conversation with the author before the 1979 election, Mrs Thatcher used the word 'evangelical' to describe her role as a political leader: 'You can only get other people in tune with you by being a little evangelical about it.' There is this strong Messianic streak in Thatcherism that her opponents, especially within the Conservative Party, gravely underestimated. Her economic theories were not technical devices but tablets of stone: she was leading a moral crusade to save the nation – which is why she would have no time for arguments with consensus or pragmatic politicians. 'Get thee behind me . . .'

Indeed, if the sobriquet of Thatcherism is to have any real meaning, it is as a description of attitude rather than policies. It is the Prime Minister's way of thinking that singles her out from her post-war political contemporaries, and why she has thus coined an 'ism' all of her own. Mrs Thatcher has always believed in simple truths; but for her they are truths, none the less. What has marked her out is her constant search for first principles, in the belief that only the vigorous application of first principles will ever change anything. Many people in Britain during the 1970s were despairing about the country's future; but more importantly, many politicians and political commentators had come to the depressing conclusion that politicians at Westminster no longer had *power* to alter the seemingly irreversible decline. Lord Young – a Labour Party supporter until 1964 – seriously considered emigrating to America in 1975, because after Heath's U-turn in 1972 he became disillusioned with the apparently impossible task of reversing Britain's economic decline. It was the sceptical, enquiring mind of liberal Britain that had presided over the country's post-war economic demise; Mrs Thatcher represented an uncompromising Messianic political approach which was in striking contrast. Her acolytes argued that only such a black-and-white approach could rescue government from the powerlessness which had seemed to grip Westminster during the late 1970s.

Other Conservative politicians arrived at virtually the same analysis of Britain's deplorable economic situation, just as they suggested the same policies of economic liberalism to remedy the situation, policies which would later come to be known as monetarism. Such politicians were Enoch Powell – he as far back as the late 1950s – and, more immediately, John Biffen. Yet Biffen, although on paper an economic soulmate of Mrs Thatcher, would always find it more congenial to talk to colleagues such as Jim Prior and Francis Pym, who shared his pragmatic, sceptical approach to politics. Just as Biffen had grown sceptical of the achievements of consensus politics in the late 1960s, so he was to grow increasingly sceptical of the achievements of Mrs Thatcher; so much so that by 1987 he was sacked from a Cabinet of which he had always been one of the few to agree with the Prime Minister on the general thrust of economic policy. Mrs Thatcher is incapable of scepticism; a policy is either right or wrong. It is remarkable how little she had changed her beliefs and first principles formed behind the shop counter at Grantham; it is her fortune that the tides of economic and social change conspired to give those views a run for their money in 1979.

Thatcherism is also about *will*, and, in particular, the willing of the means as well as of the ends. At the time of Heath's victory in 1970 most of the Conservative Party leaders wanted to make many of the changes which Mrs Thatcher made a decade later, but were not ready to take the practical steps to bring these changes about, some because they thought the means would create such political problems that the ends would not be achieved, others because they recoiled from the prospect of the suffering the means would inevitably entail. They wanted change but would not will it.

After the initial shock of the 1979 Budget, the consensus politicians settled back to rely on the coming of unpleasant economic developments to 'educate' her. For the Thatcherites the worsening economic situation that was a necessary, but hopefully temporary, consequence of monetarism, only made them more determined to pursue their policies. The divisions in the Party were soon being widely reported in the press, where the terms 'wet' and 'dry', referring to the opposing views within the Cabinet, became common usage. These two sobriquets described not only a difference in ideological approach, but also a difference in character. For Mrs Thatcher, Wets and Drys could as well be described as Talkers and Doers. She had been listening to speeches about the 'property-owning democracy' and the virtues of the 'free economy' at Tory Party Conferences ever since 1946, but subsequent Conservative Governments had only talked about these concepts, and had actually shied away from implementing them. For Mrs Thatcher, the time of talking was over, and she was actually going to 'do' something about creating this 'property-owning democracy'. The sale of council houses, which took place within her first years of coming to office, was only one step along the road. To the Thatcherites, the Wets were profoundly wet in the traditional sense of the term: not only were they distinctly suspicious of the policies themselves but they were also reluctant to put them into practice for fear of the political consequences.

Another term that quickly gained common currency after 1979 was the phrase, 'Is he one of us?' – supposedly asked by Mrs Thatcher of political colleagues with whom she might and might not work. Asked by Peter Jay what she meant by 'one of us', she replied: 'Are they hardworking, do they believe in personal responsibility, do they believe in endeavour, do they believe in the voluntary spirit? Do they believe fundamentally in the same philosophy I believe in?'

In other words, did they have her sense of mission? One group of people in her view who did not was the Civil Service, and just as her Cabinet swiftly came to realize that she was not going to conform to type and behave like any other post-Attlee managerial Prime Minister, so the Civil Service quickly discovered her reforming zeal. To her, it embodied much that had been wrong with the British Government and economy during the previous forty years: for individual civil servants she had affection and respect, but corporately, the Service seemed to her complacent, inert, pedantic and incapable of appreciating the need to devise or implement radical solutions to Britain's dire problems. The same charge had been laid at the door of the Civil Service by the radical left of Tony Benn and Richard Crossman. The problem was brought to much wider attention by the television comedy series *Yes, Minister* – one of Mrs Thatcher's favourite programmes!

Her attitude to the Civil Service before she came to Downing Street had four ingredients. Her experience at the Ministry of Education has already been mentioned. Secondly, just as she felt that the housewife frequently knew more about the day-to-day facts of life than politicians or economists, she felt that businessmen often knew more about trade and industry than men behind desks in Whitehall. Thirdly, like several other members of the Heath Cabinet – and some senior civil servants – she was disturbed by the amount of influence that Sir William Armstrong, then Britain's top civil servant, seemed to have had on the judgement and policy of the Prime Minister between 1970 and 1974. Heath's meetings with the miners' leaders, accompanied by Armstrong but by no member of the Cabinet, in the months leading up to the fateful strike, were much criticized by his colleagues, and some of

Armstrong's colleagues complained that he was involving the Service in party politics. That Armstrong's role appeared in retrospect to have harmed the Government fed the ire of those who had resented it at the time. Fourthly, she seemed to suspect top civil servants of being Labour supporters because they had for so long carried out Labour Government policies, policies fundamentally opposed to those which she proposed to implement. Bearing all these considerations in mind, it could have been predicted that when she took up residence in Number 10, she would be at her most strongminded in keeping the Civil Service in what in her view was its proper place.

Sir John Hoskyns, head of Mrs Thatcher's Policy Unit in Downing Street, told Peter Hennessy of her attitude towards the Civil Service and the general Whitehall culture: 'I think first her temperament and background make her impatient with the whole sort of establishment culture and way of thinking, even of talking. And that, I think, is extremely healthy because I happen to think the Establishment ... is absolutely at the heart of the British disease. She's gone further than that because she has been prepared to be extremely unreasonable in order to get change – impossible on occasions and many people of a more gentlemanly and old-fashioned upbringing were rather shocked at the way she carried on.'[2]

Sir John was typical of the new breed of Thatcherite men imported into the corridors of power to introduce the efficient, competitive ethos of private industry into the quiet corners of Whitehall. Hoskyns was a self-made businessman, a successful entrepreneur who had made his considerable fortune in the computer business. He had then offered his services to Mrs Thatcher in the mid-1970s and headed her Policy Unit (a small team engaged in formal thinking specifically for the Prime Minister) from 1979 to 1982. He took a tough line on most issues and was very vocal in his demands for a total overhaul of the machinery of government. Another import into Whitehall to infuse some Thatcherite rigour into proceedings was Sir Derek Rayner, whose brief was to scrutinize inefficiency in Whitehall and to propose remedies. The Rayner Efficiency Unit based at Number 10 soon reported that Whitehall was wasting £70 million per year. Large cuts were also proposed in Civil Service manpower. The recommendations of the Unit were vigorously implemented, and by 1983 the Service had shed almost 100,000 jobs, 500 'quangos' and 3,600 different types of Government forms. It was an essential piece of Thatcherite economics in eliminating waste and inefficiency. The most successful pruner was Michael Heseltine whose Department of the Environment was 29% smaller by 1983, having shed

15,000 jobs. His efficiency drive continued when he transferred to the Ministry of Defence, which found its staff reduced by 20,000 between 1983 and 1986. Heseltine carried out a reform of the higher echelons of the Civil Service management structure to make individual Departments more responsive to the Minister's wishes, introducing what was known as MINIS, or Management Information System for Ministers. Heseltine also took the initiative in recruiting businessmen into Whitehall to improve the cost efficiency of Departments.

What became obvious in Mrs Thatcher's first year of Government was that the Civil Service was perceived as the most important obstacle to her plans, and their cautious and sceptical approach often drew out the most domineering and stubborn side of her character. According to a report in *The Observer* before the public expenditure discussions in October 1979, 'Mrs Thatcher became enraged with what she considered the dilatoriness of the Treasury in coming up with the required public expenditure cuts. It couldn't be done, said the mandarins. She promptly summoned all five Treasury ministers and all five Treasury knights to Downing Street. They came out shaking from what was an unprecedented joint dressing down. A week later the Treasury came up with £1,400 million in cuts.' If the Thatcher revolution was going to happen, she was going to have to raise her voice to get things done.

She was determined not to be over-awed, or to defer to the hallowed procedures and 'wisdom' of the Civil Service and would always take them on, even on their own specialist ground. The results were sometimes disastrous. Jim Prior records that on one occasion she 'got into an argument' with one of his senior officials. 'She insisted on picking an argument without knowing the facts or the legal position on secondary industrial action. Even when Patrick Mayhew intervened in utter frustration, she still wouldn't stop ... (it) showed her at her worst.' Whatever else was going to happen to Thatcherism, it was not going to die in Whitehall.

Her treatment of her own colleagues could be just as brusque; the Cabinet of 1979 to 1982 was not only the most divided in modern British history, but it was also the most unhappy. Contrary to popular belief, there was a lot of argument around the Cabinet table, some of it quite fierce. This is because Mrs Thatcher likes to argue her case, even though she is determined that her view will prevail: 'You can only get other people in tune with you by being a little evangelical about it.'

Cabinet colleagues were used to the tradition of the Prime Minister being the chairman, weighing and evaluating everybody else's view. John Nott has commented on the 'process of combat' in Mrs Thatcher's

Cabinet, adding that she was not a 'natural chairman', but more of a 'managing director'. Her colleagues soon came to realize that she did not see the role of the Cabinet as her predecessors had seen it. To her, Cabinet members were her agents; they were there not to influence or inform Government policy, but to execute it. She saw her Cabinet more as an American president sees his. Here is one ex-minister's summary of a Thatcher Cabinet meeting:

> In Cabinet she spoke first, outlining what she proposed to do, what the policy of the Government was going to be. The dissidents came next. They did not always get a chance to complete their case because she would interrupt them, sometimes offensively in that she would tell them in very simple language that what they were advocating was simply not on. Then she would sum up. The summing up would be a restatement of the action she had proposed at the beginning of the meeting. The Cabinet minutes, when circulated to those Cabinet Ministers who had been present, would reflect what the Prime Minister had told the Cabinet what her Government was going to do.

The justification for such behaviour was simply that the Cabinet process, in its old form, held no use for a revolutionary in a hurry, as was Mrs Thatcher in 1979. The Cabinet system was also, of all the Great British Systems, quintessentially a *male* system; it was conceived as a gentlemanly debating chamber in which the Prime Minister was no more than first among equals. It had evolved to cater for politicians who wanted to carry their colleagues with them, not for politicians who wanted to get their own way. Indeed, the system had never been able to accommodate such politicians. Neville Chamberlain, the Prime Minister whom Mrs Thatcher much resembled in terms of social and political style, was similarly possessed of a confidence in his own views, which led him virtually to dispense with Cabinet Government: he ran the Government with an 'inner Cabinet' of four sympathetic senior ministers who rubber-stamped everything he did. Mrs Thatcher, as a person, was uniquely unsuited to a Cabinet system evolved to give 'colleagues' a forum in which to exchange ideas; Mrs Thatcher already had her ideas, and her forum was the country.

She also possessed an advantage in that she was a woman, and whereas she was used to arguing her case with men, so the men were certainly not used to an argumentative, competitive style from a woman. It disoriented many. Jim Prior has since written, very honestly: 'Traditionally politics has been a male preserve, and I think we did all find it difficult coming to terms with a woman leader.' There was also no doubt that she could use her sex to her advantage, by exploiting the common courtesies that are normally accorded to women by men through turning them into symbols of deference rather than mere gestures of politeness. At meetings of the traditionally powerful Tory back-bench 1922 Committee, MPs have normally remained seated when a male leader of the Party has entered the room to address them. The first time Mrs Thatcher entered the room as leader, everybody rose. According to one observer, 'She made a procession to her seat, as though she expected them to remain upstanding; and when she got there turned as though to say, "Please be seated".' It was not many months after this that Norman St John-Stevas invented the title of 'Leaderene' for her.

Her new style and earnest determination to carry through her policies were quickly on display on a world stage at the EEC summit in Dublin. The British contribution to the European Community's budget had been allowed to drift upward during the course of the previous six years to the point where there was a difference of about £800 million per year between what Britain paid in and what she received from the communal coffers. A Brussels Commission report had argued that Britain was indeed among the poorest nations of the Community in 1979 and yet was at the same time being called upon to pay the heaviest subscription.

Britain's European partners were perfectly prepared to acknowledge this situation, and went to the summit prepared to make small concessions which would appease Britain but avoid having to tackle the root of the problem. Once again, there was a yawning gulf in perception, which even the British Foreign Office failed to notice. Patrick Cosgrave, a special adviser to Mrs Thatcher at the time, has since written that she 'regarded the budgetary imbalance not as a regrettable problem which could be dealt with through good will on all sides, but a matter of fundamental difference'. She also went to the summit as a convinced Nationalist. Mrs Thatcher had very little vision of a united European Community in the sense that Mr Heath had. The EEC was only worth supporting if it was helping Britain economically; and in 1979 it plainly was not. Indeed, quite the opposite was the case. Once again, she was not interested in tinkering, but was determined to hold out for profound and lasting change.

As is always the case, she was quite certain what she was going to do and that it would ruffle some feathers. Before her departure for Dublin, she told the Conservative Foreign Affairs Committee that she was going to put her European partners 'on the spot'. This is precisely what she did. The Foreign Office was horrified to behold years of carefully orchestrated diplomatic custom being trampled underfoot. The Foreign

Office, like the wets, did not take her seriously at the start and presumed that once entangled in the subtle webs of diplomatic convention in Dublin, she would bow to pressure and be conciliatory. The opposite happened. She stuck by her guns from the first day. A one-off rebate of £350 million was offered to Britain, but she turned this down as unsatisfactory. The Foreign Office was aghast, and through the Diplomatic correspondents stories appeared in the press about her undiplomatic, dictatorial behaviour. But Mrs Thatcher was strictly utilitarian in these matters. If the niceties of diplomatic convention did not yield results, then there was no reason to observe them. On a later occasion, she was to say to the author, of her negotiations with the EEC, 'I know nothing about diplomacy, but I just know and believe that I want certain things for Britain.'[3]

This was when the world in general, and Europe in particular, became aware of the quality of the new British leader. The Dublin summit broke up in some confusion and disarray, but in the long term her tactics brought results. After further meetings during the next six months, she got most of what she wanted. In May 1980, it was agreed that Britain would be refunded £1,800 million in respect of her budget contributions for 1980 and 1981, and the EEC also undertook to explore the whole area of budgetary imbalance, and to devise a new system of working it out. Like so much of what she was to do, Mrs Thatcher's arguments and methods – and her manner – had incurred almost universal wrath (Giscard d'Estaing, the French President at the time, was wont to describe her as 'La fille de l'épicier', the grocer's daughter; Mrs Thatcher was inclined to describe him as 'that bogus count'), but she was not going to allow considerations of personal popularity to throw her off her course. This was the 'resolute' approach to politics.

If her stand in Dublin did much in the eyes of the Europeans to put a cloud above her Government, the creation of Zimbabwe after the Lancaster House Conference in 1980 went a long way to restoring her reputation as it showed that she could be persuaded to change her position in the light of reason. Lord Carrington has, rightly, been given most of the credit for the Lancaster House agreement, and a detailed discussion of it belongs to a biography of Lord Carrington, not Mrs Thatcher. Neither should the contribution of David Owen, Foreign Secretary in the previous Labour Government, be forgotten or under-estimated. What was interesting from the point of view of Mrs Thatcher's style of leadership was the fact that she changed her mind. She started out in 1979 by favouring the resignation of Bishop Muzorewa and the establishment of an Ian Smith regime which gave majority rule to the blacks of Rhodesia, but which reserved certain important levers of power for the white population – an approach not popular with the United Nations or the countries of the Commonwealth. In the course of the next four months she changed her mind, coming to the conclusion already arrived at by Lord Carrington, that there should be a Constitutional Conference in Britain involving all political parties in Rhodesia before independence was granted. How she came to this conclusion is still obscure. She certainly met Muzorewa, and, as Cosgrave tells us, formed a 'downright unfavourable opinion of him'. She also listened to Lord Carrington, who presided over the conference at Lancaster House in 1980 which, as a result of persistent diplomatic endeavour, managed to frame a new constitution for Rhodesia which would satisfy all parties, based on democratic elections and parliamentary democracy.

As the first election under this new constitution approached, it became clear that Mr Nkomo's main opponent would be Mr Mugabe, leader of the avowedly Marxist ZANU Party, and that the latter's chances were rapidly improving. Lord Soames, as the representative of the British Government, was sent out with a small peace-keeping force to oversee the election and the transference of power. Victory for Mr Mugabe would be a reversal of British desires and expectations. Mrs Thatcher came under pressure from members of her Party and from the military on the spot to 'adjust' to the new situation. Her response was categorical: the die had been cast. The principle of one man–one vote elections had been accepted. There could be no turning back or interference. If Mugabe won, so be it.

The fifteen-year-old crisis about the country's future came to a swift end with the announcement of Mr Mugabe's election victory on 4 March. It was a great coup for the new British Government; Mrs Thatcher and Lord Carrington received the plaudits of the world. The Rhodesian negotiations and the EEC negotiations had both shown that the new Prime Minister was tactically astute. She was capable both of firm resolution and cautious evaluation. She was not a dogmatist in the sense that she had a closed mind; but she was a dogmatist in the sense that having made up her mind, she would not deviate from the course of action which she had decided to follow. This was conviction politics.

Though foreign policy demanded attention during the first two and a half years of government, Mrs Thatcher's principal preoccupation was with the domestic economy. It was on this issue that she knew she would stand or fall, and it was thus important to her that the central direction of economic policy should be as far as possible in her own hands. Thus, although her Cabinet was a forum for debate, the vital issues of economic policy were predetermined from outside.

As well as the E Committee, Misc 62 (known as the 'Star Chamber'), chaired by Willie Whitelaw, was set up to settle the differences between the Treasury and the spending ministries. Whitelaw's work on this committee was to become perhaps his most important contribution of many to the success of the first of the Thatcher administrations. This arrangement for the conduct of economic policy meant that the wets in her Cabinet, in the majority for a long time, were effectively neutralized. It was a pattern of government that might have made for forthright leadership, but which could border on the dictatorial. Peter Hennessy, a keen observer of the ups and downs of Cabinet government since the war, has written about the 'battering the more reassuring notions of collective responsibility have received in the Thatcher years'. Her tight personal control might have been dubious on constitutional grounds, but it certainly ensured that the disputes between her and her Cabinet dissenters would become more bitter and irreparable. As her sole concession to collective responsibility she put Jim Prior as the representative of the wets on the E Committee. It was a shrewd move. First, Prior was a senior figure, and yet he was also tied down with onerous Departmental responsibilities which would distract him from paying too much attention to economic policy. Secondly it meant that discussion of economic policy was kept away from its two most articulate and effective critics in the Cabinet: Ian Gilmour and Norman St John-Stevas, who both had wide-ranging Government briefs and who were thus in a position to spend time and effort on gathering arguments with which to oppose her if they were given the chance. This led to increasing bitterness, and an increase in the amount of leaking from the Cabinet in order to produce pressures from outside, mainly newspaper stories and comment which would 'educate' her out of her economic convictions.

Think-Tank reports and Policy Unit reports, exploring the more radical – the more 'Thatcherite' – possibilities of Government policy were also leaked in an effort to rally public opinion against such measures in advance of any decision to carry them out. In the end, this policy of leaking, or of 'calculated indiscretions', proved to be at least in part counter-productive, as it encouraged Mrs Thatcher to operate in ever smaller groups of people whom she could absolutely trust – so that dissenters found themselves even further away from policy formulation. Jim Prior has since written: 'Margaret would give as her reason for working increasingly in small groups that she couldn't rely on her colleagues to respect her authority. I regret to say that this was true.' The wets were not only wet, but leaked as well. Moreover, the Civil Service, also under attack during these years, also became leaky in some places as a result of disaffection and occasionally demoralization. But conviction politics had not set out to provide a happy administration.

The economic policy that was pursued by Mrs Thatcher was thus kept firmly on the rigid monetarist lines envisaged by the Treasury Ministers (the Prime Minister is also First Lord of the Treasury) and Sir Keith Joseph. After the budget of June 1979, their commitment to their financial policy was further demonstrated by the public expenditure cuts agreed in Cabinet on 23 July when a £3.6 billion cut was agreed. Monetarism as a control of the money supply was only one strand in the anti-inflation strategy. The strategy also involved a change in taxation (an increase in indirect taxation), public spending cuts to lessen the PSBR, and the maintenance of tight cash limits on pay deals. The last aspect was very important, as the yearly round of public sector pay deals, which had sometimes reached as much as 20% or over in the late 1970s, had been one of the major contributors to the inflation spiral.

The Government's resolve on wages policy was soon to be tested by the steel strike, which lasted from January to April 1980. The Government sat the strike out, as it was to do on all occasions with one important exception. The eventual settlement of 14% was below the going rate in the public sector, and it was regarded as due reward for the Government's resolution in refusing to capitulate. Workers would now have to earn their pay increases through greater productivity, rather than expect them annually as a right, regardless of their economic performance. This was now part of the new atmosphere in industrial relations, an atmosphere which also eschewed tripartite or bilateral Government/union consultative talks through such agencies as the NEDC, an agency set up by the Macmillan Government specifically to solve difficulties between government, management and unions, Such talks were now seen by the Thatcherites as all part of the failed corporatist past. Corporatism was over.

The budget of 26 March 1980 continued the work of the 1979 budget, and introduced the Medium Term Financial Strategy (MTFS). This was mainly the work of the junior Treasury Minister Nigel Lawson, and was an attempt to set precise targets for the money supply, public spending and the PSBR. To meet the targets set in the MTFS for a four-year period, public spending was cut by a further £1 billion and Sir Geoffrey Howe envisaged public expenditure at being 4% lower in 1983–4.

This was a severely deflationary budget, and fuelled the growing discontent within the Cabinet and the Party – to say nothing of the opposition parties. The problem with the MTFS was held to be that the targets were hopelessly unrealistic and inaccurate; in other words, that the economic policy was simplistic and unworkable. In anticipation of just such a budget, discontent began to surface from within the Party. An unsigned piece by a 'Tory MP' appeared in *The Observer*, on 16 February 1980, claiming that 'We are suffering from A-level economics'. The problem was a 'matter of both policy and personality. Mrs Thatcher is didactic, tart and obstinate.' The author was soon identified as Julian Critchley, and he was the first of many Tories to break ranks. He has since written of the first year of Mrs Thatcher's Government that it was 'set to martial music; brass, over which her shrill contralto could be heard urging friend and foe to go over the top. There is a quality to that gritty voice which, when combined with a fierce and unrelenting glare, and the repetition of the obvious, amounts to the infliction of pain. Her supporters seem to relish her exhortations; those of us who had doubts cringed as she continued remorselessly to trample upon our susceptibilities. The genie had escaped the bottle and swallowed the cork.'

There is general agreement now that the monetary policy envisaged in the MTFS was too simplistic – that the wets were right. According to Patrick Cosgrave even Nigel Lawson would now admit that 'too much hope was invested in the whole idea, and that too much was claimed for it at the outset'. To give one example of how wayward the MTFS calculations were, the MTFS figure for the growth of the money supply was 9% for the full year 1980–81: In September 1980, it was announced that the money supply had risen in two months since the budget at a rate of 8%. Part of the problem was the technical difficulty in measuring the money supply – the amount of money in circulation in the economy. The choice of M3 – notes and coins plus bank deposits – to measure it in the MTFS proved to be highly inaccurate and unsatisfactory; it proved to be virtually impossible to operate a monetary policy if one could not reliably measure the money supply! These difficulties were grist to the mill for the wets; Jim Prior has pointed to the fact that all the monetarists were 'theorists ... none of them had any experience of running a whelk stall, let alone a decent-sized company'. However, those defenders of the MTFS could justify their strategy on the grounds of 'rational expectation', that if stringent targets were set, then 'the announcement of those target rates of growth of the money supply, etc. would induce entrepreneurs, investors and workers to adjust their behaviour to the new policy as though it were a new reality'.

This was in fact sound psychology, as people would be more likely to keep to low targets if the desired target itself was very low. Alan Walters, who was soon to join Downing Street as an economic adviser to Mrs Thatcher, has depicted such financial targets in these terms:

> It would be a great mistake to retreat from the sharp focus of setting one's sights on a particular number. The fact that one expects a wide margin of error is no argument for dispensing with the target. Just as in rifle practice, although experience shows that only a very small fraction of bullets hit the bullseye, the marksman will get a better score ... if he *aims* carefully to hit the bull, rather than if he waves the rifle carelessly in the vague direction of the target! So it is with budgetary process.[3]

A graver charge was laid at the door of the Government's economic policies during 1979 and 1980: that they were ignoring the changing economic circumstances in which those policies had to operate. The Government's most pressing problem was that it had drawn up its economic policy, and worked out how it would operate in practice, back in 1978, in time for an autumn election, before two events took place that were to make major changes in the world economy, and particularly to Britain's place in it. First came a massive explosion in the price of oil, from $13 per barrel at the start of 1979 to anything up to $40 per barrel by May of that year. It was a price explosion at least as significant as that of 1973-4. Secondly, the world economy entered a severe recession in 1980, partly caused by the rise in oil prices and partly by other factors. The rise in oil price was crucial, as it ensured that Britain, which was by then a major oil producer due to the huge reserves under the North Sea which began to come on tap in the late 1970s, would be vitally affected. It had always been assumed that North Sea oil could only be a bonus to the economy, but by 1980 it began to dawn on economists that this might not necessarily be the case. It meant that sterling virtually became a petro-currency, i.e. its value became firmly linked to the rises and falls in the price of oil. Exchange controls were abolished in 1979 as part of the drive for a 'freer' economic system, with the result that sterling began to climb rapidly against the dollar and by the autumn of 1980 it had reached $2.40. This meant that the exporting industries, mainly the staple manufacturing industries, found their competitiveness being eroded.

This deserves special comment in view of the dissent on the subject between the Prime Minister and the Chancellor in 1988. In 1979 the new Conservative ideology was taking the national fortunes into a particularly risky area. 'For the first time in his life Geoffrey [Howe] had trouble getting to sleep that night,' said a friend of his at the time. The same night Mrs Thatcher told some of her colleagues, 'Now we are beginning to be free.'

For any British company that had to compete in the international market, the high exchange rate was disastrous. The effect of oil prices led to anguished pleas from industrialists, such as Sir Michael Edwardes of British Leyland, that the Government should 'leave the bloody stuff in the ground'. One economist who warned of the dire consequences of the exchange rate was John Forsyth of Morgan Grenfell the merchant bankers, who argued that the effect of the Government's policies *combined* with the rise in sterling, was to make 'oil production a substitute for, rather than a supplement to, activity in the rest of the economy'. With the world economy in recession anyway, the wets looked on in dismay as much of British industry was decimated; Prior recalls how the exchange rate 'piled agony upon misery – our exports were priced out of markets which were already squeezed, while our home market was flooded with cheaper foreign imports'. The most alarming consequence of this economic downturn was the fast rise in the unemployment figures. In July 1980, a 1.9 million unemployment total was announced; by November this figure had reached 2.1 million and in January 1982 the politically emotive figure of three million was passed. Despite the pleadings of the Government that this was due to the fact that workers were pricing themselves out of their jobs, it was at least in part due to the Government pursuing a tight monetary policy regardless of the changing economic circumstances.

As a result of the economic depression and the steep rise in unemployment from the beginning of 1980, Mrs Thatcher faced a chorus of disappproval, not only from the expected quarters, like the TUC, the opposition parties and a wide spectrum of 'liberal opinion', but also, and more menacingly, from her putative supporters in the Conservative Party and in industry. The Confederation of British Industry (the CBI), under the robust leadership of Sir Terence Beckett, was as scathing as anyone in its condemnation of the Government's handling of the economy. In a celebrated attack in November 1980, Beckett called for 'a bare knuckled fight' with the Government – demanding a reduction in the high interest rates, a change in the Government's *laissez-faire* attitude towards the exchange rate, energy policy and public spending. A record number of industrial bankruptcies were reported – never had relations between industry and a Conservative Government been so sour. In the opinion polls, the Government began to register record lows, and Mrs Thatcher's personal rating fell steeply through 1980. The Party grew increasingly restive, but apart from sporadic attacks and coded warnings, there was little that the Cabinet wets, denied access to the formulation of economic policy, could try to do.

This could not disguise the fact that there were deep misgivings. It had always been assumed that a Government which *chose* to preside over mass unemployment would render itself unelectable. Heath's U-turn in economic policy in 1972 had signalled the return to a more Keynesian approach when the jobless total had crept above one million; Mrs Thatcher was holding to her course with the total at three million. Even some of her most loyal supporters began to desert her, since they concluded that just as the Conservative Party of the 1930s had been condemned to be the party of mass unemployment, so now in the 1980s Mrs Thatcher was committing electoral suicide.

Calls came from all sides to reflate the economy: to spend the way out of the recession. But the Thatcherites dug their heels in, reiterating their prediction that their policies needed time to bear fruit. John Biffen pointed to the economic necessity of sticking to the Government's policies: 'Overmanning has been replaced by unemployment, a change which is miserable in human terms in the short run but eventually carrying a potential for national advantage ...' The CBI, increasingly disturbed, put forward a plan for reflation which would require an expenditure of £6 billion. Mrs Thatcher turned her back on it, refusing to countenance the idea of spending to alleviate the situation, seeing it in both the narrow economic context and the wider philosophical context. On the issue of unemployment she would have said then what she said to Peter Jay in an interview five years later:

> The only way we're going to get higher employment, more jobs, is by quite simply the old fashioned way ... by companies, businesses, starting up to produce goods or services that other people will buy – the right design, the right price, the right value. I believe that we could do much better at that than we are. I believe we have lost a lot of the elements of enterprise ... I am very much trying to get that back here. It's trying to roll back a whole attitude of mind for many many years. It is going to take time. But we will only get more people employed, other than by shuffling round the money that we've got, we'll only get more people employed by the creation of more small businesses, and more self-employment.

By the autumn of 1980, the chemicals giant, ICI, the flagship of British industry, had declared a yearly deficit for the first time in its history. Their announcement seemed to encapsulate the pervading industrial misery.

It was in this atmosphere that in October Mrs Thatcher faced the Conservative Party conference at Brighton and made a defiant speech declaring that she was not to be swayed from her chosen path. She had always been a popular leader with the conference. The Party faithful liked her combative, partisan approach. It was on this occasion that she needed their support most. Adapting the title of Christopher Fry's play, and referring to Heath's U-turn in 1972, she told the conference: 'The Lady's not for turning.' She went on: 'I will not change just to court popularity ... if ever a Conservative Government starts to do what it knows is wrong because it is afraid to do what is right, that is the time for the Tories to cry "Stop". But you will never need to do that while I am Prime Minister.'

She received a six-minute standing ovation. The conviction politician was not going to make U-turns. This might have been good propaganda for the Party faithful, but it made some of Heath's old supporters wince. One ex-Cabinet Minister found her barely coded references to the former leader 'unpardonable – there was no reason for her to make a big public spectacle of *not* making U-turns ... (it) has done much harm to the Party.' Asked by an American television interviewer two years later to look back on this period she said: 'When the ratings were very bad it was an acutely difficult time for us, and nevertheless I knew that we had to do certain things economically to get things right in the long run. There are certain right ways to go, and you have to stick to it long enough to get the results.'

Beneath the rhetoric, it was clear that the Government was adrift. The MTFS was way off target; unemployment was rising much faster than expected and inflation was still at 20%. Inflation had been fuelled by the Government's rash and, in retrospect, foolhardy acceptance of the full conclusions of the Clegg Commission on wages to which it had pledged itself for prudent electoral reasons during the 1979 election campaign. It is estimated that this added about £2,000 million to the public sector costs, thus increasing inflation. It was widely recognized now that the economic policy of the Government was off course, and that the previous simplistic expectations of monetarism entertained in 1978 were no longer adequate – even to the extent that they had found the money supply itself to be virtually immeasurable. Mrs Thatcher began to cast around for new ideas and solutions to what looked like becoming an economic débâcle. For some months, economists like John Forsyth of Morgan Grenfell had been arguing that to stimulate industry and achieve growth out of the recession, it was essential that monetary policy should be relaxed, but to compensate for this public expenditure had to come down further. In an economic analysis of 1980, Forsyth had argued 'to preserve the industrial structure of the economy and encourage the growth of the non-oil sector', so Britain would 'have to run a smaller deficit and even a public sector surplus'. Forsyth recognized that the high interest rates the Government was maintaining to keep the money supply down merely limited the private sector's access to credit to do business – and it was precisely to the private sector that the Thatcherites were looking for the regeneration of the economy. The prescription now seemed to be for a relaxation in monetary supply, through a cut in interest rates and a compensatory cut in public expenditure.

This was largely the conclusion reached by Alan Walters, one of the architects of the Government's monetarist economic policy, who took up the post of Chief Economic adviser to Mrs Thatcher in January 1981. He and Alfred Sherman brought in an independent economist from the University of Berne, Jurg Niehaus, to confirm their findings, which he duly did. When he also pronounced that the Government's techniques for measuring the money supply were misleading, the experts decided that monetary policy should be relaxed, and fiscal policy (public expenditure, the PSBR) should be tightened. The first signs that a policy change was occurring came on 14 November 1980 when the Government sanctioned a cut in interest rates of 2%, and the Prime Minister announced that the Government was preparing for a fresh round of public expenditure cuts.

The change was in belated recognition of shifting economic circumstances. None the less, it signalled a change in emphasis within the broad anti-inflation strategy. It was not a U-turn – the aim of the economic strategy, the defeat of inflation, remained the same – but the technical means to achieve it were modified. Monetary control was now downgraded in importance – by the 1982 budget, M3, the fashionable measure of the money supply of 1980, scarcely merited a mention. Budgetary cuts to eliminate the PSBR became the primary method of beating inflation. There is no doubt that this shift in emphasis during the winter of 1980–81 did much to restore industrial prosperity both in the short term and long run. It also demonstrated again that behind the rhetoric was a cautious politician, amenable to argumentation – provided it came from 'one of us'. But the rhetoric was essential, since it was, to use Alan Walter's analogy, 'the Bullseye'. Even if the actual achievement was a little off beam, it would still be of considerable merit.

This was the background to the budget of 1981. Once again, its formulation was kept within the confines of the Thatcherite Ministers.

Notwithstanding his seat on the E Committee, even Jim Prior was apparently excluded from their deliberations: he did not see the budget details until the afternoon before Sir Geoffrey Howe presented them to the House of Commons. When Prior was told them by Howe, 'I told him it was awful and absolutely misjudged ... I couldn't say anything bad enough about it.' Which was presumably why the Cabinet had been excluded from the discussion. Francis Pym, like Prior, thought the budget was 'awful' and the means of arriving at it unconstitutional. As he has written:

> The 1981 budget was rigidly deflationary and thus highly controversial at a time of deep recession, yet the strategy behind it was never discussed in Cabinet and was only revealed to the full Cabinet on Budget day itself. One can guess the reason is the Chancellor and the Prime Minister concluded that the Cabinet might well insist on some changes. But that is why Cabinet exists – to make collective decisions on important issues that face individual Departments, and thus affect the Government as a whole. Collective responsibility is based on collective decision-making. Margaret Thatcher is not the first Prime Minister to circumvent her colleagues, nor will she be the last, but this habit is not the sign of a happy or healthy Government.

The budget was indeed severely deflationary and arose out of the Government's new concern with the PSBR. It was also a budget that was uniquely shaped by Mrs Thatcher. The Treasury drew up a list of proposals for cuts in the PSBR, feeling that really radical changes would not be called for. Sir Geoffrey Howe, and Sir Douglas Wass, the head of the Treasury, were, however, summoned to No 10 Downing Street to be confronted by Mrs Thatcher, Alan Walters, David Wolfson (Mrs Thatcher's political secretary) and Sir John Hoskyns. The Prime Minister told them that the Treasury's list of proposals was unacceptable, and then put forward a considerably lower PSBR figure, the Treasury figure being 'too soft'. The Treasury had provided for the indexing of income tax allowances. The lower PSBR could be achieved within the general policy by *not* indexing the allowances; in other words, the Prime Minister was now willing to see even pensions eroded by inflation for the sake of adapting to the new economic strategy. Howe and Wass both argued that the Downing Street figure for the PSBR would be too severe and that not indexing personal allowances would hit the pockets of many of the Government's staunchest supporters. After what has been described as a 'perfectly amicable' discussion, the Treasury men went away and revised their figures downwards. 'No blood was shed at this meeting, but much was shed at the subsequent Cabinet meeting,' said one who was present.

It was, even for Mrs Thatcher, a singularly bold as well as radical move – all the more so when one considers that her own team at that meeting included no Cabinet Ministers; in terms of her attitude towards the substance of the 1981 budget, she was totally isolated within her own Cabinet.

The budget presented to the Cabinet on the morning of 10 March envisaged taking £4,300 million out of the economy by reducing the PSBR from £13.5 to £10.5 billion. At the same time, it outlined increases in indirect taxation on oil, drink, cigarettes, petrol and motor cars. Howe had even contemplated an increase in direct taxation, but desisted. All Keynesian economic orthodoxy demanded that at a time of recession the Government's role was to increase spending. Howe was doing exactly the opposite: increasing taxation and cutting spending. To Keynesian economic commentators like William Keegan this was heresy: 'The extraordinary contribution of the Thatcher Government was to remove the normal Keynesian procedure and to cut public spending and raise the tax burden when the economy was already in recession.'

One thing about the budget was indisputable: it was a watershed budget. It proved that the Government was determined to press on with its radical anti-inflationary policies even when Mrs Thatcher was under almost unanimous pressure to reflate the economy. This is perhaps why her critics, both in her own Cabinet and outside, were so surprised; not only had she rejected their advice to trim or reverse her policies, but she produced her most radical anti-inflationary budget yet. The academic economic establishment were similarly shocked; it was at this moment that 364 economists put their signatures to a letter to *The Times* arguing that the Government's economic policies were unworkable and would not lead to a reduction in inflation – a prophecy that was soon to be confounded. Flying in the face of all received wisdom and opinion, Mrs Thatcher needed all her confidence in her sense of mission. For the Thatcherites, this moment brought the ultimate test of dedication to the cause.

The wets were astounded by the budget, but they failed to form an effective opposition to it. It was at this juncture that they can be seen to have failed. Behind them they had the almost unanimous backing of popular opinion, an unemployment rate of two million and rising, and the embattled economic establishment: yet they allowed themselves to be steamrollered by Mrs Thatcher. 'The wets are wet indeed,' one of her staff is reported to have said. The reason for the ineffectiveness of the wets is still not clear, but some things are plain. They never presented a coherent articulate case against Mrs Thatcher. The most charismatic and politically prestigious of their number, Lord Carrington, was immersed in Foreign Office business, and so could contribute little. They were undoubtedly restrained by the traditional Conservative ties of loyalty to the Prime Minister. They knew that if they brought her down by a mass resignation, they would hand the Government on a plate to a hopelessly divided and ineffectual Labour Party under Michael Foot. This was an alternative that none of them wanted even to contemplate. As Peter Riddell, political editor of the *Financial Times*, has written, the weakness of the wets was that they 'were never clear about what they wanted to do, nor did they have the will to press their case ... The prevailing ethos of the Conservative Party was against them; loyalty counted more than doubt. They knew that Mrs Thatcher had gauged the mood of the Conservative activists correctly and that there would be little support for any challenge.'

The one concession that the wets did get from the Prime Minister was a promise that in future, economic policy would be discussed in Cabinet. Prior has recorded how divided the Cabinet was on the first occasion that this happened and how isolated Mrs Thatcher's position had become:

> In July 1981, the controversy over the Budget was revived at the Cabinet's annual set-piece discussion of the Government's future spending plans. On this occasion, even several of those usually friendly to the overall policy could find little to favour in the Treasury's submission. Only Margaret and Keith backed the Chancellor and his Chief Secretary. The Treasury's critics included, most notably and unexpectedly, John Biffen [no longer Chief Secretary] and John Nott.

If Mrs Thatcher could count on only three committed supporters, the situation outside the Cabinet was much more serious. The popularity of the Conservative Party was at an all time low. In December 1981, a Gallup poll put the Conservatives' rating at 23% and the proportion of the electorate expressing satisfaction with Mrs Thatcher's performance at a dismal 25%. Popular discontent had been demonstrated, and increased, by the inner city riots of July when the central areas of Brixton in London, Toxteth in Liverpool, Moss Side in Manchester and St Paul's in Bristol erupted in riots, arson and looting. This was a severe blow to the nation's self-esteem. When such disturbances had happened in other western countries, notably during the 1960s in the USA, the view of the British people was that 'it could never happen here'. The eruptions in the inner cities seemed to be the ultimate antithesis of everything that 'One Nation Toryism' was supposed to stand for. Some objective observers, as well as Mrs Thatcher's critics, claimed that the poverty and unemployment which the Government's deflationary policies had induced was largely responsible.

Unemployment meanwhile continued to climb, and inflation stayed stubbornly high. During the summer of 1981, Mrs Thatcher's political stock reached its nadir. She kept her nerve; Thatcherism during the summer of 1981 was not for the faint-hearted.

If the Government's fortunes were to recover, the newly devised economic strategy had to be put into operation, and, more importantly, it had to be seen to work. The new strategy was still an anti-inflationary strategy, but the emphasis was now less on the money supply and more on the fiscal side – controlling and possibly eliminating the PSBR. The significance of this switch in tactics was not fully appreciated at the time, but in retrospect it has come to assume a significance of immense proportions. In it lay not only the seeds of the recovery of the British economy, but also the difference between 'Reaganomics' and 'Thatcherite economics'. As John Forsyth pointed out: 'Reagan never performed such a U-turn, so that Reaganomics and Thatcherite economics, which were widely regarded as two peas from the same pod, diverged fundamentally from that winter with consequences which are now only too apparent' – with the record-breaking American Federal budget deficit destabilizing the hard-fought gains of the previous six years. Behind the defiant rhetoric of 1980–81, Mrs Thatcher had once again proved her worth as an empirical, cautious politician in effecting this vital change.

However, for the new strategy to work, the PSBR, as Howe had announced in his 1981 budget, had to be reduced, and here Mrs Thatcher was up against the political difficulties of Government spending cuts. Having come to her new conclusions about the economy, she still had to demonstrate the iron resolve needed to carry the policy through. Just how difficult this would be had been demonstrated by the experiences of Sir Keith Joseph at the Department of Industry – where his apparent inability to cut anything had at least been partly responsible for the fact that by October 1980, the Government had exceeded its public spending forecasts by nearly £1.5 billion for the *first half* of the financial year 1980–81. Standing firm in the face of strikes such as the steel strike of 1980 and the prolonged Civil Service strike of 1981 was not going to be enough.

At the Department of Industry, Sir Keith, the 'arch-monetarist', was confronted by a series of unpalatable choices between spending money

112

on the despised nationalized industries or seeing them go bust, with all the political uproar and social distress which that would cause. The problems for Sir Keith were very much worsened by the world recession and the high pound, since an admittedly uncompetitive manufacturing industry became even more so when it had to fight the same recession as its competitors. There were no grandiose plans of privatization in the 1979 manifesto. Sir Keith's task merely came down to, as he describes it, 'stopping the haemorrhage' in the nationalized industries, that is, preventing them from going bankrupt during the recession. Joseph had to do it, unwilling as he was: Jim Prior has described how the conscientious Minister of Industry would sit in Cabinet in 'the most appalling agony' wrestling with 'the dilemma between doctrine and pragmatism'. This might have given the wets some ironic amusement, but it endangered the whole of the Government's economic strategy.

A good example of Sir Keith's dilemma was provided by the steel industry, which suffered from chronic overmanning and inefficiency and by 1980 was losing £2 million per day. To make the industry efficient and save it during the recession, on Sir Keith's advice the Government imported Ian MacGregor, a Scottish American industrialist, from the New York firm of Lazard Brothers, at a 'transfer fee' of £1.8 million. This caused protests, but there came a storm when after his first few months as British Steel Corporation's chairman, Mr MacGregor announced that 20,000 jobs would have to go, and that capacity would have to be reduced so that BSC could aim for profitability by 1982–3. Profitability was an enticing prospect, but MacGregor also asked for a Government cash injection of £6.6 billion to enable him to carry out his corporate plan. Faced with the prospect of handing out the money, or presiding over the wholesale collapse of the industry, Sir Keith chose the very un-monetarist first option. In the end, much like the Government's MTFS, MacGregor's break-even predictions were way off beam, but in the course of making his error he further lowered the Government's already sinking popularity by the closure, with all its attendant social miseries, of steelworks at Corby, Port Talbot and Scunthorpe.

British Leyland posed another dilemma when Sir Michael Edwardes similarly held out the enticing prospect of a return to profitability if the Government was prepared to fund *his* corporate plan for the ailing car giant. Sir Keith resolved this dilemma as he had that presented by BSC, and consequently the launching of the new Metro and Maestro range of cars was supported by a handout of £990 million. To the surprise of many, the Government also disbursed £9 million to save the Meriden Motor Cycle Corporation, a co-operative workers' enterprise

113

that had been the cherished child of Tony Benn from his days at the Department of Industry; for Sir Keith Joseph to be bailing it out seemed most incongruous. Similarly, £200 million was given to the computer giant ICL to prevent liquidity, £13 million was assigned to write off the debts of the National Film Finance Corporation and most controversially of all, the Government gave a hefty grant to the American car producer John DeLorean to start making sports cars in Belfast. These hand-outs were glaringly at odds with the declared policy of encouraging competition rather than using public money to lengthen the life of lame ducks.

Sir Keith Joseph was, in fact, the prime victim of the Government's monetarist policies. Industry was the hardest hit sector of the economy, and there was little doubt in the minds of most industrialists that Government policy, not the world recession, was mainly largely responsible for their predicament. The high level of interest rates, essential to the Government's tight control of the money supply up to 1981, and the contemporaneous high exchange rate led to the liquidation of much of manufacturing Britain. A number of economists have agreed in their estimates that between one third and a half of the unemployment created during the first two years of Mrs Thatcher's Government was directly attributable to Government policy. The monetarists had predicted unemployment as a necessary and, in the long term, therapeutic consequence of their policies – but none of them had predicted publicly that it would top three million by the beginning of 1982.

With the shift in policy during the winter of 1980–81 specifically designed to help industry beat the recession by bringing both interest rates and exchange rates down, so the Government was now looking for Government spending cuts to compensate for the laxer monetary control to keep on the course of their anti-inflationary strategy. Yet it was obvious that the industrial sector was not going to provide those cuts, and that Mrs Thatcher was thus going to have to look elsewhere, which meant the big spending Departments. The crucial problem here was that they were in the hands of the wets – most notably Francis Pym at Defence, Patrick Jenkin at Health and Social Security, and Michael Heseltine at Environment. Lord Carrington at the Foreign Office could also organize a powerful lobby in defence of his own Department's interests, such as the BBC External Services, the cost of which many Government supporters wanted cut.

With the switch from monetary to fiscal policy in the winter of 1980–81, the wets now came directly into the firing line. Until then they may have been unhappy with Mrs Thatcher's economic policies, but they had also had precious little chance to influence or mitigate them. Now, by defending their Departmental interests, they could for the first time effectively obstruct the Government of which they were part. The irony of the situation was that in doing so, they were obstructing a policy that was designed to alleviate the problems of industry and unemployment about which they were so vocal. But as Mrs Thatcher never discussed economic policy with them, and since they were all oblivious to the economic reshaping that was going on in Downing Street at that time, there was no reason why they should have appreciated this!

Battle was joined in November 1980 when the Treasury ordered public spending cuts of £1,000 million – £500 million from the Ministry of Defence and the rest from the Department of Health and Social Security (DHSS). Pym treated this threat to his budget as a resignation issue, and leaks to the press made this threat perfectly clear. Defence was always an emotive issue for the Conservatives and it proved easy to rally many of the Party faithful and the press to his side. As he has since described this episode:

> The one occasion when I might have resigned was in 1980 when, as Secretary of State for Defence, I had a major row with the Prime Minister and the Treasury over their proposed cuts in defence expenditure. I was convinced they were wrong on both defence and political grounds, and I think subsequent events proved me right. As it happens, I won the argument. Had I lost, I would have resigned, because the Cabinet would have overruled me on a fundamental matter for which I was primarily responsible . . .

On this occasion he won. The Treasury, having demanded £500 million worth of cuts, got only an almost token £170 million saving. Mrs Thatcher's and the Treasury's encounter with the wets over the DHSS was no more successful. The Treasury's proposal to cut the DHSS budget was that the coming year's old age pensions would not be increased in line with the rise in prices. Prior has given a description of this particular joust: 'But I went to Cabinet armed – as was Patrick Jenkin, the Social Services Secretary – with copies of Geoffrey Howe's and Keith Joseph's own personal election addresses in their constituencies at the 1979 election, in which they had specifically pledged to protect pensioners against inflation. So that idea was soon thrown out – Margaret was too good a politician to allow that to happen.'

The Treasury emerged from these 'discussions' with only half the savings that they had sought. (To compensate, they duly raised the cost of the employee's insurance stamp by 1% to raise the extra £1,000 million needed.) The next day, the 'Victory of the Wets' in the confidential Cabinet discussions was extraordinarily well publicized in the national press.

The 'new' or 'modified' economic policy, whatever the name given to it, meant that there would have to be a political showdown within the Cabinet, and such there was. Up to now, by concentrating on the monetary side of the anti-inflationary strategy, Mrs Thatcher had been able to pursue her economic policy without having to seek recourse to the Cabinet table, where she was outnumbered, because the tight control of the money supply need not involve her Cabinet colleagues. Now, the switch of emphasis to the fiscal side and the need to reduce the PSBR involved her in confrontations with those of her Cabinet colleagues in charge of the spending ministries. This issue could no longer be excluded from Cabinet, as the new economic policy had to involve *all* her ministries. She had to choose between two options: she could either capitulate, and abandon the economic strategy; or she could sack some of her Cabinet.

Not surprisingly, conviction politics require the latter approach. In the New Year (1981) she undertook her first Cabinet reshuffle. It was designed to bolster her position in the Cabinet and remove the recalcitrant wets from the spending ministries. Thus Francis Pym was removed from the MoD to become Leader of the House of Commons, and John Nott, a very arid dry, replaced him. Leon Brittan, another dry, became Chief Secretary of the Treasury, John Biffen went to the Department of Trade and Norman St John-Stevas, a most unThatcherite wet, given to making witty but spikey cracks about her, was sacked altogether. This reshuffle gave her much more power around the Cabinet table but was, as usual, a cautious move – the principal wets (Prior, Gilmour, Pym, Carrington, Walker and Carlisle) were still in place but they had been served notice. The replacement of Pym at the MoD had immediate results, as John Nott immediately set about trying to cut the MoD budget, and in 1981 he produced his controversial defence review which threatened the existence of the Royal Navy's surface fleet to an unprecedented degree, and which prompted the resignation of the Navy Minister, Keith Speed. Fortunately, General Galtieri decided to invade the Falklands before this review could be put into effect – it would have left a much reduced Navy to retake the Falkland Islands. ·

The reshuffle also meant that, outraged as the wets were, the 1981 budget got a better ride in the Cabinet. As we have seen, one of the concessions they won in the wake of the budget was the opportunity to discuss economic policy. Prior has described how the first meeting to do this, in July 1981, exposed both how isolated Mrs Thatcher had become and how divided the Cabinet was. To Mrs Thatcher, her isolation had to be ended, especially if more public expenditure cuts were to be implemented. This July meeting was the first, and last, look the wets would get at economic policy. As the economic gloom of the summer darkened, this only seemed to fuel her resolve to implement her policies to the greatest extent possible. It was probably perceived in Downing Street that the anti-inflationary strategy was not being allowed to work because of the obstructionists in the Cabinet. The PSBR had to be cut, and it was still evident that she did not have a Cabinet ready to do this.

In September 1981, therefore, the really big sweep came: Peter Walker remained Minister of Agriculture; otherwise the wets were either sacked outright or removed to where they could do no harm. Lord Soames, who was mistrusted for having tried to negotiate the Government's way out of the Civil Service dispute, was sacked, as was the most antagonistic and articulate wet, Ian Gilmour. Jim Prior, despite his protestations, was exiled to Northern Ireland. Lord Thorneycroft, who had admitted to 'rising damp', was sacked as Party Chairman. Mark Carlisle withdrew to the back benches. To replace them, the younger generation of Thatcherite junior ministers were now promoted to take their place. Nigel Lawson, who had been one of the principal architects of the Government's MTFS, became the Minister for Energy; Norman Fowler went to the Department of Health and Social Security; Cecil Parkinson became Party Chairman; Norman Tebbit became Employment Minister, and Jock Bruce-Gardyne and Nicholas Ridley went to the Treasury to inject it with a little more enthusiasm for Thatcherism. Other changes included Sir Keith Joseph becoming the Secretary of State for Education and Patrick Jenkin going to the Department of Transport. Jock Bruce-Gardyne has since written: 'It was indeed a sea-change. For the first time since she had come to office the Prime Minister had built herself a clear majority in the Cabinet.'

It was *indeed* a sea-change, and must have considerably bolstered her confidence to force through the reforms she wanted. The two remaining wets, Francis Pym and Jim Prior were both neutralized: Prior, although he retained a seat on the E Committee, was, as was expected, so busy in Northern Ireland that he was effectively removed from criticizing economic policy. Pym, as Leader of the House of Commons, was also removed from the nexus of economic decision making. The only constant factors throughout these reshuffles were Willie Whitelaw and Lord Carrington. Whitelaw, despite his undoubted sympathies for the case of the wets and his former mentor, Ted Heath, put loyalty to the Prime

Minister at a premium. As her position looked increasingly precarious through 1981, Whitelaw's loyalty – coming as it did from the most senior, balanced and respected politician in the Party – was probably her greatest asset. Lord Carrington likewise sympathized with the wets, but his role as Foreign Secretary effectively excluded him from paying much attention to the detailed economic arguments.

Mrs Thatcher's resolve, demonstrated by her Cabinet changes, was once more on display at the Party conference in October 1981, when she once again declared herself against any change in policy when the Government was 'within an ace of success'. It was evident that she was indeed a singular politician and many now began to admire her merely for her resolution – no matter what she was being resolute about.

The replacement of Prior by Tebbit was another indication that she regarded the pace of her reforms as too slow. The nation was not being 'saved', in her view, because her policies were not being implemented with sufficient vigour. Trade union reform had been one of the major pledges in the Conservative manifesto. The appointment of Prior as Minister for Employment when the Party came to power had given encouragement to the wets that the Government would not rush at this objective as Heath had done in 1971 with his ill-fated and unworkable Industrial Relations Act – drafted as it so happens, largely by Sir Geoffrey Howe. Prior fully agreed with this approach (it became known as the 'Softly, Softly' approach) and as a result he became the regular whipping boy of the right wing of the Party who all remembered the ignominious collapse of the Heath Government at the hands of union militants and who now wanted to pass punitive legislation against the unions as fast as possible while, in the aftermath of the winter of discontent, they still had the chance and popular opinion was on their side. Mrs Thatcher often made it clear that she counted herself amongst the ranks of these more urgent reformers.

Prior was thus caught in an awkward vice between the right wing of his own Party and the unions themselves who were naturally suspicious of any legislation. In the end, he handled both sides very well and managed to go at his own pace in his own time. His Employment Bill that was eventually passed in July 1980 went some way towards correcting the most obvious union abuses that had been on display during the winter of discontent, without totally alienating the unions. It outlawed secondary picketing; allowed money to be given to unions from Government funds to hold their own ballots on strikes; restricted coercive practices of union recruiting; and it limited the closed shop.

The philosophic premise underlying the Conservative Party's

approach to the unions was that by passing such legislation they were giving the unions back to their members. The thesis was that the ordinary union members had for years been oppressed by the tyrannical, self-interested 'union barons', and, consequently, by encouraging elections and by discouraging union monopoly practices, the Government was now giving back to the union rank and file their 'freedom' and their 'right to choose', rights that had been usurped by politically motivated militants. Once again, as with the sale of council houses, Mrs Thatcher was tapping a rich vein of popular feeling that proved to be electorally rewarding. The number of 'working class' voters for Mrs Thatcher has been one of the most striking features of her election victories. The Thatcherites deemed Jim Prior to be too 'corporatist' in his approach to those very union leaders to whom the Thatcherites were most antagonistic. As well as arguing for inflation of the economy in Cabinet, Prior would also argue 'for a public sector wages policy, combined with a form of national economic forum'. Mrs Thatcher consistently resisted this, for – as Prior himself observed – 'It would have involved giving too much credibility to trade union leaders'. The Thatcherite ethos was populist in the sense that it was releasing the workers from their thraldom to the union leaders. The new Minister, Mr Tebbit, a self-made man in the new Thatcherite mould, was much more in tune with this line of thinking, and his taking over from Prior in September 1981 gave a good indication of where Mrs Thatcher wanted to go – and how fast – so far as the unions were concerned.

The vanquishing of the wets and the maintenance of the anti-inflationary strategy, despite the unprecedented chorus of disapproval, mark the year 1981 out as the watershed year of Mrs Thatcher's three successive Governments. That she could go on to give millions of people shares in industry, let alone fight the Falklands War in 1982, was indeed a minor miracle considering the buffeting the Government took the previous year. In the summer of 1981, she was almost isolated, not only in the Cabinet, but in the country as well. To say she had the courage of her convictions is an understatement. What appeared to some to be supreme resolution was to others sheer bloody-mindedness. What neither group realized was that behind the rhetoric she had effected the necessary economic and personnel changes that were to ensure her survival. She was resolute about putting into practice the new economic strategy; that the new economic strategy had been allowed to evolve showed that behind the resolution was a cautious, calculating, empirical political mind.

In 1981 the wets were effectively neutralized as a political force within

119

the confines of the Conservative Party, though the argument between the two wings of the Party is still very much alive, and it is perhaps too early to foresee what may happen in the future to the cleavage between them. Meanwhile, much of what the wets and the drys perceived to be the difference between them in general terms is expressed by Francis Pym: 'In my case, I never seriously considered resigning from Margaret Thatcher's Government over issues of general policy. As I have already made clear, I do not like the style of the Government, nor the tone it adopts in presenting and debating policy, and I disagree with certain aspects of policy. But I remain a firm supporter of the Government's objectives and of much that it has achieved.'

It would thus seem to be more the methods which Mrs Thatcher has adopted rather than her objectives which have angered the wets. Of her objectives Ian Gilmour has written:

In their defence of the individual against Socialism and excessive State power, Conservatives rely chiefly upon the family and private property ... If there is no private property, there will be no freedom. The State will be unchallengeable and supreme. On similar grounds, Conservatives support the system of private enterprise. State monopoly spells tyranny ... Conservatives value private property and private enterprise primarily as the protectors of the family and of freedom.

The wets were the generation of Ted Heath and they supported him in his quest for the 'Quiet Revolution' when he was elected to power. What Mrs Thatcher was trying to do in 1979 was almost exactly what Heath set out to do in 1970. The means were perhaps different, but the ends were the same. And yet the whole idea of a quiet revolution is self-evidently contradictory. Revolutions are not quiet. Mrs Thatcher's tone and style of policy implementation are a necessary, indeed vital, part of the Thatcherite revolution. What the wets learned was that you could not have one without the other. By the same token, Mrs Thatcher could only succeed if she was possessed of the Messianic and moral zeal to introduce the property-owning democracy; only if she was possessed of the notion that she was saving the country from the tyranny of Socialism could she have succeeded in seeing through the gloomy years of 1980 and 1981. Hers was a frame of mind very alien to the traditionally sceptical and pragmatic high Tory political thinking.

Furthermore, just as the prospects for the Government looked at their dullest during the autumn of 1981, there were the first faint glimmerings that the economic rewards for the devotion to the anti-

Margaret Roberts (*front row, fifth from right*) at primary school.

Margaret Roberts married Denis Thatcher in 1951.

Before her marriage, she worked as a research chemist.

Campaigning as Conservative candidate in Dartford, 1951. She lost to Labour.

Six-year-olds Mark and Carol with the newly elected MP for Barnet, Finchley, 1959.

The new leader of the Conservative Party, 1975, with two key supporters: (*above right*) Airey Neave and (*below*) Sir Keith Joseph.

With two former Prime Ministers: (*above*) Ted Heath and (*below*) Harold Macmillan.

Britain's first woman Prime Minister, May 1979, with her Cabinet: (*left to right*) Michael Jopling, Norman Fowler, John Biffen, David Howell, Norman St John-Stevas, Humphrey Atkins, George Younger, Michael Heseltine, Nicholas Edwards, Patrick Jenkin, John Nott, Mark Carlisle, Angus Maude and Sir John Hunt; (*seated*) Sir Ian Gilmour, Lord Soames, Sir Keith Joseph, Lord Carrington, William Whitelaw, Margaret Thatcher, Lord Hailsham, Sir Geoffrey Howe, Francis Pym, James Prior and Peter Walker.

With the Governor of the Falklands, Rex Hunt, during the crisis, April 1982, and (*right*) aboard a Polaris submarine the same year.

With her despatch box and (*below*) during the 1983 general election campaign, which won her a second term.

With friend and ally President Reagan in June 1984.

After the church service following the IRA bomb explosion which killed five people during the Party conference in Brighton, October 1984.

At the 1985 Bonn summit meeting of the world's leading industrialized nations: Helmut Kohl, Margaret Thatcher, Jacques Delors, Yasuhiro Nakasone, Ronald Reagan, Bettino Craxi, Brian Mulroney and François Mitterrand.

Visiting police and troops in South Armagh, Northern Ireland, 1986.

On holiday in Cornwall.

inflationary strategy were beginning to come. For in the autumn, inflation began to fall, as it continued to do for the next eighteen months until it reached below 5% by the time of the 1983 election. As well as this, it was announced that productivity for the year 1981 had been the best since the war and that the supposedly insurmountable 'British disease' of endless strikes had been cured as British industry reached the lowest strike rate since 1939. None the less, during the autumn and winter of 1981 the Opposition Parties were riding high in the polls; a finding confirmed spectacularly by the victory of Mrs Shirley Williams of the newly founded SDP at a by-election in Crosby when she won the seat by overturning a Tory majority of 18,000. Roy Jenkins won an equally spectacular victory for them in Glasgow. It was obvious that many Conservative moderates were deserting to the more consensus style politics of the SDP and Liberals, and the telegenic leadership of the SDP began to distribute the portfolios of Government between themselves in anticipation of their coming general election victory.

But by the New Year, with the brightening economic news, the Government's stock was slowly recovering from the very low point of 1981. By March 1982 inflation was falling rapidly. It began to look as though there might be some reward for what John Biffen described as the previous 'three years of unparalleled austerity'. The March 1982 Budget stuck to the economic strategy whilst some electorally popular tax cuts were also included. Industry was cheered by it, and by the continuing notable absence of the tight monetary control that had characterized the budgets of 1979 and 1980. M3 and money supply were now barely mentioned. Furthermore the value of the pound against the dollar was now falling, from $2.40 to a much more manageable $1.50, adding to industrial competitiveness. To those critics who complained that by its own standards of 1979 public expenditure was still far too high, the Government could rightly claim that having staggered through the worst recession for nearly fifty years, it was a remarkable feat to *contain* spending as they had done – considering that all other political and economic wisdom pointed to the old Keynesian remedy of spending its way out of the recession. And in this probably lay the Government's trump card. All the old remedies had been tried in the past and had been seen to fail, merely producing runaway inflation and in the end uncompetitiveness and unemployment. Jim Callaghan had warned everyone as long ago as 1976 that the days of spending your way out of a recession were gone. Mrs Thatcher was taking him at his word.

Even so, with unemployment at over three million and the opinion polls showing a recovery for the Conservatives in so far as they were now neck-and-neck with Labour and the SDP/Liberal Alliance, the Government's prospects still looked perilous. Then, suddenly, things changed: the precipitating factor being the news on 2 April 1982 that the Argentinians had invaded the Falkland Islands.

# 9

# THE FALKLANDS WAR

Today, Mrs Thatcher's admirers claim that in the field of foreign policy she is Britain's most effective and influential Premier since 1945. There is no doubt that her international standing is the envy of many other middle-ranking powers. She is, above all, a leader whom other powers can trust: there is unlikely to be any arms-for-hostages dealing while Mrs Thatcher remains at Downing Street.

Before considering her conduct at the time of the Falklands crisis, and the better to understand the effect she has had on Britain's international standing, it would be useful to reconsider Britain's place in the world as seen a decade ago by the vastly experienced and objective Sir Nicholas Henderson, former British Ambassador to Poland, West Germany, France and later the United States. On giving up his post in Paris in the spring of 1979, Sir Nicholas composed a valedictory despatch for the benefit of the Foreign Secretary, a convention observed by all retiring envoys. The dissertation which Sir Nicholas submitted to Dr David Owen, Foreign Secretary in Mr Callaghan's Labour Government, intentionally went well beyond the bounds of polite reminiscence characteristic of such documents. The theme that urged Sir Nicholas 'to go beyond the limits of an Ambassador's normal responsibilities' was that of Britain's precipitate economic decline since 1945, resulting in the country's standing in the world being at a distressingly low point. The note accompanying the report to the Foreign Secretary read as follows:

Sir – Since Ernest Bevin made his plea a generation ago for more coal to give weight to his foreign policy, our economic decline has been such as to sap the foundations of our diplomacy. Conversely, I believe that, during the same period, much of our foreign policy has been such as to contribute to that decline. It is to the interaction of these delicts, spanning my time in the Foreign Service, that this valedictory despatch is devoted.

Whilst accepting that it was inevitable that Britain's influence would be outstripped by that of her two wartime partners the USSR and the USA, the retiring Ambassador, having been able to make such comparisons from the advantage of postings to Madrid, Warsaw, Bonn and Paris, wrote:

It is our decline since 1945 in relation to our European partners that has been so marked, so that today we are not only no longer a world power, but we are not in the first rank, even as a European one. Income per head in Britain is now, for the first time for over 300 years, below that in France. We are scarcely in the same economic league as the Germans or French. We talk of ourselves without shame as being one of the less prosperous countries of Europe. The prognosis for the foreseeable future is discouraging. If present trends continue we shall be overtaken in GDP per head by Italy and Spain well before the end of the century.

Britain no longer counted in Europe, let alone on the world stage, said Henderson. Even the Americans, when they wanted to deal with Europe, tended to bypass London and go direct to Bonn or Paris because the governments there were not perpetually being plunged into economic crisis and so could deliver political action. Henderson also warned of the enveloping complacency that still permeated the British. Through continental eyes 'the British people do not give the impression that they are fully aware of how far Britain's economy has fallen behind ...', nor did they seem to be aware of 'the efforts needed to reverse the trend'. Henderson concluded by saying that what was needed was 'a considerable jolt' if the trend was to be reversed.

Two months after this was written Mrs Thatcher became Prime Minister, and shortly afterwards made a visit to Paris accompanied by the new Foreign Secretary, Lord Carrington. By then *The Economist* had acquired a copy of Sir Nicholas's despatch and had published his conclusions. In Paris Mrs Thatcher gave a press conference at which she was asked by David Lawday of *The Economist* if she agreed with Sir Nicholas's assessment of Britain's international standing. She replied that his despatch had said, 'Some of the things which Peter Carrington and I have been saying with much less panache and much less style. . . . One could not quarrel with that analysis, I'm afraid. It's all written there in figures. What I am determined to do is to get the position turned. That, after all, is why, I believe, we were elected.'

For the next three years she carried out the 'jolting' policies she thought necessary to restore Britain's strength on the domestic front, and by March 1982 the first fruits of this painful treatment had appeared with the fall in inflation, the central objective of the Government's economic policy. This achievement did not make her a heroine in the eyes of the majority, who were more aware of the industrial and social dislocation which had come in its wake. Few people in the early days of 1982 would have put money on the return of a majority Conservative Government at the next general election. The problem lay in what Henderson had seen as the lack of public awareness over Britain's problems; the British, a proud island race, were unwilling to see just how low they had sunk in the eyes of the world by 1979, and how far they were destined to keep on falling unless the process were reversed. The blame for this national state of mind, a psychological malaise, was fixed by Henderson upon Britain's position at the end of the Second World War: 'Although we were victorious we were only marginally victorious: we did not have the spur that defeat might have provided, nor did we have the strength with which victory should have endowed us.' In the war, he said, France, Germany and Japan had been humiliated and devastated and it was out of this very humiliation that the astounding national regeneration of those countries had come. They had consciously sought national salvation as a means of wiping clean the humiliating slate of 1939–45. Henderson believed that for Britain to undergo a similar regeneration, a similar sense of 'national purpose' had to be stimulated.

For all Mrs Thatcher's efforts during her first three years of office, she had not succeeded in generating a sense of 'national purpose' or a 'national will'. Unpalatable economic policies were not enough. What was needed was a national humiliation. Only then would the British people as a whole feel, as Henderson had written of the Germans since 1945, 'the dire need to rise from the ashes'. Such a national humiliation was provided by the Argentinian invasion of the Falkland Islands; the rise from the ashes was provided by Mrs Thatcher.

It was from precisely such a foreign perception of Britain as a sick, declining, dozy nation that Henderson had outlined to David Owen in 1979 that Argentina viewed Britain in the early 1980s. Not only did the Lion have no claws; it seemed asleep as well. This was the Argentinian junta's most fundamental mistake: they did not realize that much had changed since 1979; that by 1982 Mrs Thatcher was in power and that Britain had never had a political leader better able to take the national pulse. The intention of the Argentinians to invade the Falklands was based on the fundamental misconception that Britain no longer had the political will or national conviction to defend a small patch of land so remote. The whole of Britain's post-war history, with its systematic shedding of colonial responsibility, seemed to them to ensure that they would have nothing more to fear than the languid Lion's roar. Throughout April 1982, as the British task force steamed towards the Falklands with the declared object of repossessing the islands by force if necessary, those who had to negotiate with the Argentinian junta saw with increasing despair that its leaders would not heed Mrs Thatcher's outspoken intentions. Alexander Haig, the American Secretary of State, who tried hard to negotiate a settlement which would prevent a war, later wrote of one of his last encounters with the Argentine rulers:

> Even after all that I had said to the contrary I feared that Galtieri and his colleagues were unable to believe that the British would fight. In one final attempt to convince them I sent Dick Walters (a State Department official and former Deputy Head of the CIA) to see Galtieri alone and tell him in crystal clear terms ... that if there was no negotiated settlement, the British would fight and win – and the United States would support Britain. Galtieri listened and replied: 'Why are you telling me this? The British won't fight.'[1]

Though the Argentinians based their strategy on a false premise, they had good reason for doing so. The malaise afflicting Britain, which Nicholas Henderson had identified, was compounded by the country's specific attitude towards the Falklands and seventeen years of desultory negotiation with Argentina that preceded the invasion. The dispute over the islands was historic, and the virtues of each side's case will not be discussed here. What was important to the Argentinians was the conclusion they had reached as a result of the negotiations from 1965 to 1982: that the British Foreign Office were willing to divest themselves of responsibility for islands which no one in Britain seemed to be greatly concerned about. The collective sagacity of the Foreign Office, as expressed by an endless succession of officials and junior ministers who had to deal with the problem, seemed to suggest that ultimately some form of leaseback arrangement would have to be negotiated with the Argentinians if the Falkland Islanders were to enjoy a secure economic and social future. The problem with this policy was that it foundered on the rock of the islanders' fervent wish to stay British. The alternative was a 'Fortress Falklands' policy which the prudent dismissed as un-

realistic, especially on the grounds of cost. If successive British Governments had entertained any doubts on this score, they were to be
disillusioned by the very voluble 'Falklands lobby' in the House of
Commons – mainly composed of right-wing Conservative MPs – who
prevented any government from trying to sneak through any compromise on the question of sovereignty as part of a wider package of co-
operative measures with Argentina.

If the Argentinians thus gained a perfectly understandable impression
that Britain would not only not defend the islands, but in typical post-
Colonial fashion, actually wanted to divest themselves of responsibility
for them, the British similarly based their negotiating strategy on the
false premise that the Argentinians would never fight for the islands.
This assumption was not unwarranted. On the only previous occasion
when a post-war British Government had sensed an armed threat from
Argentina to the Falklands – when in 1976 a group of Argentinian
'technicians' had landed on South Thule in the South Sandwich group
of islands – the British needed to do nothing more than make mild
diplomatic protests. It should have been recognized by the Foreign
Office that the prestige-hungry military dictatorships which ruled Argentina from 1976 to 1982 might be readier to resort to force in the South
Atlantic than the governments which had preceded them. In 1977, the
British Government despatched a nuclear submarine ready to 'deter'
threatening Argentinian moves towards the Falklands if they materialized, but its existence in these waters did not become known to
the Argentinians, so that it never became a factor in Argentinian
calculations.

British strategy was based on the premise that the Argentinians
would never launch an invasion to enforce their claims – despite mounting evidence to the contrary. The problem for the Foreign Office was
that they never mobilized opinion in Britain in support of their leaseback plans. However sensible and rational these plans might have been,
the Foreign Office left the field to the 'Falklands lobby' so far as the
more irrational and emotive arena of public debate was concerned. As
Simon Jenkins has written:

> A compromise settlement was never achieved because the British Foreign
> Office proved far more competent at negotiating with another government
> than with its own. Successive Cabinets regarded the political price of compro-
> mise as always just too high. American diplomats take it for granted that
> an essential function of their job is to lobby politicians, to sell policies that
> they consider desirable or essential to those who have the power to implement
> them. In Britain, the Foreign Office existed in a world of its own. Diplomats

failed to mobilize any constituency of political opinion for a compromise over the Falklands. Their ministers, whose responsibility they believed this to be, were never in office for long enough or were never sufficiently interested to do the job for them ... The flaw was that a political strategy was never evolved to complement the diplomatic one. Diplomacy without policies is ultimately impotent.[2]

When Mrs Thatcher came to power, the Foreign Office did not change its attitude to the Falklands problem. The new minister with responsibility for the Falklands was Nicholas Ridley and he, having been duly briefed by his officials came down firmly, as all his predecessors had done, in favour of leaseback. Negotiations went on as before, except that Ridley persuaded the Foreign Secretary, Lord Carrington, to seek Mrs Thatcher's permission to put his leaseback plan to Parliament. This is the first time that Mrs Thatcher is recorded as expressing a view on the subject of the Falklands: when Lord Carrington told her about the plan, her reaction has been reported as being 'thermonuclear'. She was firmly in line with the Falklands lobbyists in rejecting any deal that would infringe the islanders' rights of sovereignty, which effectively meant retaining the status quo in perpetuity. Ridley persisted, and, despite Mrs Thatcher's apparent attempts to stop him, won the support of the Cabinet's important Overseas and Defence Sub-Committee. On 2 December 1980 he laid his leaseback option before Parliament, but the Falklands lobby was out in force and the hapless minister was savaged. Not only was he attacked by such Falkland stalwarts as Julian Amery, but he was also hounded by Opposition politicians such as Peter Shore (Labour) and Russell Johnston (Liberal) who attacked the Foreign Office's 'shameful scenes ... festering for years.' Ridley is reported to have left the chamber 'pale and trembling'.[3] Lord Carrington found it necessary to give an assurance that nothing would be done against the wishes of the islanders.

The last hope of a compromise had failed. The Argentinians now calculated that if they occupied the islands by force, and Britain was faced by the prospect of mounting a full-scale invasion to repossess them, the British Government would not have the nerve to act, and the small but vocal Falklands lobby, after initial remonstrations, would find itself ignored. What they seem not to have taken into account was the attitude of Mrs Thatcher, which, admittedly at that stage, would have been hard to discern. The Argentinians had their eyes on Ridley and the Foreign Office, who seemed to be continuing the previous course of British concessions. They did not know that Mrs Thatcher, unlike previous Prime Ministers, was firmly opposed in principle to any leaseback or other arrangements that involved concessions on the question of sovereignty. They assumed that she would, like any other British Prime Minister in a similar situation, make some threatening noises, and then lay aside her convictions and bow to the inevitable 'education of events'. The Argentinians were not the only ones who had made this miscalculation; so had the Foreign Office in 1979, the majority of her political opponents and most members of her Cabinet.

Having rejected a compromise settlement, the British Government now, in its turn, gravely miscalculated, since it refused to give substance to the only alternative proposal, the Fortress Falklands option. In so doing, the Government was trying to get the best of both worlds. On the one hand, it resolutely nailed its colours to the mast of sovereignty and self-determination, and on the other hand eschewed the responsibility that such a policy entailed; it actually cut back on the cost of its commitment to the Falklands. On the one hand, it shut the door in the face of any Argentinian hopes of eventual control of the islands, and on the other hand encouraged the Argentinians to use the only possible alternative, armed invasion, by signifying an apparent willingness to leave the islands unprotected out of a desire for a reduction in Government spending. For this policy, Mrs Thatcher bore direct responsibility. She was thinking one policy but seemed to be carrying out another.

It was the withdrawal of the armed ice patrol vessel HMS *Endurance* which probably did most to embolden the Argentinians to attack. Apart from the minuscule detachment of Royal Marines on the Falklands, *Endurance* represented the only permanent tangible deterrent to invasion. The decision to withdraw *Endurance* arose out of the Prime Minister's desire to stem Government spending – a task that became manifestly more urgent after the switch in economic tactics described in the last chapter. The removal of Francis Pym from the Ministry of Defence in January 1981 had seen his replacement by the more monetarist John Nott precisely to make those defence cuts which Pym had refused to carry out. Nott's wide-ranging Defence Review in June 1981 singled out for particularly heavy cuts the Royal Navy's surface fleet, most of which was now considered superfluous for patrolling the North Atlantic, which was the Navy's primary NATO concern. Any vessels extraneous to this role were thus vulnerable, no more so than *Endurance*, and they included the aircraft carriers, *Hermes* and *Invincible*, and the assault ships that were to make the Falklands campaign possible. The imminent withdrawal from active service of *Endurance* represented a saving of £2 million a year; it was quietly announced in the House of Lords by Lord Trefgarne on 30 June.

The Foreign Office argued strenuously against the withdrawal of *Endurance* on the grounds that it removed any viable defence from the Falklands. Lord Carrington wrote several letters of protest to John Nott, but to no avail; in the ensuing argument Mrs Thatcher backed the Secretary for Defence against the Foreign Secretary whereas Callaghan when Prime Minister had done the opposite. So, the financial dogmatism of the MTFS meant the sacrifice of *Endurance*. The price that Mrs Thatcher had to pay for sticking to her guns over the Government's economic strategy was the loss of those very guns that would convince the Argentinians of Britain's continued commitment to the Falklands. The Falklands were such a peripheral issue in the overall scheme of Government thinking that the Foreign Office objections were overruled, distinctly ironic in the light of future events when Lord Carrington felt compelled to resign over the loss of the islands whilst John Nott survived. Another piece of legislation that the Government now passed without any consideration of the effect it might have had on the excitable minds of the Argentinian military junta was the British Nationality Bill which deprived about 800 Falkland Islanders of British citizenship. To the junta, this Act, together with the proposed withdrawal of *Endurance* at the end of its 1981–2 tour of duty, seemed to indicate a final weakening of British interest.

As a result, all the Government responses that might have indicated a different frame of mind came too late. When in February 1982 intelligence reports in London indicated an increase in Argentinian military activity in the South Atlantic, a meeting at the Foreign Office was convened on Monday 8 March at which old contingency plans for the recapture of the islands were brought off the shelf with no apparent thought that it might become necessary to use them. Events now began to move fast. On 20 March, an Argentinian scrap metal merchant hoisted his country's flag on South Georgia, which prompted *Endurance*, still on station, to evict the intruders with a section of Royal Marines from Port Stanley. By 28 March the reports from the Joint Intelligence Committee had become so grave that Mrs Thatcher and Lord Carrington agreed to the despatch of three nuclear submarines to the South Atlantic: *Spartan, Splendid* and *Conqueror*. The news was duly leaked to the press (intentionally or unintentionally it is hard to say) and it was thus only at the very last moment that the Argentinians received a signal, somewhat obfuscated, that the British were prepared to defend the Falklands. The sending of the submarines was, however, only a gesture, as the first one to arrive was only able to take up station off the Falklands more than a week after the occupation.

On Wednesday 31 March it became clear that an Argentinian fleet was sailing towards the islands and that an assault could be expected within forty-eight hours. The forecast was correct: Argentinian forces went ashore on Friday morning, 2 April.

For Mrs Thatcher that Wednesday was undoubtedly the most disturbing day of her premiership. Britain was left militarily impotent in the face of an invasion of her territory by a man whom many would now disdainfully refer to as a 'tinpot dictator'. It was a humiliating moment. As the news grew worse throughout the day, Whitehall moved rapidly into action, and in the evening worried senior officials and politicians streamed into Mrs Thatcher's room at the House of Commons. By all accounts it was a gloomy occasion. The Civil Servants supported the Ministry of Defence in emphasizing the logistical, administrative and economic difficulties of launching an expedition which could recapture the Falklands. They suggested an approach to Ronald Reagan to ask the American president to warn General Galtieri that he must not invade islands that were British territory.

The atmosphere of the meeting was changed by the late arrival of Admiral Sir Henry Leach, the First Sea Lord and Chief of Naval Staff. The previous Monday, when the three submarines had been despatched to the Falklands, Leach had begun not only to examine the possibility of sending a task force to recapture the islands, but to plan its composition, and was now able to present a positive plan of action. After the gloom and scepticism of the previous twenty-four hours, Leach threw the Prime Minister a military and political lifeline. It was a political lifeline in so far as few doubted that if she failed to respond to the Argentinian initiative, after allowing the débâcle of the actual invasion itself, she would have to resign. It was also, to a certain extent, a military lifeline for Leach himself, since what he now proposed vindicated the existence of precisely the type of surface fleet which his own Minister, John Nott, had tried to eliminate in his 1981 defence review. It is impossible to discern how much this consideration influenced Leach's naval plan; the least that can be said is that the conflict cannot have happened at a better time for a First Sea Lord not only trying to save the bulk of his surface fleet, but also keen to show what the Navy could do if it were allowed the appropriate equipment.

Leach also realized that if the Navy did not respond positively to the challenge as the only service capable of delivering men and munitions 8,000 miles to the South Atlantic, then the pervading logistical difficulties would probably preclude any military response. As Leach has told one author of his thoughts on that Wednesday:

Knowing that there was no conceivable means of any UK agency doing anything about it unless they got there by the Navy and protected by the Navy when they got there, it seemed to me that it was the wrong naval attitude to tell Ministers what we couldn't do: we should at least say what was possible. That was not the tenor of the brief which had been prepared for Mr Nott that day. I thought it had taken the wrong slant ....[4]

There is no doubt that Mrs Thatcher was impressed by the positive attitude of Leach, and by the chance of a way out of her predicament. Leach proffered the advice that a task force would be able to sail by the weekend and that it would have to be large, with full logistical support.

The Navy saw the projected Falklands expedition as an opportunity to demonstrate its skills; the RAF and Army were, initially, somewhat less than enthusiastic.

The next day, orders were put in motion for the task force to be assembled. As usual, the Prime Minister had responded positively to a man of similar temperament – a man who preferred to emphasize what could be done, rather than what could not. Simon Jenkins is probably correct in writing of Leach's bravado that Wednesday night that 'certainly without his personal dynamism it is unlikely that the fleet would have sailed so soon, and as a result more cautious counsels might have gained wider currency'.[5] It might be said in retrospect that Mrs Thatcher saved the Falklands, and Leach saved the Navy.

The invasion began on 2 April. The following day, Mrs Thatcher had to face an outraged House of Commons in an emergency session. It was the first Saturday meeting of the House since the Suez crisis in 1956. If the Government had been hitherto only dimly aware of the passions in Britain, which the Argentinians had stirred up by their unprovoked aggression, now it could not fail to register the fury expressed in the House. Julian Amery characteristically spoke of the nation's wounded pride now that Britain, 'the third naval power in the world, and second in NATO, has suffered a humiliating defeat'. Michael Foot, the Labour leader, denounced the invasion in the strongest possible terms from the Opposition front bench:

The rights and circumstances of the people of the Falkland Islands must be uppermost in our minds. There is no question in the Falkland Islands of any colonial dependence ... It is a question of people who wish to be associated with this country and who have built their whole lives on the basis of association with this country ... They are faced with an act of naked, unqualified aggression, carried out in the most shameful and disreputable circumstances.

Mrs Thatcher's announcement that a large task force would be sent that very weekend to put pressure on the Argentinians to leave the islands was greeted with acclaim, but the Foreign Office became the scapegoat, being branded as a nest of appeasers – evoking memories of earlier national humiliation. It was partly these bitter words that persuaded Lord Carrington to resign as Foreign Secretary (together with his entire Ministerial team) on Monday 5 April. Carrington was replaced by Francis Pym. The appointment was not ideal but Mrs Thatcher had little choice. Pym was the only experienced, senior Conservative Cabinet Minister without a vital portfolio of his own at the time who could restore the necessary stability and sang-froid to the tottering Government.

From the very start, Mrs Thatcher saw the Falklands campaign as action on principle: the British Government was going to war to defend the principle of self-determination. Her outspoken stand clearly appealed to countries whom Argentina had expected to side with them, and not even the normally friendly Organization of American States could overcome its scruples and bring itself to declare support for Argentina.

The most impressive diplomatic victory for Britain came at the United Nations in New York. As experience had shown, it was one thing to establish one's theoretical rights at the UN but another to have those rights embodied in UN resolutions. On this occasion, Britain was able to achieve both. Its representative, Sir Anthony Parsons, brilliantly marshalled into line the smaller, more volatile states, who composed the shifting temporary membership of the Security Council; the Council – the Soviet Union abstaining – then passed Resolution 502 exactly as drafted by Britain. The Resolution called for the 'immediate withdrawal' of Argentinian forces from the islands as a prelude to any negotiations. It exhorted the two sides to seek 'a diplomatic solution to their differences and to respect fully the purposes and principles of the Charter of the United Nations'. Most importantly, it also gave Mrs Thatcher the use of Article 51 of the United Nations Charter, which expressed 'the inherent right of individual and collective self-defence if armed attack occurs ... until the Security Council has taken measures necessary to maintain peace and security'.

Resolution 502 was passed only two days after the invasion, and was effectively to sanction all Britain's subsequent actions over the next two months. Mrs Thatcher had frequent recourse to Resolution 502. Although she had never been among the UN's most enthusiastic admirers, she was to benefit greatly from the Resolution which obviated a great deal of complex diplomatic and legal work which might otherwise have been needed to justify Britain's case. In contrast with the ill-fated Suez expedition, which isolated Britain and France in world opinion, the Falklands crisis found the world apparently united in condemnation of the Argentinian action. This early and almost unanimous support from the international community for her defence of the principles of sovereignty and self-determination were to sustain the Prime Minister throughout the coming weeks of crisis.

At no time did Mrs Thatcher see the Falklands War as an issue confined to Britain and Argentina. She always saw it in a global context, as a test of the Western nations' resolve to stand up to aggressors, and of the will and abilities of democracies to fight against dictatorships. The historical parallels haunted the proceedings, as they had done during the Suez crisis. Just as Mrs Thatcher was, after her early uncertainties, committed to sending the task force, so she was never in any doubt that it would have to be used. At the Cabinet meeting on 2 April to announce its despatch, her first words were a very calm and controlled, 'Gentlemen, we shall have to fight.' From the beginning she was under no illusions as to whether Argentina would withdraw unless they were forced to. Her assessment of General Galtieri's state of mind and of the popular pressures on the Argentinian military junta proved to be absolutely sound.

One person who had plenty of time to discover the Prime Minister's reasons for reacting so firmly was the American Secretary of State, General Alexander Haig, who appointed himself the international emissary between the two sides to try and bring about a negotiated peace. Haig has written of her view of the conflict:

> ... almost Messianically, she viewed it as a test for Western fibre and determination. In this she was correct ... Had Britain collapsed in the face of this petty aggression, it would, in Mrs Thatcher's words to me, have sent a signal round the world with devastating consequences. Had the United States, for reasons of selfish advantage retreated from the principle that the status quo must not be changed by use of force, and, however subtly, connived at rewarding aggression, it would have confirmed the corruption of the West.

The British Prime Minister was asserting the ancient principle that aggression must not be allowed to pay. The historical parallels were acute. On 8 April, on the first leg of his shuttle diplomacy between Buenos Aires and London, Haig was taken into the drawing-room at No 10 Downing Street. According to his account Mrs Thatcher:

rapped sharply on the table top and recalled that this was the table at which Neville Chamberlain sat in 1938 and spoke of the Czechs as a faraway people about whom we know so little and with whom we have so little in common ... She begged us to remember this: Do not urge Britain to reward aggression, to give Argentina something taken by force that it could not attain by peaceful means and that would signal round the world with devastating consequences. Before dinner Mrs Thatcher had shown me ... portraits of Wellington and Nelson. She was in a forceful mood, embattled, incisive and with the right indisputably on her side.[6]

These sentiments found frequent echoes in the House of Commons. Winston Churchill, grandson of Sir Winston, summed up this mood in the Falklands debate on 7 April:

The objective of our policy is clear. First and foremost it is to liberate the Falkland Islanders from the Fascist dictatorship; and, secondly, to restore British sovereignty and administration to the Falkland Islands and their dependencies ... The failure to achieve these objectives would have repercussions far beyond the fate of the Falkland Islanders and the Falkland Islands themselves. Britain's standing and credibility in the world, in the eyes of both her adversaries and her allies will be judged by the resolution and determination with which we meet this challenge.

Haig's negotiations foundered on the issue of sovereignty: both sides refused any concessions on this point. They had not managed to come to any agreement about it during the course of the previous 150 years, so it was even less likely that they could do so now. As with everything Mrs Thatcher does, having decided where her principles lay she applied them with total conviction and unremitting vigour. To those who did not appreciate her earnestness about both the specific and general principles she was asserting, the whole affair could look farcical; at the outset Haig probably shared the Washington State Department view of the conflict as a 'Gilbert and Sullivan battle over a sheep pasture between the choleric old John Bull and a comic dictator in a gaudy uniform'.[7] After talking to Mrs Thatcher personally about the Falklands crisis, Haig saw the conflict in a different light.

The launching of the Falklands expedition not only evoked famous historical parallels but raised an infamous ghost, a ghost that had to be laid to rest. The humiliating fate of the Suez expedition of 1956 was regarded as having done more than anything to break Britain's nerve in the post-war world, and Willie Whitelaw later confessed that he lay awake at night during the Falklands crisis trying to exorcise the demons of Suez. Members of the Cabinet and senior Civil Servants – and generals and admirals – wondered how Mrs Thatcher would stand up to the same kind of terrible strain which had brought Antony Eden low, and if she did not, how long it would be before she cracked. She did not crack. The crippling weakness of the Suez expedition was indecision, about its objects and about the means by which they should be achieved. There was consequently a lack of will to see it through, with the result that the British Government ended up with the worst of all worlds: universally hostile condemnation, and failure to secure its objectives. In the case of the Falklands there was no weakness of will. There was clarity about the objectives and about the means by which they would be achieved. Having committed herself to a military option, Mrs Thatcher accepted the responsibilities that went with it, including allowing the task force commander to sink the *Belgrano* if he considered it a threat to his ships. For the armed services, this political will to support the military option was her outstanding contribution to the enterprise. The Chief of the Defence Staff, Admiral Sir Terence Lewin, who saw or spoke to her every day during the ten weeks of the crisis, gave this assessment of her when asked by an interviewer whether she was cautious:

> I think cautious is the wrong word – determined, prepared to weigh up the risks and make a judgement and make a decision and stick by it. She was a decisive leader, which is what of course the military want. We don't want somebody who vacillates, we want to be able to put the case to her, the requirements to her, and say this is how it is, this is the decision we want, we want it now and we want it quickly and we don't want a wishy-washy decision, we want a clear-cut decision. She was magnificent in her support of the military.[8]

With this political will at the top, generated by a small and positive War Cabinet consisting of the Prime Minister, John Nott, Whitelaw, Pym and Cecil Parkinson (chairman of the Conservative Party), the military were assured of all the financial, diplomatic and political support they needed, and which their predecessors had crucially lacked in the Suez operation.

To provide this firm political resolve Mrs Thatcher had to exercise great self-control and self-discipline. As had been forcibly impressed on her in the fateful meeting of 31 March in her room at the House of Commons, to embark on an amphibious operation 8,000 miles from home against an enemy with local air superiority of anything up to four or five to one was a hazardous undertaking. Behind her display of iron determination in public was anxiety and apprehension. David Owen, who saw her not only in the House but in private on Privy Councillor terms of confidentiality, has described her going into her testing time:

[She was] terribly vulnerable. At home her political position was weak. A
bad reverse in the early days and her leadership might have to be terminated
… She knew she was playing for enormous stakes. But once she faced them,
she behaved outstandingly well … Mrs Thatcher's personal behaviour in the
House of Commons was neither self-confident nor jingoistic. She was a very
worried woman and by no means certain of herself.

The Prime Minister was fortunate in having a number of men around
her, civil servants as well as Cabinet Ministers, who had been in action
in the Second World War and knew what fighting was about. They
were able to help prepare her mind for the casualties that were bound
to come. Lewin had served on the Arctic convoys to Russian ports;
Willie Whitelaw and Francis Pym had both won the MC. Lord Hailsham
had served in the Army in various theatres throughout the duration;
Sir Frank Cooper, Permanent Under-Secretary at the Ministry of
Defence, had distinguished himself as a pilot in the RAF. Whitelaw later
told one interviewer: 'I was always very clear on one simple point: that
those at the top must be prepared to accept casualties. And I took it
upon myself to say to her how important it was to steel oneself when
there were casualties. And she was marvellous.'[9]

Expressions of sentiment on her part, more natural coming from a
woman than a man, could have had a bad effect on the commanders in
the field, possibly inducing, if not hesitation, then a degree of caution
which could have led to even greater casualties. One senior civil servant
said that 'from the point of view of the officials and military involved
in the direction of the fighting, it was up to a point a good thing that
the Prime Minister had no experience of bloodshed and had a relatively
detached view of the loss of life in war. They could get on with their
job'. He drew a hypothetical comparison with Eden: 'He could never
forget the slaughter in the trenches of the Somme. He would have
agonized whenever another platoon was sent into action.'

On 2 May the Argentine cruiser *General Belgrano* was torpedoed by
a British submarine, and sank with heavy loss of life. On 4 May HMS
*Sheffield*, a Type 42 destroyer, was hit by an Exocet air-to-sea missile,
with the loss of twenty lives; she sank six days later. These grim events
seemed to change the atmosphere. Until then there had been something
unreal about it. From now on, it was war indeed. This was a moment
when the eyes of the world were on the Prime Minister to see how she
would react. Had these two disasters shaken her resolve? There was no
sign of it, and the war entered a new and deadly phase.

Mrs Thatcher, more than anyone, saw the Falklands as an opportunity for Britain to respond to Henderson's warnings of 1979 and 'rise from the ashes'. David Owen encapsulated what many people felt about the crisis when he said that for him 'it convinced many people in and outside the country that we were not played out as a nation'. This was a ready-made theme for Thatcherism – the proclamation of Britain's salvation from its post-war Socialist decline. There were frequent echoes of this theme during the Parliamentary debates on the Falklands and in the press. Alan Clark, a right wing Conservative MP, spoke for many when he told Parliament on 7 April that he believed 'that this is the last chance, the very last chance for us to redeem much of our history over the past twenty-five years, of which we may be ashamed and from which we may have averted our gaze'.

Clark was articulating a resentment at Britain's post-war history; and Mrs Thatcher had presented Britain with a chance to purge this resentment. It was a theme that she consciously expanded and built on. It was not a phoney theme, nor one she had produced for the transient political task of capitalizing on the Falklands War. It was at the centre of her long-term political thinking. While the task force were regrouping off the Falklands to begin their amphibious operations, on 14 May Mrs Thatcher addressed a Conservative rally in Perth. The words she delivered with the greatest feeling were as follows: 'What we have seen in the last few weeks is this ancient country rising as one nation to meet a challenge that it refuses to ignore. Perhaps we have surprised even ourselves, and I know we have surprised all those who didn't think we had it in us ... Too long submerged, too often denigrated, too easily forgotten. The springs of pride in Britain flow again.' This was not jingoism – in which some popular newspapers indulged – but a robust patriotism that had lain dormant in the hearts of many since the Second World War, and which she now succeeded in awakening. It was this personal empathy with the most basic instincts of the electorate that laid the foundation for a landslide election victory a year later.

The negotiations between Britain and Argentina to try and seek a peaceful solution to the crisis came to an abrupt end with the sinking of the *Belgrano*. If General Haig, who had undertaken to act as an arbiter between the two combatant countries, had entertained hopes of a speedy resolution of the crisis, he was disabused by his first visit to London, where he was first exposed to the Prime Minister's strength and feeling. Sir Nicholas Henderson, the British Ambassador in Washington at the time, met Haig on his return from London, and has since written of his encounter with the rather perplexed Secretary of State:

'I think that his first round in London made a strong impact on Haig. He had been left in absolutely no doubt that London required the Argentines to withdraw as the essential first step. Mrs Thatcher was prepared to negotiate but not to yield to force, and she was "very tough", to use Haig's words to me, to which he added, "I wish we had more like her".'

The member of the War Cabinet with whom she clashed most frequently on her attitude towards war was the new Foreign Secretary, Francis Pym. He was the most reconciliatory of the War Cabinet and also the most cautious. This attitude could frequently raise her ire, particularly if, as on one occasion, Pym's more even-handed stance was applauded by politicians unsympathetic to her such as Edward Heath. Haig has left a record of one clash between the Prime Minister and the recalcitrant Foreign Secretary:

> At one point, during a discussion about the capabilities of the British task force, Pym murmured, 'Maybe we should ask the Falklanders how they feel about the war.' Mrs Thatcher heatedly challenged him: Aggressors classically try to intimidate those against whom they aggress, saying that things far worse than the aggression itself could happen.[10]

As the crisis deepened, her resolution could at times border on the obsessional. Haig had noted 'Messianic' convictions on the subject, and as the pressure on her increased during April, she at times appeared over-wrought and overbearing, even to her most loyal colleagues.

Was the Prime Minister's resolution such that it precluded the possibility of a negotiated settlement before unconditional surrender? Had she been sincere in declaring that the task force should be merely a military back-up for her diplomatic efforts and not the replacement for them? The full story of the attempts to find a negotiated peace before the fighting ended, and of Mrs Thatcher's part in them, will not be known until the official files are opened under the thirty-year rule in 2012, but even now it is possible to see a continuing desire for a negotiated settlement being pursued throughout the crisis.

The clearest evidence of this is the last British peace offer, drawn up at Chequers by Mrs Thatcher and Sir Anthony Parsons, Britain's representative at the United Nations, on Sunday 16 May, two weeks after the first shots had been exchanged and when hundreds of lives had already been lost. Behind the rhetoric of resolution, required by the military, can be seen Mrs Thatcher's readiness for a remarkably generous compromise settlement. The Parsons proposals included the offer of a mutual withdrawal of forces; the installation of a UN administrator on the Falklands with his own staff; and the undertaking that further negotiations would be 'without prejudice' and would be completed 'with a sense of urgency' by the end of the year. Thus, to bring about a negotiated settlement and stop the inevitable bloodshed, Mrs Thatcher was willing to concede titular sovereignty to the UN and further negotiations on all issues, including that of sovereignty.

This is the general context in which the sinking of the *Belgrano* has to be seen. There would be little point in Mrs Thatcher permitting the sinking of the aged Argentinian cruiser in order to scupper the 'Peruvian Peace Plan' which had been presented to the Foreign Secretary in Washington on the morning that the ship was sunk, if she were planning to propose even more generous terms of settlement to the Argentinians only two weeks later when the task force was poised for victory. The *Belgrano* was sunk because the Prime Minister was advised by her service commanders that it represented a threat to the task force. Only the day before the sinking, a large force of Argentinian Mirage jets had tried to sink the British frigate HMS *Glamorgan*, only the skill of the task force preventing the disaster. To the task force commanders, Argentinian aggression was real and threatening – it was obtaining results every day. The Admiralty planners in Command Headquarters at Northwood sought the sinking of the warship to prevent a massive blow at the task force. The Prime Minister could not contradict the opinion of the military commanders on the spot; once she had taken the decision to send the task force she had irrevocably committed herself to the duty of protecting it. It may be that the military opinion on the spot that the *Belgrano* was a potential threat was unsound; but it is impossible to fault her decision to take the advice of the Chiefs of Staff that the cruiser should be attacked when the military commanders on the scene had asked for this protection. The Prime Minister recognized from the start that having sent the force in the first place she had to follow the advice of its commanders about how it should be protected. She was perfectly sincere in her account of the sinking of the *Belgrano* to the House of Commons on 4 May, during which she described the anxieties bedevilling any political head of a military force:

> May I make it perfectly clear that the worry that I live with hourly is that attacking Argentine forces, either naval or air, may get through to ours and sink some of our ships ... There was clear aggressive intent on the part of the Argentine fleet and Government. It could be seen first in their claims. They previously claimed that they had sunk HMS *Exeter*, that they had damaged HMS *Hermes* ... The Right Honourable Gentleman may also remember the persistent attacks throughout the whole of Saturday on our Task

Force, which were repelled only by the supreme skill and courage of our people.

It was this 'hourly worry' that task force ships, especially the two precious aircraft carriers, might be sunk that was the reality of political control of the force. As Michael Foot later privately acknowledged, faced by a military request to sink the *Belgrano* for the defence of the force, no Prime Minister could have refused it. It is a cynical but perhaps correct argument that if HMS *Glamorgan* had been sunk on 1 May, then Mrs Thatcher would have been saved facing such a hostile reception when the *Belgrano* was sunk on 2 May.

Her other, most personal contribution, to the war was her strong Atlanticist bias, which was always going to make it hard for the Americans to do anything else eventually but come down heavily on the side of Britain. It was widely recognized in Washington during only the second year of Reagan's presidency that Mrs Thatcher was the staunchest supporter that the US had in Europe – and so US policy *vis-à-vis* the Falklands was, to a certain extent, conditioned to keeping her in power, which inevitably meant giving the British as much covert help as possible in order to ensure her Government's survival as the victors of the conflict. US support was not always a foregone conclusion, however, as there were vociferous elements in Washington politics who wanted to keep the links with Argentina that Washington had been slowly and patiently building up over the previous five years. The US representative to the UN, Mrs Jeane Kirkpatrick, was the most pro-'Latinist' of all the senior American politicians, and many feared that her arguments for keeping on good terms with Argentina might find a sympathetic reception in the mind of Ronald Reagan, with whom she was known to be very close. The counsels of Caspar Weinberger and Haig prevailed. The President eventually came down firmly and decisively on the British side at the end of April, thus legitimizing the covert help that the British had already been getting from the US. Sir Nicholas Henderson has since written:

> ... some measure of the significance of American support for Britain over the Falklands can be gathered by imagining what it would have been like for Britain to have been detached from its most powerful ally as we were at Suez. From my discussions with service leaders since the event, I conclude that it is difficult to exaggerate the difference that American support made to the military outcome.[11]

It was largely due to Mrs Thatcher that such support could be mobilized, just as it was she who could put the conflict in global terms to General

Haig in a way in which the Americans could hardly ignore. It was another aspect of her handling of the war which made the months of April, May and June 1982 a personal triumph. David Owen's verdict was that although her conduct of the Falklands issue before the invasion was open to criticism, 'during the war her leadership had been superb'.

The British task force entered Falklands waters on 22 April. Four weeks later, on 20 May, Mrs Thatcher gave the House of Commons details of the final offer made to the Argentinian Government, and reported that it had been rejected. The House thought the terms were fair and reasonable, though Mr Foot urged further attempts at a peaceful settlement. Fighting began the following day, when, in spite of heavy attacks from Argentinian aircraft, British forces established a bridgehead on East Falkland at San Carlos Bay. In the first few days of the fighting, the frigates *Ardent* and *Antelope,* and the supply ship *Atlantic Conveyor* were sunk, five British warships were damaged, and the destroyer *Coventry* had to be abandoned, shortly to sink. In the next three weeks other ships were lost or damaged. British troops rapidly made ground, however, and on 14 June the Argentinian forces surrendered. British casualties – 255 servicemen and civilians – had been relatively light, damage to planes and ships could have been much worse, but there had been many anxious moments during the brief hostilities, and the question of whether at some stage the bombing of the Argentina mainland or acceptance of stalemate would be necessary was never far from the Government's mind.

When the fighting ceased, Mrs Thatcher's reputation was higher than it had been at any time since she came to office three years previously. But there was criticism of her. Her exclamation, 'Rejoice, rejoice!' at the door of Downing Street when success was assured was censured by her political opponents as insensitivity if not bellicosity; her friends considered it an expression of relief that further bloodshed had been prevented. It was alleged by her critics that she represented the Argentinian surrender more as a victory for the Conservative Party than an achievement for the armed forces. Some said that the salute of the task force marching through the City of London on its return, a parade arranged by the Lord Mayor, should have been taken by a member of the Royal Family, not by Mrs Thatcher. It was said that she took some exception to parts of the service of thanksgiving in St Paul's Cathedral, particularly because prayers were said by the Methodist leader, Dr Kenneth Greer, who had expressed misgivings about the sending of the task force. These criticisms did not amount to much.

When on 3 April, the day after the Argentinians attacked the islands,

Mrs Thatcher had informed the House that the British task force was on its way to the South Atlantic, there was an immediate demand for an inquiry into why the invasion had not been foreseen. Three weeks after the war was over she announced that a committee of Privy Councillors under the chairmanship of Lord Franks would inquire into the Government's discharge of its responsibilities in the period leading up to the beginning of the war.

Lord Franks had been an eminent Ambassador to the United States, subsequently holding many important posts in public life. Three members of the committee had served in Labour Cabinets, two in Conservative Cabinets; the other member was an eminent former civil servant.

The Franks Committee submitted its report six months later on 3 January 1983. It said that two of the questions it had had to consider were 'crucial': First, could the Government have foreseen the Argentinian invasion? The answer was No. Secondly, could the Government have prevented the invasion? The answer to that question, said the Committee was 'more complex', and had to be considered in the context of the period of seventeen years covered by the report: 'there is no simple answer to it'. The British Government *could* have acted differently in several ways – the Committee listed them – and 'fuller consideration of alternative courses of action might, in our opinion, have been advantageous . . .' Even so, the Committee concluded, 'There is no reasonable basis for any suggestion – which would be purely hypothetical – that the invasion would have been prevented if the Government had acted in the ways indicated in our report.'

Some of Mrs Thatcher's critics claimed that reading between its lines revealed serious shortcomings in the Government's conduct in the eighteen months before the attack, and that even what the report had said did not justify its final conclusion. Some claimed that the Franks Committee 'whitewashed' the Government's record on the Falklands. Of those who inclined to that view the best informed, by virtue of his experience as Foreign Secretary from 1977 to 1979, was Dr David Owen: 'They gave the Government the benefit of the doubt. They did so, I suspect, as practical people knowing that there had been a famous victory and that the majority of public opinion approved of what the Government had done and did not want a bitter retrospective row.'

It is often argued that Mrs Thatcher is, above all, an extremely lucky politician. This may be so, but politicians often appear lucky only in retrospect. Galtieri gave her a chance to display all her outstanding qualities to the full on a world stage: resolution, determination and coolness in a crisis. She might have been lucky in the fact that Galtieri had crossed her bows at all, but it could also be said that a political leader without her qualities might have been swept away by events to join those in history who did not measure up to their ultimate challenge – Asquith, Baldwin, Chamberlain, Eden. The last word on her conduct at the time of the Falklands crisis might for the time being be left with Dr Owen:

> She knew she was playing for enormous stakes. But once she accepted them, she behaved outstandingly well. Some potential Prime Ministers might have accepted the invasion, decided not to throw the Argentine out, and worked out some compromise. I have never doubted that such a course would have been absolutely devastating for this country. Mrs Thatcher recognized that from the start, instinctively, and deserves credit for it.

# 10

# IN CONTROL

T he outcome of the Falklands crisis gave Mrs Thatcher a much more visible and influential presence on the stage of world affairs. On a relatively minor level she at once secured the postponement of negotiations with Spain for the reopening of the Gibraltar frontier, and – a major coup – her visit to Peking in September ended a period of tension with an agreement with the Chinese Government securing the reversion of Hong Kong to China in 1997 on the expiration of the century-old leasing agreement. But more important in the eyes of the world was the enhanced stature of her relationship with President Reagan.

She was fortunate in that her *réclame* in the United States for her handling of the Falklands coincided with the beginning of a decline in confidence in the President's capability as a world leader. Nobody questioned the power of the United States, but how fit and capable was Mr Reagan to direct it? It was at this point that Mrs Thatcher was able to lay the foundations of a reputation as an international leader soon surpassing that of any European since President de Gaulle. The basis of this was her relationship with the United States. She showed herself loyal but also independent; affection and partnership would coexist with candid advice and, where necessary, criticism. Without talking about 'a special relationship', and never irritating or alarming American opinion with implicit expectations of preferential treatment, she established a relationship between the two governments closer than at any time since the post-war period of Attlee and Truman.

Resentment against the Reagan regime mounted in 1982 for a number of reasons, not least in his own country. The American economy did not come up to his promises. More than 12 million were unemployed, more than 30 million were living below the poverty line. He was forced to revise his economic policies and disown some of his ideas. He introduced camouflaged tax increases to reduce budget deficits fast threatening to go out of control. American citizens deplored the rise in expenditure on defence, the more since Congress questioned the President's judgement on new weapons he wanted to produce. Outside America there was resentment against the international effects of America's high interest rates in the first nine months of the year, at the President's support for right-wing regimes in Latin America, his alleged intolerance towards several Third World countries, and his intransigence on nuclear issues. His frequent statements of policy on international problems without proper consultation with America's allies reduced confidence in his judgement and diminished his personal popularity. As a result the United States Government and American public opinion had not got as much credit as they deserved for the support they had given Britain in the Falklands crisis, support which if it had not immensely impressed the people of Britain had put a severe strain on the President's relations with the countries of Latin America. In these circumstances it was not difficult for Mrs Thatcher to stand out as President Reagan's loyal friend: she did not have much competition. But she had the will and courage to do it, and the style and persona to carry it off.

The President's stock had fallen in Europe particularly as a result of his ban on all exports to the USSR of material which could be used in the building of the oil pipeline which the Russians proposed to construct into Western Europe, a ban which he extended to European firms, threatening them with reprisals against their American trade if they did not comply. The British Government protested against this as 'an unacceptable extension of American extra-territorial jurisdiction which is repugnant to international law', and, under the Protection of Trading Interests Act, forbade British firms to comply with it. The Prime Minister endorsed her Government's resistance to the ban, but, tactfully affecting to speak in sorrow rather than in anger, said: 'I feel particularly wounded by a friend.' The President's rescinding of the ban in November on condition that his European allies would not trade in any way contributing to the purposes of the Warsaw Pact was generally seen as a climbdown. Again Mrs Thatcher was tactful. 'As so often before,' she purred, 'the alliance has risen to the needs of the time.' She displayed the same forbearance a few weeks earlier when the United

States had to compromise with the EEC on the export of European steel, having sought virtually to embargo it on the grounds that European producers were illegally subsidized. Her tone when she got her way with the Americans was noticeably different from her tone with the Europeans.

As her standing as *the* American ally grew, so did her reputation as the hammer of the Europeans. Her success over the Falklands invested her with a new authority; friendly Europeans saw her as wearing the mantle of Churchill: Galtieri was not another Hitler, but once again Britain had gone to war on the principle that aggression must be resisted. Mrs Thatcher went on behaving much the same way in the EEC, but the perception of her was different. Her success had made her seem more important. The year 1982 was not a good year for her in Europe, but she cut a bigger swathe. 'I intend to go on being stubborn,' she had said in March on the subject of the British rebate. In May the Community successfully withstood strenuous attempts from the Minister for Agriculture, Peter Walker, to improve the terms, and Britain had to settle for a sum much less than it had demanded – 'A sad and damaging day in the Community's history,' said Mr Walker. But Mrs Thatcher nevertheless seemed to have dominated the EEC, and her failure to get her way yet seemed like a success. As she told the author five years later, 'I know nothing about diplomacy, but I know I want certain things for Britain.'

If the Falklands victory had enhanced her stature abroad it did not make progress easier on the domestic front, and one of her problems was a growing suspicion in Britain of American policy on nuclear weapons. Cruise missiles were to be installed at the Greenham Common base. On 6 June a large demonstration took place in London in which, according to the Campaign for Nuclear Disarmament, nearly a quarter of a million people participated. Picketing of the base by 'Women for Peace' got wide publicity. It seemed probable that nuclear armament would be an important issue at the next election, but nobody could have foreseen that the issue would turn out to favour Mrs Thatcher.

It was soon clear that though the Falklands victory had done the Government's reputation much good abroad, it had not relieved it of the longstanding criticism of its economic policies. The Confederation of British Industry, which at the time of the Budget in March had asked for £3,000 million to be spent to help industry and reduce unemployment, continued to demand Government action. They reported growing loss of business confidence, the most depressing feature of the industrial scene being the outlook for manufacturing. In July, the Chancellor announced that he was taking two measures to deal with the unemployment problem. First, the number of 'enterprise zones', areas of declining industrial activity where tax and rate reliefs, capital grants and planning easements were available to stimulate industrial investment, would be doubled from eleven to twenty-two. The second measure was for the extension and co-ordination of the existing schemes for community service by the unemployed, and their incorporation in a new community programme, providing 130,000 new jobs at a cost of £185 million.

The new community programme was launched on 5 October by the Manpower Services Commission. The trade unions denounced the Chancellor's measures as a device to improve the unemployment figures, and to provide cheap labour. The CBI said that the measures were ameliorative, but what was really wanted was 'a fundamental improvement in the economy'. In August Mr Prior said publicly: 'I do not believe that any government or any country can sustain these levels of unemployment.' At the Conservative Party conference at Brighton in October, Sir Geoffrey Howe rejected all suggestions that the Government in the light of these criticisms and suggestions should change its course. 'We are not going to pile up problems for the next Government because we intend to be the next Government.'

By then the Government had sustained a particularly damaging blow, the effects of which were all the worse since a general election seemed likely within six months. On 18 September a highly important document drawn up by the Government's Central Policy Review Staff, the 'think-tank', was leaked to the press, precipitating speculation that Mrs Thatcher intended to dismantle the Welfare State. The think-tank's proposals were aimed at the replacement of State by private spending, and the encouragement of personal choice. They would have cut public spending on higher education and social security benefits, but they incurred most opposition for proposing to substitute personally paid-for health insurance for a national health service that was free. The compulsory minimum health insurance which the think-tank's report proposed would relieve the NHS annual budget of an expenditure of about 3 million pounds a year.

The leak of the CPRS report occurred two weeks before the annual Labour Party conference: the conference would have made hay of it. The Government promptly dissociated itself from the report: Mr Norman Fowler, the member of the Cabinet primarily concerned, said on 23 September that there were no plans to change the existing system. The controversy continued, and just before the Conservative conference opened Mr Heath made a public statement in which he asked Mrs Thatcher to disavow the think-tank's proposals. In her speech at the conference she said that the Government continued to support the principle that people's health should be looked after whether or not they could afford to pay. She went on to say that the Conservative Party would go forward without compromise or false promises to accomplish what it had set out to achieve. But there was a widespread feeling that she had back-tracked when she saw the public reaction to the leaked CPRS report, that she had handled the affair clumsily, and that this was another occasion when she had seen discretion to be the better part of valour. The general feeling was that she had repudiated as undesirable a course which in fact she wished to take, and which indeed she was to resume in 1987.

Of greater importance for the Government and more central to Mrs Thatcher's political mission as she saw it then was the Employment Bill which became law on 28 October. Bitterly contested inside and outside the House of Commons, it allowed for civil damages of up to £250,000 in actions against unions for 'unlawful industrial action', a definition which embraced sympathetic strikes, damages for workers dismissed as a result of the closed shop, and the right of employers to dismiss strikers. It provided government funds for union ballots on wage disputes. There was great opposition to the Bill. Mr Callaghan went so far as to say of it: 'If the law is a bad law, there is always a contingent right to take action that you would not otherwise take.' Conservatives up and down the country, and according to opinion polls many non-Conservatives, claimed that the Employment Bill had not gone far enough. They called for compulsory secret ballots both before strikes and in the election of top union officials; for the banning of strikes called before dispute procedures had been implemented; and a return to contracting-in from contracting-out of political subscriptions to the Labour Party.

In the early autumn there was an expectation that another Trades Union Bill to satisfy these demands would be announced in the next Queen's Speech. But Mrs Thatcher, as she told the author a few months later, thought that enough had been done to date; time must be allowed for digestion and 'persuasion'. To the surprise of some and dis-appointment of others, a third bill was not after all included in the Royal Speech. Mrs Thatcher made it clear in the interview that there would be a third Employment Bill after she had won the next general election. And there was.

The Queen's Speech, delivered on 3 November, created controversy by including bills for the reduction of public ownership or the removal of monopoly in various industrial fields, such as telecommunications, shipbuilding and electricity supply. These bills heralded the expansion of the process soon to become famous as privatization, dealt with in a later chapter. But the legislative programme outlined in the Queen's Speech was light, supporting growing opinion that there would be a general election in the first part of the following year.

When 1983 opened, few people would have gambled on Mrs Thatcher winning an election six months later with an overall majority of 144 seats. The outlook for the economy was dark. Anticipation of a fall in North Sea oil prices had weakened sterling; in January the bank rate went up to 11%. Industrial output was lower than it had been for nearly twenty years, unemployment had risen to a new record of nearly $3\frac{1}{4}$ million, and the Public Expenditure White Paper in February indicated an outlay £500 million less than had been projected. The budget on 15 March was described as 'neutral' by the commentators, but irritated the public with increased taxes on drink and tobacco, and higher car licence fees. The Labour Opposition attacked the growing rich-poor, North-South division. The Confederation of British Industry demanded a vast programme for the resuscitation of manufacturing and the reduction of unemployment, a campaign which, to Mrs Thatcher's annoyance, they maintained until the eve of the general election three months later. The Government was embarrassed by the public outcry provoked by the Serpell Committee's report on the future of Britain's railways foreshadowing extensive reductions in services, by a four-week national strike in the water and sewage industry, the first in its history – nearly eight million people were advised to boil all water – and by continued controversy over privatization.

Though much was to be made later over divisions within the Labour Party, particularly over nuclear weapons policy, as a factor in Mrs Thatcher's election victory, such developments in her favour were not so clear at the time: on the contrary, in March and April the pressure for nuclear disarmament mounted, receiving support in varying degrees and kinds from the Anglican, Roman Catholic and Methodist churches, from a British Medical Association report, and from ecological and environmental organizations. In particular there was a demand for 'dual-key' control of all Western nuclear weapons, a system whereby American weapons sited in Britain could not be used without the consent of the British Government. Mrs Thatcher was moved by the agitation to launch a publicity campaign to neutralize it, and to put pressure on thirty Conservative MPs to withdraw their signatures to a

House of Commons resolution calling for dual-key control.

When Mrs Thatcher announced on 9 May that she had asked the Queen for a dissolution, and that the general election would be held on 9 June, her chances of success were by no means rosy: a poll just before her announcement showed the Conservatives rating 46% support, but Labour's 34% and the 18% of the Alliance, bearing in mind the number of marginal seats, could well mean that she would not get an overall majority.

Three weeks before the announcement, in an interview with the author Mrs Thatcher had said that in the next year or so there would virtually be only four possible dates for a general election, and that the main consideration was uncertainty having a bad effect on the economy and in particular causing fluctuations in the value of the pound. In the event she decided on the first of the four dates. Michael Foot, leader of the Labour Party, called it 'a helter-skelter, hugger-mugger, dis-creditable decision . . . a cut-and-run election . . .' Mrs Thatcher replied: 'It was in the national interest to end the uncertainty and therefore I acted swiftly. If I had wanted to cut and run I would have done it a very long time ago. You are bound to be accused of *something*. If you go between four and five years you are accused of cutting and running. If you *don't* decide, you are dithering. If you continue to go the whole year, you are clinging to office.'

The election was remarkable in many respects. In their introduction to *The British General Election of 1983*, twelfth in the series of British general election histories sponsored by Nuffield College and published by Macmillan, the eminent political historians, Dr David Butler and Professor Dennis Kavanagh, give the following assessment of it:

> It revealed that the traditional bases of the British party system and of British political ideas were in ferment. It presents as great a challenge to the analyst as any British election this century. Looking back on the election of 1983 and the events preceding it, one figure stands dominant. Margaret Thatcher, to an increasing degree, towered over the political scene, over a government that lacked any strong alternative figures, and over an oppo-sition that was in disarray. Unlike other recent Prime Ministers, she gave her own name to a comprehensive set of ideas and attitudes. Thatcherism and Thatcherite means very different things to different people and were used as terms of praise and as terms of opprobrium. But they were the terms and ideas on which the election was fought. They were perceived and, in varying measure, responded to, by the British public: 'Victorian values', 'paying your own way', 'no easy solutions', 'reducing the size of government', 'making Britain great' were all pursued with seeming relentlessness by an

151

Iron Lady, a Boadicea, TINA ('There is no alternative'). In material terms there was little outward sign that her policies were succeeding. But her resolute approach, clearly symbolized by her Falklands leadership, had come to be generally recognised at the end of the four years. More than Harold Wilson in 1966, more than Harold Macmillan in 1959, perhaps as much as Churchill in 1945, she is the central figure of the 1983 election story. Yet two years earlier it did not look like that. She was more unpopular than any post-war Prime Minister and she seemed to be presiding not only over economic disaster, but also over the break-up of the old two-party system.

The election manifestos of Mrs Thatcher's opponents made unemployment their major issue. The Alliance's appeared first, and promised to reduce unemployment by a million in two years by investment in public works, subsidies and re-training schemes. There were proposals for preventing pay awards becoming inflationary, if necessary by a statutory incomes policy. The Alliance's policy for nuclear weapons leaned towards the disarmers but was cautious and non-committal – for instance, there should be no decision on the future of Cruise missiles until current disarmament negotiations had been concluded. The Labour manifesto also featured an emergency cure for high unemployment involving an immediate investment of £6,000 million. The next Labour Government would come out of the EEC, move towards a non-nuclear defence programme, and take steps to ease out independent schools.

The Conservative Party manifesto was the last to appear. Broadly speaking it promised the mixture as before – 'a remarkably anodyne document' commented Butler and Kavanagh – with the pledge of trade union legislation already referred to, and with the commitment to privatize British Telecom, Rolls-Royce, British Airways, British Steel, British Shipbuilders and British Leyland. There was also a pledge, very near Mrs Thatcher's heart, to abolish the Greater London Council and other metropolitan councils, a 'wasteful and unnecessary tier' in the structure of local government and the main begetters of 'exessive and irresponsible rate increases'.

As the campaign developed, though unemployment remained a major issue, the topic most talked about was defence. The longer the campaign went on the more clearly revealed were the bitter divisions within the Labour leadership on the subject of nuclear weapons. One of the Party's election publications referred to Britain becoming 'the first nuclear weapons State to renounce unilaterally such weapons'. Several Labour speakers repudiated this, and Mr Callaghan said in a speech at Cardiff on 25 May: 'Our refusal to give up arms unilaterally has brought better and more realistic proposals from the Soviet Union ... Britain and the West should not dismantle their weapons for nothing in return.' Alex Kitson, a former Labour Party chairman, denounced Callaghan publicly for the speech, which he said could cost Labour the election. The following day Tony Benn announced, 'No individual is going to divert the Labour Party from carrying out its policy ... No Trident, no Cruise, no bases, no Polaris'.

The Labour Party took further knocks on defence from remarks made by some of its leading figures about the Falklands victory, a subject which the Conservatives played down. When Mr Healey said that Mrs Thatcher 'glories in slaughter' he was so much criticized, outstandingly by Dr Owen, that he withdrew the word 'slaughter' and substituted 'conflict'. Neil Kinnock also had to explain what he really meant when he responded to a heckler who had shouted, 'Mrs Thatcher has guts' with, 'It's a pity that people had to leave theirs on Goose Green in order to prove it'. There were protests from some of the families of those servicemen who had been casualties in that area.

Mrs Thatcher visited constituencies up and down the country and appeared on radio and television, but she concentrated most on the morning press conferences at Conservative Party headquarters which, however many Cabinet Ministers were present, she presided over and dominated, answering most of the questions herself. In the first week her colleagues wondered if she seemed to be too 'headmistressy', but by the second week the feedback was that she was doing well. When asked if she minded being called 'headmistressy' she replied that she did not mind at all, adding: 'I have known some very good head-mistresses who have launched their pupils on wonderful careers. I had one such myself. I am what I am. Yes, I do believe certain things very strongly. Yes, I do believe in trying to persuade people that the things I believe in are the things that they should follow ... I am far too old to change now.'

At the press conferences she commented on or criticized what her Cabinet colleagues said without inhibition, or mercy. When her Foreign Secretary, Francis Pym, suggested that the sovereignty of the Falklands was negotiable, she interrupted and said that it was not, and two days later, after he had said on television that too great a majority for the Conservatives might be undesirable – 'Landslides on the whole don't produce successful governments' – she dismissed what he had said as 'the natural caution of the Chief Whip. He is a member of that small club of former Chief Whips who always wonder how they would cope in the Commons with a large majority of Conservative MPs.' She later explained that her intervention was due to concern about the discouraging effect Pym's remark might have on Conservative candidates fighting in marginal seats. 'We want as many Conservatives as we can possibly get. I think I could handle a landslide all right.' This most unusual public correction by a Prime Minister of a senior Cabinet Minister (by now she was known to be generously given to such practice in private) did not seem to harm her. Male voters did not take exception to it, apparently, and women voters seemed to enjoy it.

A few days before polling day the Conservatives led by 15%. Their spirits rose, but the Party leaders remembered the shocks of 1970 and 1974 and knew that many Conservatives had said they might vote for the Alliance if they came to the conclusion that the Alliance had a chance. The Party analysts were not sure how seriously the electorate had taken Mr Healey's charges that the Tories had a 'secret manifesto' of social and economic measures to be implemented if they won the election, including the alleged 'dismantling' of the National Health Service, as adumbrated in the leaked think-tank report of 1982. Mrs Thatcher berated Mr Healey for trying to start 'a cruel, callous scare ... I have no more intention of dismantling the health service than of dismantling Britain's defences'.

On the eve of the poll a Conservative victory looked predictable. The unsuccessful leadership of Michael Foot, a longtime loyal supporter of the Campaign for Nuclear Disarmament, and the division of opinion between him and his deputy, Denis Healey, on major aspects of defence policy, had clearly damaged the prospects of the Labour Party, while an attempt during the campaign by the leader of the Liberals, David Steel, to replace Roy Jenkins as titular leader of the SDP-Liberal Alliance seemed to have badly flawed the Alliance image.

It was said at the time and it is frequently said today that the 1983 election was not won by Mrs Thatcher but lost by her opponents. That may be so, but there could be no argument about what the result did for her position in the House of Commons, in the Cabinet, in the Conservative Party and in the country. The 397 seats she won, the largest number any party had won since the war, gave her a majority of 144 over all the other parties put together. The Labour Party had 209 seats, 49 less than in any post-war election, and the Alliance won 23 – in 1979, when the SDP did not exist, the Liberals had won 11 seats. The Conservative share of the vote was 42.4%, which was low, but the Labour Party won only 27.6% of the vote, less than in any election in sixty-five years. The Alliance share was 25.4%. Had there been a system of proportional representation with seats awarded in direct ratio to votes cast, the Conservatives could have claimed only 276 seats, Labour 179, the Alliance 165, the rest 30.

However it was described, analysed and interpreted, the result of the election had palpable effects on each of the three contending parties. Michael Foot announced that he would not stand again for the Labour Party leadership; the divisions in the Party opened up by the campaign showed that it would face a long and bitter conflict between left and right before it could hope to present an appearance of unity. The Liberal leader, David Steel, considered resigning. Roy Jenkins, leader of the SDP, resigned to make way for David Owen. For Mrs Thatcher the outcome was a personal triumph; her already dominant position within her Government was patently strengthened, and as we shall see she took swift advantage of the fact. Her devotees could claim that her reputation for uncompromising, decisive, honest conviction government, as opposed to consensus government, had prevailed over the electoral hazards of high unemployment, rumours of the end of the Welfare State and threats of economic and political disruption by desperately embattled trade unions. The result of the 1983 general election made Margaret Thatcher the strongest Conservative Prime Minister for a hundred years.

# 11

# SHOWDOWN WITH THE MINERS

T he story of Mrs Thatcher's first administration, 1979–83, is of her acquisition of the reality, as against the appearance, of political power. The story of her second is of how she used it. The first tells of success, of her remarkable achievement in rising, with the odds against her and with less support and good will than any newly elected prime minister since Baldwin, from a position far from strong in Cabinet, Party and country, to one of ascendancy in all three. The story of the second is of some singular successes but of some disturbing failures too.

As well as establishing her power, in her 1979 administration she had carried out a significant part of her programme, keeping promises made in the election campaign which even members of her own Party had thought over-optimistic if not rash. She had not kept them all, so far, but enough to show she had meant what she had said, and more than enough to prove those Conservative leaders wrong who had said that much of what she promised was 'politically impossible'. Whether they approved of what she had done or not, people felt that under Margaret Thatcher there had been activity, movement, challenge and change; and an attempt to relieve the country of many inhibiting, and some dangerous, constraints. In the 1983 administration too there was pro-gress, and significant success; but much of it was below the surface, and much of it that was above the surface was not spectacular. By its end her supporters could claim that the economy had strengthened steadily; productivity had increased; inflation, tumbling from 21% in 1980 to

4% in 1983, had been brought down to 3% in 1987; the number of strikes, official and unofficial, had been reduced. But on the whole, though she held to her course, and made port near where she had steered for, the story of the second Thatcher administration is of a rough crossing.

The first thing which became clear after the election was that in spite of her new strength the Prime Minister had no intention of relaxing her discipline over her Government: when she reshuffled her Cabinet the day after the result was declared, she fired her Foreign Secretary, Francis Pym.

The removal of Pym disturbed the Conservative Party greatly. Here was a highly regarded, popular and loyal senior member of the Party who had been a respected and liked Chief Whip (a rare achievement), Minister of Defence, Leader of the House, and then Foreign Secretary. *The Times* spoke of him as 'an accomplished parliamentarian ... as a House of Commons man he has few superiors'. Though newspapers carried stories that he was not a success as a Departmental Minister, the general impression was that Mrs Thatcher wanted to be rid of him because he was not 'one of us'. He was a wet, and he had compounded his wetness by his remark during the election about a landslide victory not being a good thing. Many Conservatives not only deplored his removal but the circumstances surrounding it. Newspapers reported that the Prime Minister had repeatedly made it known that Pym had been asked to become Speaker of the House of Commons – a distinguished post but a dead end for an aspirant to political power – though she had been aware all along that he had declined the job and wished to remain in the Cabinet, preferably as Foreign Secretary.

A few days after his dismissal he spoke in the House, a loyal speech, asking for no changes in domestic or foreign policy, but urging more concern for the plight of the unemployed. 'Mr Pym', said *The Times*, 'is not offering an alternative policy, merely an alternative attitude.' Its editorial went on to say prophetically: 'if in one and a half to two years' time the economic revival has petered out, unemployment is still rising, the unions are less docile and public hope is fading, then the Prime Minister will know that behind her on the Conservative back benches there is a critic with the parliamentary skills to mount a rebellion and no sense of personal obligation to prevent him from doing so. But that is a risk that she took deliberately when she sacked him.'

*The Times* deserves credit for its prescience of events which turned out almost exactly as it had predicted. In May 1985, with unemployment still rising and the bitterness and violence of the miners' strike still in everybody's minds, Pym did indeed launch the only 'rebellion' against Mrs Thatcher from within the Conservative Party when he announced the launch of a new ginger group within the Party called 'Conservative Centre Forward'. It was an attempt, in his own view, to re-establish the centre ground of politics within the Conservative Party and recreate the 'One Nation' brand of politics championed by Macmillan and Butler.

The new effort barely lasted a week, rapidly disintegrating in the teeth of clear intimations from the Party Whips that membership of the new group would be neither forgiven nor forgotten. Conservative Centre Forward itself proved to be a one-weekend sensation; but the idea behind it and the fact that Pym had felt confident enough to put himself at its head demonstrated that even after the sweeping success of the 1983 election there was still a great deal of resistance to Thatcherism within the Party. Many were worried that if the Party, under Mrs Thatcher, veered off too much to the right, so politicians of the centre like David Owen would be able to capture the hearts and minds of many moderate Conservative voters alienated by her robust and crusading style of politics. Although in retrospect these worries can be seen to have been exaggerated, they were very real at the time.

The debate in which Pym registered what *The Times* described as 'not an alternative policy but an alternative attitude' was wound up by the new Lord Privy Seal and Leader of the House, John Biffen, and his speech too was the subject of measured comment in the same editorial. Of Pym the paper had said: 'Above all, he was warning Mrs Thatcher not to interpret her election triumph as a licence to be harsh or extreme.' Of Biffen, in the next sentence, it said: 'Mr Biffen may have given an impression of reinforcing that warning when he wound up the debate. It is not an accident when a senior minister used such Conservative code phrases as "a sense of continuity that is the hallmark of British public life". This followed a more explicit statement by Mr Biffen last week that the new Tory majority will not mark an increase in the ideological tempo.' But, *The Times* concluded, 'it is far more likely that Mr Biffen was sending a message not to Mrs Thatcher but to the Conservative Party and to the country. He was in all probability not telling her that she should be careful but telling us that she would be. That would accord both with the style of her election campaign and with the reshuffling of the Cabinet. In neither respect has she shown much evidence of preparation for a sweeping programme of radical reform.'

It might have been better for her if she had. Had she appeared to be embarking on a vigorous and controversial programme, requiring maximum support from her Parliamentary Party, she might have encountered less trouble throughout the whole of her second administration. The blandness of the programme, the absence of challenges to her own Party, the lack of a need for unity and discipline, was to dog her fortunes almost to the eve of her election victory four years later.

Her immediate post-election strategy was clearly designed to consolidate her power at the very top, notably in the Treasury, and thus permeate and influence all government policies by using the power of the purse. The number of loyal Thatcherites in the economic departments was accordingly increased. Nigel Lawson became Chancellor of the Exchequer, Geoffrey Howe going to the Foreign Office. The Party chairman, whom she spoke of as the architect of the election triumph, Cecil Parkinson, became Secretary of State for the merged departments of Trade and Industry. The general effect of the reshuffle at junior as well as senior level was that loyal and active Thatcherites now occupied all the key economic posts. Other moves added to her strength in the Government. Whitelaw left the Home Office and went to the House of Lords. David Howell was removed from Transport. Peter Rees became Chief Secretary to the Treasury. John Wakeham became Chief Whip. Jim Prior remained bogged in Northern Ireland. Sir Douglas Wass, the Head of the Treasury, reaching retirement, was succeeded by Sir Peter Middleton, thought to be more committed to monetarism than Sir Douglas, and an enthusiastic collaborator with Nigel Lawson in his early days at the Treasury in 1979. The new regime, and especially the Cabinet, looked distinctly more Thatcherite than its predecessor, which could not be said of its programme.

The programme, indeed, in contrast with the rhetoric which had introduced it and now accompanied it, presaged a cautious advance. If the frontiers of the State were going to be rolled back, very little was being said about where, when and how far. This was understandable. If Mrs Thatcher was going to deliver what her supporters believed she had promised, she would have either to make large cuts in expenditure on welfare or continue to provide benefits much as before, which would involve increases in taxation and borrowing. Saying so in public so soon after the election would not be to sound a clarion. The Conservatives had come to power in 1979 promising to reduce taxes at all income levels and, it was generally accepted, to cut public spending as well. In the event, taxes in teal terms increased for all but the richest, and as a proportion of Gross Domestic Product public expenditure rose by 3%.

On these fundamental matters, and on others such as trade union reform, the Government said very little. Meanwhile the question was posed and re-posed: what does Mrs Thatcher intend to do with her immense majority in the next four years?

A trailer of things to come appeared two days after the election: Arthur Scargill, president of the National Union of Mineworkers, made a speech amounting to a declaration of war on the Government. His description of the election result echoed *Pravda* – 'an unprecedented manipulation of public opinion' – but the chief culprits, he said, were the leaders of the Labour Party, 'who in some cases actually undermined the vital unity around our manifesto by speaking against key elements of Party policy', and he cited Mr Callaghan's denunciation of the Labour Party's promise of a non-nuclear defence policy. But Scargill was more concerned about the domestic front. The workers could not expect any protection against Government policy from the Labour Party, he said. They would consequently have to resort to 'extra-parliamentary action'. The re-election of Mrs Thatcher was 'the worst national disaster for 100 years.' Unemployment would reach eight million. He predicted 'social violence on the streets, aggravated by a paramilitary police force'. There was no alternative for the working man: 'We must resolve to fight in the trade unions and all other democratic bodies inside and outside Parliament to bring about another general election as quickly as possible to get rid of this vicious government.'

This was the classic call for a political strike, the withdrawal of labour not to press a claim for more pay, better terms or better working conditions, but to change the policies of a government democratically elected by the will of the people. The trade union movement had turned its back on such a stance ever since the débâcle of the General Strike of 1926.

Scargill's challenge did not escape the attention of the Prime Minister. She had expected it. If the miners had been ready to bring down the consensus Government of Ted Heath in 1974, they would be even readier to bring down a conviction Government one of whose main convictions was that the unions had to be brought to heel. There was nothing new about Scargill's attitude; what was new was hers. If he wanted a political strike, let him have one: it would be just as well to have one, because the Government would win that strike, and as a result the trade union movement would be put back into its proper place for the first time since the end of the Second World War.

Because she was convinced that it would be a waste of time, she spent little thought on how to accommodate the demands which were the ostensible reason for the coming dispute. She knew that Scargill would not in reality strike for better terms, but for power. She concentrated her mind, therefore, on how to win what was not merely another battle but the one which she intended to be the last in an overly long war. The story of Mrs Thatcher and the miners is recounted later, but it is relevant here to mention the preparations she made immediately after the election to introduce her third bill for the curbing of trade union power, which, when it became law the following year, was to be of great importance in breaking Scargill's power.

In the interview with Mrs Thatcher on the eve of the election, referred to earlier, the author had reminded her that when she took office she had said that 'the balance of industrial power was far too tipped in favour of the unions'. How did she feel about that now? She answered:

> We have as you know passed two acts which have made a very good start. One was much concerned to deal with picketing and the second to make the unions responsible for action which would have been illegal if done by an individual. Both were concerned with the closed shop. Another bill is to come. There is a Green Paper out on whether ballots for the election of union officials should be secret. I personally think that's the most important thing. . . .

Four weeks after the election victory, and three weeks after Mr Scargill had thrown down his gauntlet, Norman Tebbit, Minister for Employment, issued the Government's White Paper on 12 July 1983. The next day, *The Times* singled out as the most important of its legislative proposals the one which Mrs Thatcher mentioned on the eve of the election. 'The proposal to enable members to enforce the use of fair and secret ballots in elections to union governing bodies is the most far-reaching of the new plans,' concluded *The Times*. 'It will be hard for the unions to raise much of a head of indignation against a commitment so prominently presented in the campaign, especially when it takes the side of the average trade unionist against the chief holders of power in his own union.' The following Sunday, 17 July, the *Observer* said that 'Mr Tebbit has produced an ingenious and modest package which may even be welcomed on the shop floor. It provides rank-and-file union members with the opportunity to exercise their rights through the secrecy of the ballot box for the election of their governing bodies.' The *Observer*, frequently very critical of Mrs Thatcher's policies, took the view:

> Britain's trade union leaders have only themselves to blame for Norman Tebbit's latest set of legislative proposals designed to strengthen trade union

democracy. The misuse of the block vote system, the reluctance of union leaders to consult their members on vital issues, and the enormous gap that has grown up between the minority who runs the unions and the millions they claim to represent have all helped to make union democracy an urgent subject for reform. In their initial, negative response most union leaders are behaving like the last of the Bourbons.

Other important changes in the law were foreshadowed in the White Paper, including the holding of secret ballots before strikes could be regarded as legal, the calling or endorsing of a strike without ballot forfeiting immunity. Without immunity, the trade union might risk an injunction, its funds becoming liable to an action for damages. The new legislation would substitute 'contracting in' of trade union members to subscriptions to the Labour Party for the existing practice of 'contracting out'. These and other important changes were to receive much publicity when the House of Commons came to debate them the following year. What is to be noted now is the setting of the stage for the completion of Mrs Thatcher's structure for the curbing of union power, to be of great significance in the coming struggle with the miners, the test of whether she was determined enough and politically strong enough to do what above all she had been elected to do in 1979, after the winter of discontent, to confront and solve the greatest of Britain's problems since the Second World War, and restore the trade unions to their proper place in British society. Meanwhile, in the summer of 1983, Mrs Thatcher got on with her more immediate business.

This, considering that the morrow of such an electoral triumph might have been one of unusual joy and gratitude, was troublesome. After their circumstances had been studied by the Top Salaries Review Body, Members of Parliament had been awarded a pay increase which mounted to about 31%, an award to which the MPs had given an enthusiastic welcome. Mrs Thatcher had not, and now made it clear that she would try to limit the increase to 4%. There was such fury among Conservative MPs that there was speculation about the Government being defeated when the issue came to the vote. As it was, the Government was defeated on an amendment to the bill, but the main provision, a compromise under which there would be five annual increments of 5.5%, was carried. Controversy also reared its head when it was announced that the Commons would debate the restoration of capital punishment. Mrs Thatcher and the Home Secretary were known to be in favour of hanging, and it was predicted, correctly, that the majority of the new intake of Conservative MPs were also in favour of it. The debate was preceded by much public discussion, some of it acrimonious, but the move to bring hanging back was defeated.

In the second week of July came news of an emergency package of large cuts in public expenditure amounting to £500 million in 1983–4, nearly half in defence, but, much more controversially, a quarter in the health service. 'Only four weeks into the life of the new Government and already the axe falls on health services and social benefits: no wonder that its opponents have returned to the election theme of a secret manifesto,' observed *The Times*. 'Only two days before the election, Mr Norman Fowler declared that it was out of the question that a re-elected Conservative Government would cut NHS spending: where are those promises now?' *The Times* pointed out in defence of the Secretary of State for Social Services (Mr Fowler) that he had spoken about levels of expenditure agreed whereas the cuts would be made in overspending above those levels, but warned him that the public might not read 'the small print', and that 'an assault on social services when the new Tory recruits in the Commons have scarcely been sworn in risks creating an impression of lack of heart, and also of frankness'. The following day, the *Observer* weighed in. 'The announcement of £500 million of public spending cuts within a month of the general election undoubtedly leaves the Government with egg on its face ... And it cannot but feed the worst suspicions of those many members of the public who were concerned about possible threats to the Welfare State from a Mk. II Thatcher administration.' The *Observer* also pointed out that it was over-spending that would be cut, adding that the Chancellor could reasonably claim that total spending in real terms would rise in 1983–4. 'The most disturbing aspect of Mr Lawson's package and threats of future packages is the confirmation that, in the name of prudent housekeeping, the Government intends to carry on down the same deflationary road it pursued in the first four years.'

Ministers in charge of spending departments were disturbed by the Treasury's sudden demand for cuts coming only three months into the fiscal year and so soon after the election. That it could be interpreted as the new Chancellor making a show of his strength and resolution made it no easier for them. There was dissidence within the Cabinet. The most outspoken was the Minister who bore the brunt of the assault, the Secretary of State for Defence, Michael Heseltine. The Chancellor also met with resistance from the Minister for Energy, Peter Walker: the Chancellor wanted to speed up the repayment of capital advances made to the electricity and gas industries, and Mr Walker objected since this would mean higher prices for the consumer.

The Government came under new fire, directed by many of its own party, when on 1 August its White Paper appeared announcing early legislation enabling it to impose ceilings on expenditure and rate increases on every local council in England and Wales. The Government's case was that high rates and extravagant spending put unfair burdens on many individuals, and especially on industry and commerce, who shouldered 60% of the load and had no vote with which to defend themselves. Though Conservative-dominated councils also joined the protest, the most vociferous were the high-spending Labour councils, well aware of being the Government's prime target. The Conservative-controlled Association of County Councils denounced the Government's policy as a threat to local democracy. This, with the threat of 'rate-capping', was the beginning of a debate about rates which was to last for several years and then merge into Mrs Thatcher's highly controversial scheme for the abolition of rates altogether and the substitution of a national poll tax.

As the summer recess approached there was more and more argument about the cutting of public expenditure, and more criticism of the Government's apparent lack of a clear strategic approach to the problem. The Government's sale of £500 million worth of shares in British Petroleum 'to keep its borrowing nearer forecast is a cosmetic device that should fool no one', warned *The Times*. 'As Mrs Thatcher's housewifely economics might have it, the Government is selling off the family heirlooms to pay the grocery bills.' The chief grocery bill, said the paper, was the cost of unemployment benefits, 'which is undermining the Cabinet's most strenuous efforts to keep down public spending', the direct result, according to her critics, of Mrs Thatcher's misguided economic policy. Be that as it may, 'The issue of public spending is obviously paramount,' observed *The Times*,

> both because of its effect on the economy and because it determines the whole political climate in which the Government will be operating ... The next five months or so will determine the fate of this Government at the next election ... Unfortunately there is no real sign that this Government has yet developed either the strategic mentality to take a long view, or the machinery to put it into effect. The fortunes of this Government will not ultimately depend on mastering departmental briefs. They will depend on a combination of strong nerve and clear argument, neither of which has been obvious since the election.

That leader appeared on Thursday 28 July, the day of the Penrith by-election, occasioned by Whitelaw's elevation to the House of Lords. The result of the poll was bad news for the Government: the Conservatives held this hitherto impregnable seat with a majority of only 522, an astonishing fall of 15,000 since the general election in June. In a leader headed 'Evaporation' *The Times* said, 'It looks like the shortest honeymoon in political history', though it cited several reasons why the Penrith result should not be taken to show much more than the resentment of the electors at having to revisit the polls so quickly. Though it was a great 'humiliation' for the Government, there was no question of 'a sudden reversal of a tide flowing strongly Torywards: there wasn't one'. In a leader with the title 'An Unpropitious Start' the *Observer* commented:

> Summer recesses nearly always come as a relief to governments. Seldom, though, can an administration have felt a greater sense of deliverance than Mrs Thatcher's evidently did last week. The fact that it should have come within a hair's breadth of losing one of the safest seats in the country at the first by-election of the new Parliament tells its own tale of just how fully 'the glad, confident morning' mood of Friday, 10 June, has vanished in a bare seven weeks.

In early October, on the eve of the annual Conservative conference at Blackpool, out of the blue came another blow for the Government. The stage had been set for a celebration of the general election victory, to which, next to the Prime Minister, the most effective contributor, particularly in her view, had been the chairman of the Party, Cecil Parkinson, whom as leader she had personally selected, and who was now an influential member of the Cabinet as Secretary of State for Trade and Industry. On 5 October, Mr Parkinson's solicitors issued a lengthy statement describing his longstanding relationship with his former secretary, Miss Sara Keays, acknowledging that he had once wished to marry her and that the child she was now expecting was by him. Eight days later, on the evening of the day in which Mr Parkinson had made a well-received speech to the conference, Miss Keays issued a long statement to *The Times* in which she claimed that three times over a period of four years Mr Parkinson had said he would marry her but had three times changed his mind. Mr Parkinson went to see the Prime Minister that night and resigned, leaving Blackpool in the small hours, accompanied by his wife. After consultation with his constituents he decided not to resign his seat.

Two weeks later, on 25 October, President Reagan ordered United States forces to invade the Caribbean island of Grenada. With the aid and encouragement of the government of Cuba, a left-wing military group on the island had murdered Mr Maurice Bishop, the Prime

Minister, and had established their regime. Mr Reagan said that the intervention of American armed forces had three objectives: 'to protect innocent lives, including up to 1,000 Americans ... to forestall further chaos ... to assist the restoration of conditions of law and order and of democratic institutions in the island of Grenada, where a brutal group of leftish thugs violently seized power.' His justification was the treaty of mutual support signed by eastern Caribbean nations in 1981. Britain was invited to co-operate. Not only did Mrs Thatcher refuse; she had a telephone conversation with the President in which she urged him not to sanction the invasion. The day after American forces had landed, there was an emergency debate in the House of Commons, in which the Foreign Secretary said that the (limited) amount of consultation possible with the Americans was to be regretted, but that the outcome must not be allowed to compromise the alliance. As well as diatribes from the Opposition there was much criticism of him from his own party.

Sir Geoffrey made the best of a bad job. Under pressure, and when it was clear that the invasion had achieved its purpose, he became more outspoken: on 30 October he said that the invasion was not justified on grounds either of threats to American lives or to the amount of Cuban presence on the island. Mrs Thatcher, too, became more critical. In a broadcast in the BBC World Service the same day she said: 'If you are going to pronounce a new law that wherever communism reigns against the will of the people the United States shall enter, then we are going to have terrible wars in the world.'

Grenada having been made safe, the United States troops were withdrawn in a short space of time, and the affair soon blew over. Comparatively little was heard of it at the Commonwealth Conference in New Delhi the following month. Mrs Thatcher's tolerance of an invasion of a sovereign state within the British Commonwealth could be explained by her knowledge that there was nothing she could do to stop it.

If she sensibly appeared to be tolerant – to the Opposition, overtolerant – of an event that she could have done nothing to prevent, the next challenge to be met was one that she had been planning to meet and overcome for several years – the challenge of the miners.

As we have seen, the miners' leader, Arthur Scargill, had sounded a clarion call for resistance to Thatcherism immediately after the 1983 general election. In October through a special delegate conference he declared an overtime ban. It was thus obvious that he meant what he said, and that the miners and the Government would soon be locked into confrontation.

Scargill was displaying exactly the same attitude towards the Thatcher Government as he had taken towards the Government of Edward Heath a decade earlier. Scargill had made his name during the victorious miners' strike of 1972 as the leader of the 'flying pickets' which had done so much to bring British industry to a halt and thus precipitate the fall of the Government. In an interview with the *New Left Review* in 1975 Scargill had boasted of his celebrated closure, through the sheer weight of flying pickets, of the Saltley coking plant, an event which many commentators saw as the decisive turning point in the miners' struggle against Heath. To a man schooled in unadulterated Marxism via the Young Communist League, such action was an integral part of the class war. He told interviewers: 'I believe in a class war you have to fight with the tools at your disposal ... You see, we took the view that we were in a class war, not playing cricket on the village green like they did in 1926 ... We were out to defeat Heath and Heath's policies because we were fighting a government.' Never again were Scargill's motives to surface so plainly as they did in this interview. Many people, including some in government, at first underestimated the revolutionary political implications of his actions. Mrs Thatcher, though, was in no doubt as to what he intended; she described the miners' leader to Ian MacGregor, the new chairman of the National Coal Board as 'a Marxist revolutionary – going under the guise of a normal trade union official'. For Scargill, the miners were the shock troops of the class war; the proletarian vanguard that was to bring about the fall of the capitalist puppet, Mrs Thatcher. Considering Scargill's political colours, it was thus not surprising that he had good connections and backers in the Soviet Union and Libya. Estimates by the secret service later put the Soviet contribution to the miners' cause during the 1984–5 strike at £7 million.

The only problem with Scargill's plan was that the miners themselves refused to adopt the role for which he had cast them. On three occasions before the 1984 strike Scargill had tried to get the miners to down tools, but each time he had failed on the ballot to get a majority in favour of strike action. This taught him that if there was to be a strike he would have to avoid a ballot of his members. This he did, and consequently was able to engineer a strike, to begin in March 1984. Coalfields, such as Nottingham, which did not want to strike, were simply closed down with the aid of his well tried weapon the flying pickets.

For the Government's part, the coal industry, like the rest of the nationalized industries, represented all that was worst about British industry. Over-manned, unproductive, archaic and unprofitable, it was a bottomless pit into which Governments had poured vast sums with no economic return. Due to the opening up of new coal reserves throughout the world and the ever-cheapening oil as an alternative fuel, Britain was producing far more coal, at a far higher cost, than was needed and which was affordable. It was not a problem peculiar to Mrs Thatcher's Government; 346,000 miners had left the industry between 1960 and 1968 as Harold Wilson's 'white heat' of technology had brought about a necessary slimming down of the industry in the face of competing forms of modern fuel such as nuclear power. By 1984, the plight of British coal had increased further. The report on the industry by the Monopolies and Mergers Commission in 1983 had commented:

> The longer the problems are left, the worse they will become. Unless there is a significant reduction in the numbers of high-cost pits the NCB's finances will deteriorate even further. The industry's ability to invest in modern capacity in the short and medium term will be jeopardized, for, if the problem is not dealt with, there must come a time when it will be quite impossible for any government to justify to the public the large and growing expenditure of public funds that would be needed.

Mrs Thatcher was well aware that the coal industry would have to be dealt with. The key phrase in the above report was 'the numbers of high cost pits': it was the Government's demands that uneconomic pits should be closed in order to make the industry as a whole profitable again that sparked off the 1984 strike. Furthermore, once Arthur Scargill was elected president of the National Union of Mineworkers (NUM) in 1982, it was realized in Government that such restructuring of the industry, with the concomitant loss of jobs, would inevitably lead to a clash with him. For the president of the NUM, there was no such thing as an 'uneconomic pit'. In his view coal should be mined wherever it was and whatever the cost. Asked to explain his view to a Government Select Committee, Scargill replied: 'Where there are resources of coal ... even if there is a loss on the production of that coal, then that coal should be produced.' When questioned further about the level of loss that might be acceptable in a mining operation, Scargill replied: 'As far as I am concerned, the loss is without limit because I am more interested in the investment our men have put into this industry.' For Scargill, economics did not come into it; an attack on the coal industry was simply class warfare.

The Government had already made one attempt to close uneconomic pits in 1981. On that occasion, Mrs Thatcher decided reluctantly to withdraw after earnest advice from Jim Prior, Willie Whitelaw and Lord Carrington that at that particular moment the Government could not win a strike. She found this humiliating, but she displayed a self-control and patience, and a sense of timing, which won her some new admirers. She resolved not to let the Scargill problem go away but to take it on at a time of her own choosing. There was never any doubt in her mind that a pit closure programme would lead to a massive struggle with the miners: that such a struggle was sooner or later inevitable if Britain was to be 'saved'; and that her task was to go into such a conflict equipped to win.

Ultimately, the issue at stake was the 'right to manage' the industry; the Government was seeking to restore the management's right to manage – a right which they saw as having been eroded by the growth of trade union power. It was a familiar Thatcherite theme, and one of the cornerstones of the Thatcherite revolution. As such, it had to be fought for.

From 1981, therefore, the Government began to plan for a successful confrontation with Scargill. The key to success and failure in any coal strike was the level of stocks in the country to ensure that the coal-burning power stations could continue to operate. By the spring of 1984, stocks had reached the unprecedented level of 50 million tonnes. The man who was appointed to lead the revolution in the coal industry, as chairman of the National Coal Board, was Ian MacGregor, who had already achieved a remarkable slimming down of British Steel as chairman of the British Steel Board from 1980 to 1983. Ian MacGregor already had a special place in the demonology of the Labour movement because of the job cuts he had forced through at British Steel. It was not surprising that his appointment to the Coal Board in September 1983 was seen by Arthur Scargill as a declaration of war on the National Union of Mineworkers.

The personalities of the two protagonists had much influence on developments. MacGregor was at home in the boardroom, but eschewed contact with the press and the public. Scargill was a powerful orator, skilled communicator, a natural showman. MacGregor was a hard-nosed financier and skilful negotiator: Scargill did not negotiate, and despised finance. The clashing of these two characters was the centrepiece of the struggle.

As a major element in her campaign against Scargill Mrs Thatcher made possibly the most astute political appointment of her time as Prime Minister: in the 1983 Government reshuffle she made Peter

Walker the Minister for Energy. The coal issue was one on which every Conservative could unite; by appointing a distinguished, articulate and sophisticated wet to be the political head of the coal industry, she ensured that the Government's case against Scargill would not be put primarily in the simplistic and aggressive terms favoured by Mr MacGregor. Walker was admired for his skills as a communicator – not least by the Prime Minister – and as a telegenic Minister, unlike MacGregor who was neither sympathetic nor persuasive in front of the cameras. According to Peter Walker's account of the interview with Mrs Thatcher in which she asked him to take his job, she was quite candid about what it would involve:

> During the next Parliament, she said, the Government could be challenged by Arthur Scargill. He would use the industrial clout of the miners to achieve his Marxist objectives . . . she said that if that did happen she felt there would be no one more experienced or better at communicating the Government's case. I accepted the responsibility.[1]

The scene was thus set. On 6 March 1984 MacGregor presented his plans for the closure of uneconomic pits (involving a cut in coal production of four million tonnes per year) to the NUM. Scargill, wholly predictably, rejected them and declared a strike. As mentioned earlier, and for the reason given, there was no ballot of the rank and file; the decision was a decree by the leadership. The circumstances in which the strike was declared, and the authority for it, were to assume greater significance as it went on, and to become crucially important in bringing it to an end. The strike was legitimized by reference to Rule 41 of the NUM Rule Book, which applied only to local disputes – no national ballot was ever taken on the strike. By 18 March all but 30 of the 171 pits were not working; but many of these had been picketed into submission. Some balloting had taken place at the beginning where nine regional areas decided to hold a vote; only one area, Northumberland, was in favour of a strike, and by a margin of only 52% to 48%. From the very beginning it was clear that Scargill could rely on an effective national strike only by imposing his will by force on the coalfields who were opposed to it or were not wholehearted about it. Once this force was effectively resisted, the strike would inevitably begin to collapse.

The decisive intervention of Mrs Thatcher's Government in the strike was to ensure that the physical force of the flying pickets deployed in various parts of the country was resisted with the aid of unprecedented numbers of police moved in to keep them at bay. The pitched battles of the strike were thus those fought between the police, protecting the 'right to work' and the pickets who realized that their strike could only succeed if they managed to close by force as many pits as possible.

Tactically, Scargill's timing of the strike was most inept; he chose to fight his battle at the beginning of the summer, when energy needs would be at their lowest and inconvenience to the public would be minimal. As it was, coal stocks were so high that it would probably have made little difference when he chose to strike; despite all the efforts of the miners, no electricity cuts occurred even during the peak of winter some nine months into the dispute, a testimony to the careful tactical planning of the Coal Board and the Electricity Generating Board under Lord Marshall.

Contrary to some reports at the time, Mrs Thatcher, applying her precept of non-interference in industrial disputes, intervened little during the strike. MacGregor was largely left to get on with the ceaseless rounds of abortive negotiations with the N U M in his own way. According to his own account:

> Considering the scale and importance to the nation of the strike, it will surprise many people to learn that the Prime Minister and I had so little contact with each other ... for the most part our encounters were for the purpose of bringing her up to date on the situation. We had some fairly wide-ranging discussions; but I recollect her giving me a specific order on only one occasion in the entire year of the dispute.[2]

What Mrs Thatcher did was to provide Ian MacGregor with everything that he asked for to beat the miners. Early on, he pointed out that with only local police forces of limited size available, the flying pickets had almost a free hand to close any pit they chose. The Government responded at once by setting up the National Reporting Centre at Scotland Yard in London, to enable police from different local forces throughout the country to be transferred to wherever they might be needed. Sufficient police were thus on hand outside pits and power stations to ensure that miners and workers who wanted to go to work could do so. This was crucial in an area like Nottinghamshire, since the highly visible police presence there ensured that large numbers of miners, who had been pressured into withdrawing their labour, began returning to work once their safe passage was guaranteed by the police. The continued working of the Nottingham coalfield was crucial to the whole outcome. The miners there had least to gain by a strike since they were working in the most profitable coalfield with a secure future. As Ian MacGregor himself has since written: 'The key to the whole strike was Nottinghamshire and its 31,000 miners'. Nottinghamshire's twenty-five pits could produce a quarter of the National Coal Board's total output, thus ensuring that the existing large coal stocks would remain high throughout.

Mrs Thatcher put the strike in its political context, most famously in her speech to the 1922 Committee on 19 July 1984 referring to the Scargillites of the NUM as 'the enemies within', as opposed to the Argentinians who had been the 'enemies without'. She made no bones about it: Scargill was a totalitarian Marxist trying to subvert democracy. As no ballot had been taken before he declared the strike, this charge was easy to sustain, while the bullying tactics of the flying pickets helped to project an image of Scargill and the other members of the 'troika' who ran the NUM – Mick McGahey and Peter Heathfield – as totally undemocratic.

The right to manage was an industrial right to be asserted, but Mrs Thatcher also sought to mobilize popular opinion on a broader and more ambitious front, in support of her brand of popular democracy against the extremist left-wing autocracy of Scargillism. To begin with, this element rarely surfaced, but there can be little doubt that it was in these terms that she ultimately saw the strike. To a certain extent, she also had the Party-political duty of exorcizing the ghost of defeat at the miners' hands in 1972 and 1974. This time there would be no drawing back, and there would be victory. The resources of Government, in terms of policing, importing coal, publicity and lost revenue could be deployed in 1984–5 in a way that would not have been dreamt of in 1972 and 1974.

The Nottinghamshire miners were the heroes of the conflict for the Conservatives. They dared to work in the face of physical and verbal abuse from the NUM pickets, and eventually went on to form their own breakaway union, the Union of Democratic Mineworkers, totally independent of the NUM. If the NUM was the unacceptable face of unionism, the new UDM became torch bearers of a new approach to it.

Given Mrs Thatcher's iron resolve to see the strike through, Ian MacGregor could take advantage of the knowledge that all the economic and other resources of the State were at his disposal; he could sit out the strike for as long as he wanted. He did so. During May and June 1984 Scargill tried to repeat his victorious coup in forcing the closure of Saltley in 1972, this time by securing the closure of the coking plant at Orgreave. Plants like Orgreave would have to be closed if the strike was to have any substantial effect on industry; the police ensured that Orgreave would not be closed. The climax came on 18 June: Scargill had amassed 10,000 workers from all over the country to picket the plant. There was widespread violence, but Orgreave stayed open. The event epitomized the defeat of Scargill's only effective weapon, the mass picket. Orgreave was the turning point. There was to be no Saltley, and no more victories for the miners.

What did most to alienate support for Scargill, particularly within the Labour movement, was the level of violence which the pickets seemed to precipitate and which Scargill repeatedly refused to condemn. This was grist to the mill for the Conservatives, as the NUM leader had not only rejected the ballot box but seemed also to be condoning violence as a legitimate political weapon. The pitched battles between the pickets and the police were projected daily via television into the living-rooms of the nation, and however much Scargill tried to blame the police the unmistakable impression remained that it was the pickets who were almost entirely to blame. The climax came on 30 November when a concrete slab was dropped by miners on a taxicab taking a miner to work at Merthyr Vale colliery in South Wales, killing the driver, David Wilkie. But this was only the tragic highlight of daily violence that disfigured the strike, from which Scargill did nothing to dissociate himself despite repeated invitations to do so.

The violence, and the undemocratic nature, of the strike told heavily against any effective support Scargill might have won within the wider trade union movement. Labour leader Neil Kinnock and Norman Willis, the General Secretary of the TUC, felt unable to lend Scargill any positive support whilst the violence continued. The difference between Kinnock and Scargill was quite apparent on the day of the death of David Wilkie. The two men addressed a Labour rally at Stoke-on-Trent. Scargill made no reference to Wilkie's death; Kinnock began his speech by saying: 'We meet here tonight in the shadow of an outrage.'

Kinnock and the majority of the Labour Party leadership were quite aware that as a potential Government they could not be seen to be condoning industrial or political violence. Whereas the miners' strike found the Conservative Party unusually firm and united behind Mrs Thatcher, Labour was split; for every supporter of Kinnock's approach to the strike, there were those, like Tony Benn and Eric Heffer, who felt that Kinnock was only lukewarm in his support of the miners and that he was thus betraying the Labour movement. Scargill had set out to destroy the Conservative Government; he ended up splitting his own union and the Labour Party.

Just as the NUM was divided on the strike, so was the trade union movement as a whole. Scargill could find only scant practical support for his cause amongst his fellow trade unionists – an indication both of his own unpopularity within the union movement and of the political changes which Mrs Thatcher had brought about in the country during the previous five years. Crucially the Transport Workers refused to support him in numbers, so that during the height of the summer in 1984 the NCB were still able to move 400,000 tonnes of coal a week by rail or road, thus ensuring continuing supplies for the power stations. The most dangerous moments for the Government were when it looked as though sympathetic action by other unionists would help make the strike effective. In July the dockers briefly went on strike, and in August, much more significantly, the Mining Engineers' Union, NACODS, who carried out daily maintenance work and safety checks on the pits, followed suit. But the NCB swiftly pre-empted such action by agreeing terms with them, leaving the miners isolated.

By the autumn, the NUM's own members, mainly in Nottingham, were using the courts to have the strike declared illegal, and successive legal actions eventually led to the sequestration of the union's funds, thus crippling its ability to finance the strike. It was an astute move by Mr Walker to prevent any use of the Government's own much-vaunted but controversial employment laws by the NCB or other employers; such action might have united the union movement behind the miners. As it was, individual miners were encouraged to use common law and existing laws to cripple their own union; this was exactly what the Government desired, as the litigious Nottinghamshire miners were perceived as the populist, democratic unionists fighting the tyrannical Titans who had hijacked their own union.

With effective policing guaranteeing the right to work, the desultory failure of the pickets to close any power stations, and the mounting legal quagmire in which the NUM found itself, by the Christmas of 1984 it was obvious that the game was up. By the New Year, 54,000 NUM members had gone back to work, and only thirty-five pits were still solidly out. In March 1985, Scargill was forced to call off the strike as more than half of his own members had returned to their jobs. The Government had won – at an estimated cost of £3 billion, to say nothing of the mental and physical damage to Britain's mining communities.

Was it worth it?

Mrs Thatcher saw the strike as her biggest test on the industrial front; her whole economic system was built on the right of management to manage, and it was this principle that was now seen to be vindicated. It was a crucial political victory and reversed the verdicts – and consequences – of 1972 and 1974. It was also a moral victory; from now on the market philosophies which she had espoused could be implemented throughout industry, since the Government's economic case for the coal industry was adjudged to have won the day. In the last quarter of the year 1985–6, the NCB made an operating profit on deep-mine operations for the first time since 1977; since the middle of 1983, a total of 60,000 men had voluntarily left the industry.

The most important effect of the strike was on the trade union movement as a whole. Mrs Thatcher's message was that the restrictive practices of old style trade unionism, which virtually isolated whole industries from the harsh winds of international competition, would have to go if those very industries were to survive. Of no industry was this truer than mining. The lack of public support for the miners can be interpreted as a public endorsement of Mrs Thatcher's harsh but necessary medicine. The unions themselves had begun to change, as they increasingly found themselves to be beleaguered relics of an unlamented corporatist past. Separate unions now began to adjust themselves to the realities of the market place and to tailor their working practices to the demand of the technological and management changes of the 1980s. In the forefront of this new unionism was the electricians' union, the EETPU, led by Eric Hammond, who had described the NUM strikers as 'lions led by donkeys'. He claimed to see the way ahead by signing the no-strike agreements with employers to guarantee his members jobs with new technological enterprises such as Nissan. Such an agreement would have been unthinkable only a decade before, but such was the change wrought by Mrs Thatcher on the industrial scene in the wake of the miners' strike that similar agreements are becoming increasingly common. Unions such as the Engineering Workers and the new-formed UDM have also followed this path, although not to the extent of the EETPU. As two of the most respected observers of the Labour movement, John Lloyd and Martin Adeney, have written: 'The strike cauterised all illusions that the leadership and activist groups who necessarily run unions necessarily speak for their members. The Tory challenge to the unions' hegemony over the working class, for so long unquestioned, met its greatest test in the pit dispute and won.'[3]

The outcome of the miners' strike, which had put a severe strain on relations between the TUC and the NUM, and on relations between the unions and the Labour Party, was a noteworthy step forward to the realization of Mrs Thatcher's idea of the proper role for trade unionism in British society. The author had asked her in the interview on the eve of the 1983 election previously referred to if she had 'a conception of the role you would like to see trade unions playing in the future, as opposed to their past role?' she replied:

Yes. There's nóthing wrong with trade unionism, but I don't think the unions should be considered a sort of Fourth Estate of the Realm. In all workplaces you've got to have some means of communication and co-operation between those who work on the shop floor and those who work in management, whether it's through a works council or through the unions. But I don't regard a great big national conference, or a Fourth Estate, as the means of getting that co-operation. That communication is something that should happen on the shop floor.

She was then asked: 'It wouldn't matter to you, then, if the TUC didn't exist?' Her reply was: 'I've never thought about the TUC *not* existing. And frankly, I'm not *going* to think about it – it's not going to happen. What *would* matter to me, it would please me immensely, was if the TUC was *not*, and the trade unions were *not*, a part of the Labour Party, or the Labour Party a part of the trade union movement. That connection I must say I think is wrong.' Why was this wrong?

Because people in trade unions have different political views. They're not all Labour. And it doesn't matter really what their political views are: the essential thing is that there should be co-operation between scientists, designers, salesmen, technicians, skilled and unskilled workers, managers – *everybody*. It's the enterprise in which you're working which is the important thing. And its success. It's got nothing to do with the trade union movement, or the Labour Party.

The role of the trade unions came in for public attention again as a result of the bitter Wapping dispute in the winter of 1985–6. Once again, powerful unions, this time printers' unions, were locked in battle with an obdurate employer seeking to transform technologically the fortunes of an ailing industry, in this case Rupert Murdoch of the newspaper industry. Murdoch was not the first employer to have taken on the print unions on the issue of new technology – Eddie Shah had done that with his *Stockport Messenger* group – but the dispute over Murdoch's sacking of 5,000 print workers to allow him to move to a totally new and technologically modern newspaper plant in Wapping, in East London, became the pivotal test of power between the Fleet Street managers and one of the most powerful and privileged unions in the land. Once again, there was little Government intervention; but the massive numbers of police that were used to keep the Wapping plant open and to defy the pickets was fresh evidence of its determination to uphold the rights of management. After a year, the print unions gave up their unequal struggle and the rest of the Fleet Street newspaper proprietors found themselves able to introduce the new technology on their newspapers, thus cutting costs but entailing substantial redundancies.

The 'right to manage' was again vindicated, and the print unions seemed to enjoy even less public support than the miners. The battles at Orgreave and Wapping were ugly and violent, but they were battles that had to be fought to bring Britain, kicking, into the late twentieth century.

In political terms, the defeat of Scargill represented the defeat of the greatest threat to Thatcherism during her second term of office. But there was another foe that had to be tackled if Thatcherism was to make any headway in the country, and that was the high-spending Labour controlled local councils. These councils represented a new political phenomenon at the beginning of the 1980s, and were symptomatic of Labour's leftward lurch in the wake of their 1979 election defeat. The most celebrated politician of this kind was Ken Livingstone, who became leader of the Greater London Council (GLC) after an internal *coup d'état* in May 1981. Livingstone was really the first 'child of the sixties' to reach the top of the political ladder, and as such he managed to embrace a bewildering variety of causes which were weekly chronicled in the 'Agitprop' pages of *Time Out* magazine – anti-racism, nuclear disarmament, homosexuality, ecology, pro-Sinn Fein and many more. This was a new type of Socialism. In the view of Peter Jenkins, 'In more senses than one they were endeavouring to create Socialism without the working class, for the Socialism they preached and practised bore no relation to the wishes and needs of most ordinary people.'[4]

Livingstone, and his colleagues in Liverpool, Sheffield and Manchester spent money on a massive scale, for his own declared objective was 'to use the Council machinery as part of a political campaign both against the Government and in defence of socialist policies'. He was as good as his word, and under his leadership the GLC disbursed £8,878 billion. The 'Militant Tendency' politicians who controlled the Labour Council in Liverpool were equally generous with the ratepayers' money, virtually bankrupting the city by 1986. Municipal Socialism had come a long way from that of Herbert Morrison in the 1930s.

The GLC, however, achieved very little. The only radical measure that it tried to implement that might have touched the lives of Londoners in general was its proposed blanket reduction in underground and bus fares – the 'Fares Fair' campaign. This was declared illegal by the House of Lords. What the GLC did achieve was to incur the ire of Mrs Thatcher, who saw its behaviour as a threat to national Government, and to the interests of the people that lived under it and likeminded councils. As a result, in 1984, the Government moved to curb their free-spending ways with the Rates Act of 1984, which brought in rate-capping which made it illegal for a local council to set rates above a certain level. The councils most affected by this legislation were the free spenders in the Greater London area such as Haringey, Lambeth, Brent and Hackney. The Minister with responsibility for the legislation was Patrick Jenkin, who had the difficult task of allaying fears that it was profoundly undemocratic. His burden grew heavier when Mrs Thatcher, insisting that rate-capping did not go far enough, proposed the abolition of the municipal city councils altogether. It fell to the hapless Mr Jenkin to steer the bill through the House of Commons.

Paradoxically it seemed the Prime Minister, who had most associated herself with the devolution of political and industrial power, was now centralizing political power on an unparalleled scale. The paradox was explained by the move to eliminate the local Far Left power bases in the inner cities. The Government rightly calculated that although there would be a passing political storm, in the long term its electoral popularity would not be severely harmed, since those people who supported and worked for organizations such as the GLC would always vote Labour whatever the Government did. Nevertheless the GLC raised their abolition to the status of a *cause célèbre* in the eyes of the public, and inflicted great damage on the Government's credibility with a long and expensive advertising campaign before it disappeared in a blaze of fireworks (costing £250,000) on 31 March 1986.

The Government's tussle with the local councils exhibited some intolerance. David Blunkett's leadership of Sheffield City Council made it as sober, successful and popular a local City Council as it was possible to have, and yet Blunkett, like Livingstone, found himself swept away by a central Government that had nominally pledged itself to the cause of local democracy. These events added to a growing feeling that for all the economic advantages that Mrs Thatcher conferred on large parts of the British Isles, there was an ungenerous, intolerant, undemocratic element in her regime which was never far beneath the surface.

During the war of attrition against the miners and the local councils, public sympathy for Mrs Thatcher and her Government was aroused when the IRA bombed the Brighton Conservative Party conference in the autumn of 1984. The bomb that shattered the Grand Hotel on the penultimate night of the conference was clearly intended to eliminate Prime Minister and Cabinet at one blow. It failed in this, but among those killed was the wife of the Chief Whip, John Wakeham, whilst Mr and Mrs Tebbit were both badly wounded, she being paralysed for life.

Mrs Thatcher herself escaped unhurt. She was probably saved by her lifelong devotion to hard work. When the bomb went off, during the early hours of the morning, she was busy on her keynote speech to be delivered later in the day, working in a room which escaped the main thrust of the blast. Her response was typical: in a calm and utterly controlled manner, less than twelve hours after her narrow escape, she reaffirmed the Government's determination to withstand and eradicate terrorism wherever it was to be found. That resolve might well have been at the back of her mind when she came to support President Reagan's bombing of Libya.

# 12

# THE USE OF POWER

I n their coverage of Britain's economic scene in the 1970s the media seem in retrospect to have given most attention to industrial relations – negotiations between the Government and the TUC, the vicissitudes of national wage policies, actual or threatened unofficial strikes, the activities of shop stewards. Today, the emphasis seems to be on City news – a rocketing success, a sudden crash, the revelation of a scandal, the latest share issue. The shift in interest is a result of the most significant of all the changes which Mrs Thatcher's regime has introduced so far: the change from the corporate society of the sixties and seventies to the 'property-owning democracy' of the 1980s.

For Mrs Thatcher, this has been her most personal vision of the future, envisaging a 'Britain where everyone has a financial stake and a commitment to Britain's success'. The most obvious and appealing ingredient of the 'property-owning democracy' was home ownership, and this attraction was one of the factors contributing to her first election win in 1979. Since that year, the Government has engineered the sale of more than one million council homes throughout Britain, with sales peaking at 181,200 during the last year of that first term of office. Treasury statistics suggest that the value of the public sector controlled housing so far sold exceeds £20 billion. During Mrs Thatcher's first term of office, home ownership thus rose from 52% to 58%.

Her second term of office saw a far more spectacular and controversial contribution to the property-owning democracy – the creation of 'popular capitalism' by the selling of State assets. This programme came to be known as privatization, and is widely regarded as one of her most prominent achievements. Privatisation is often called 'the flagship of the Thatcherite fleet'. It is definitely her most exportable model; privatization programmes based on the British experience have now been implemented in France, Italy, New Zealand, Malaysia and Jamaica. As Melvyn Marckus, Business and City Editor of the *Observer*, has written: 'It is hardly surprising that the art of privatization holds international appeal. Any art which can raise funds, reduce the public sector deficit, improve efficiency and capture votes, is an art worthy of pursuit.'[1]

Although privatization and popular capitalism came to dominate the Conservative Party's economic approach during Mrs Thatcher's second term of office, the first sale of state-owned assets had been made before Mrs Thatcher came to power, though this did not at all have the objective of producing a property-owning democracy. The 'letter of intent' to which the Labour Chancellor, Denis Healey, subscribed in order to secure the IMF loan of December 1976, not only introduced monetary targets and public expenditure cuts but also included an undertaking to sell £564 million of Government shares in British Petroleum (BP) for the purpose of reducing the burgeoning Public Sector Borrowing Requirement. This idea, reputed to have been supplied by the Labour Cabinet Minister, Harold Lever, was received without enthusiasm by the Labour Party as a whole, as was the rest of Healey's rescue package. But when he revealed its details in the House of Commons, the Tories, on the other hand, gave the proposal a hearty welcome. Sir Geoffrey Howe, the Shadow Chancellor, took pleasure in urging Healey to face up to the fact that the sale 'makes a nonsense of the argument previously advanced by the Government that nationalization has no adverse effect on the Public Sector Borrowing Requirement'.

But Sir Geoffrey did not leave the matter there. He expressed great concern about to *whom* the BP shares would be sold. Healey was later to compare attacks on him by Sir Geoffrey to 'being savaged by a dead sheep', but on this occasion he momentarily found himself at a loss for a suitable answer. Another Tory asked a more pointed question; Kenneth Baker, now Secretary of State for Education, who, saying he had no idea to whom such shares should be sold, added that he could see only pitfalls ahead:

Is it not an extraordinary indictment of his record that a Labour Chancellor of the Exchequer has even to consider disposing of such valuable assets as the BP shares? To whom does the Chancellor expect to sell them? Whom has he in mind? If they go to overseas interests ... is it not possible that control

181

of this company will escape not only from the Government's hands but from the country's hands?

This was indeed a question, and it has hung over the privatization programme ever since,

What was accepted at an early stage by the Conservatives, as it was with the Labour Government, was one potential of privatization as a means of raising revenue. The proceeds to the Government of asset sales from the privatization programme have always been deducted from the vital figure of the PSBR. As we have seen in Chapter 4, just as the necessity of reducing the PSBR figure became a central feature of Mrs Thatcher's successful attempt to rescue her financial policies after 1981, so asset sales became of the greatest relevance to reducing the PSBR, but the prime object of *her* privatization was not revenue.

Two years previously the 1979 election manifesto had not talked much about privatization. The concept was referred to only once. All that Mrs Thatcher committed herself to was to 'sell back to private ownership the recently nationalized aerospace and shipbuilding concerns, giving their employees the opportunity to purchase shares'. When she came to power, her Chancellor, Sir Geoffrey Howe, before allocating the new Government's crucial economic tasks to the members of his Treasury team, asked them what they would like to do. Nigel Lawson, the new Financial Secretary, asked if the privatization programme could be included among his responsibilities. He was given it. From Lawson's time on, privatization has continued to be, under the Chancellor, the particular responsibility of the Financial Secretary to the Treasury, passing from one to the other, being today in the portfolio of Norman Lamont. The assignment was and remains very important: privatization was and is at the heart, if it is not the very core, of the change Mrs Thatcher had dedicated herself to bring about in British society.

In passing it might be noted that the application of privatization has been particularly significant in the field of energy. After his stint as Financial Secretary, Lawson was promoted to be Minister for Energy, Norman Lamont had a spell at Energy, and the mammoth privatization project of today, electricity, (to be dealt with later), is, subject to the Chancellor, in the hands of the Minister for Energy, Cecil Parkinson, who also from the beginning had been dedicated to the Prime Minister's mission to establish popular capitalism.

Accounts of the unfolding and implementation of the Thatcher Governments' privatization programmes have varied, differing emphases having been put by different critics – and admirers – on different aspects of a long and complicated privatization process. As mentioned earlier, from the first years of the post-war Labour Government's success in nationalizing Britain's basic industries, Conservative Party leaders had committed themselves to a programme of denationalization and had promised to make Britain 'a property-owning democracy'. Mrs Thatcher's predecessors had not proved to be ardent denationalizers and had registered only limited success in their attempts at the multiplication of the number of property-owners; but Mrs Thatcher, with her denationalization given a new lease of life, provided a degree of enthusiasm for the extension of property-owning which no post-war Conservative Party leader had displayed before.

When Mrs Thatcher became Prime Minister, therefore, she brought with her a resolute commitment to 'roll back the frontiers of the State' and to push forward the frontiers of the property-owning democracy to occupy the vacated ground. The vast inflationary effects of public expenditures necessitated by nationalized industries would be reduced by denationalization. The burden on the Treasury of administering the nationalized industries – and of subsidizing them – would be removed, and the sales of national assets would help an Exchequer hard pressed to fund inescapable liabilities such as the maintenance of social security payments. Inefficiency would be eliminated and consumer choice would be restored by breaking up the monopolies which nationalized industries created, a process which would stimulate the country's economic performance as a whole. But beyond all these in ultimate importance ranked the propagating of the property-owning democracy, not only as a Thatcherite objective in itself, but because Mrs Thatcher and her Treasury team believed that the best guarantee against renationalization by a future Socialist government was to widen private ownership to the maximum, and especially to make employees in the denationalized industries into private shareholders, since they would then have a strong vested interest in preventing their industries from being renationalized.

Presenting his first budget to the House on 12 June 1979, the new Chancellor made clear what the Government's position on the sales of State assets was:

As I have already indicated, we are only just embarking on our review of the plans we have inherited and of the scope for reducing the size of the public sector. But it is already clear that the scope for the sale of assets is substantial.

Sales of State-owned assets to the private sector serve the immediate purpose of helping to reduce the excessive public sector borrowing requirement with which I was faced. This is all the more necessary this year, given the difficulty of cutting back public sector requirements once a year has already begun.

But such sales are not justified simply by the help they give to the short-term reduction of the PSBR. They are an essential part of our long-term programme for promoting the widest possible participation by the people in the ownership of British industry. This objective – wider public ownership in the true meaning of the term – has implications not merely for the scale of our programme but also for the methods of the sales we shall adopt.

To begin with, the Government's aim was simply to divest the Government of a moderate number of shares that it held in smaller industries. For years before the British Telecom sale in 1984, which ushered in the era of popular capitalism, the Government had therefore been engaged in a consistent and discreet sale of assets; selling its shares in various industries to the management of those industries, and/or their employees or private industrial bidders. These sales yielded a small but significant stream of revenue to the Exchequer; the most successful, for instance, yielding £7 million when the management and employees of the National Freight Corporation bought their business back from the Government in February 1982. The coffers of the Exchequer were also filled by sales of BP stock in November 1979, July 1981 and September 1983. The most important asset sale was the Government's 50% holding in British Aerospace in February 1981, an offer that attracted almost 155,000 new investors and which raised £43 million for the Government. Throughout these sales, there was no great attempt to market the shares widely to the general public; selling was mainly to institutional investors or combinations of the management and employees of the firms involved. The Government had already learned that selling shares on a large scale to the general public would be fraught with technical problems and political risks – for instance, managements did not like their companies being broken up – and, though this was the prime object, it was best to go slowly, learning the lessons on the way.

However, by the time of the 1983 election, these modest ventures looked like being followed by more ambitious projects. The experiences of the first Thatcher Government had provided the Conservatives with powerful incentives to privatize as it became clear how burdensome the monolithic, inefficient nationalized industries had become. In 1981, Sir Geoffrey Howe told a Conservative audience:

> It is only since the election that the issue of privatization has moved to the very forefront of politics. Our experience since we have been in Govern-

ment has convinced us of the need for privatization, competition or, at least, private sector financial discipline in the nationalized industries is even greater than we imagined in opposition.

So, by the time one gets to the 1983 Conservative manifesto, the privatization programme rates a much larger mention. Under the heading 'Nationalized Industries', the manifesto proclaimed: 'A company which has to satisfy its customers and compete to survive is more likely to be efficient, alert to innovation, and genuinely answerable to the public.' It went on to promise to transfer to 'independent owner-ship' British Telecom, Rolls-Royce, British Airways and substantial parts of British Steel, of British Shipbuilders and of British Leyland.

Jaguar was sold in August 1984, as a prelude to British Telecom, raising £297 million for British Leyland. The big sale came in November 1984 when British Telecom (BT), which had been hived off from the Post Office in 1980, was transferred from the public sector to the private sector in a transaction worth £3,916 million. It was seven times larger than the biggest previous UK share issue. The private investor was offered an unparalleled range of inducements, including bonus shares and vouchers that could be offset against telephone bills, to tempt him into participating in this extraordinary sale. To the amazement of the City, and even to some members of the Government, the public response was overwhelming; the offer was four times oversubscribed with the private investor putting up more than £6 billion for shares worth £1.5 billion in a partly paid form. The response had exceeded all expectations, and the Government's undue caution was demonstrated in the first day of trading of the new BT shares when the excessively low price doubled in value. Over two million people became shareholders, half of them as direct investors for the first time. Mrs Thatcher's popular capitalism had hit the big time.

The way in which BT was privatized was also reflected in later asset sales. For all the free market rhetoric, public monopoly was exchanged for private monopoly. The reason for this was simple, as the sale of a monopoly, with the guaranteed return on the investor's money that that market position implied, would prove the most attractive form of sale to the investor and therefore maximize the Treasury's profits accruing from that sale. As a result, the privatized industries retained their monopoly market positions, thus casting doubts on the Government's professed intentions to encourage competition and efficiency. British Gas, which was privatized in December 1986 for £5½ billion, was also sold as an intact industrial monopoly, mostly at the insistence of Sir Denis Rooke, its chairman.

The same conflict of interests, between the demands of the industry to retain its existing monopoly in the private sector and the demands of the free market right to encourage competition, dominated the argument about the privatization of the Central Electricity Generating Board, the biggest privatization programme planned so far, and not easy to value. The CEGB, like the Gas Board before it, having previously been a private monopoly, lobbied vigorously to remain intact as a public one. In this case, the free market right seems to have prevailed, backed and guided by the Secretary of State for Energy, Cecil Parkinson, one of the Prime Minister's closest colleagues, a great believer in competition as the enhancer of choice, and now again a power within the Government. Parkinson's plan for the CEGB divides the industry among a handful of private operators who will compete with each other and force down the price for the benefit of the consumer. Treasury Ministers fully support the proposed post-privatization electricity industry, and have said so.

The 1984 British Telecom sale revealed that there was an unexpected army of small investors waiting to buy shares in the sort of safe, instant profit-making asset sales offered to them by the Government. Further sales, such as the Trustee Savings Bank (TSB) in September 1986, British Airways in February 1987, Rolls-Royce in May 1987 and BP in October 1987, were accompanied by ever-more spectacular and expensive marketing campaigns to attract the private investor. The advertising focused on the small investor and the attractions of owning shares, stressing that the City and share ownership were no longer restricted territories but open to all. This was symbolized by the 'Bowler Hat' campaign of TSB and the 'Tell Sid' campaign for British Gas. In the end 4.5 million Sids applied for British Gas shares. Each new share issue was oversubscribed and the public appetite for the Government's asset sales seemed never ending. Even the unfortunate BP share offer of October 1987, plagued by the Stock Market collapse of that month was, eventually, adjudged to have been a success.

Given this unprecedented level of private share buying, it was not surprising that the number of shareholders in Britain has risen from about three million in 1979 to more than nine million today. The Conservative Party and independent analysts agree that whereas in 1979 the proportion of the population owning shares was 7% (a figure that remained the same throughout the 1979–83 Government) by 1987 it had risen to 20%. This makes Britain the second biggest share-owning democracy in the world, behind America, but well ahead of the French, the Germans and Japanese.

Furthermore, it is also evident that the economic performance of the industries privatized by the Government has improved. This has always been central to Mrs Thatcher's vision of privatization. As she told the House of Commons in February 1983:

> Privatization, through exposing former State-owned companies more fully to the disciplines and opportunities of the market ... improves the efficiency of businesses that are crucial to our overall economic performance. As such it forms an important part of the Government's overall strategy for long-term economic growth ... further reinforcing the enterprise culture that is essential for economic success.

There is no doubt that some of the privatized companies have made spectacular turnarounds, while those that were always financially secure have seen steady growth. The jewel in the crown must be Jaguar Cars, which was sold off in August 1984. As part of the British Leyland group it was making a loss of £32 million on a turnover of £224 million in 1981, whilst in 1985 the company was making a profit of £121 million on a turnover of £747 million. Sales in 1986 were up 11% on the previous year. British Telecom increased its profits from £990 million in 1984–5 to £2 billion in 1986–7. There is thus considerable evidence to suggest that exposing these companies to market discipline does lead to greater efficiency. The same could also be somewhat perversely claimed of BT, which has recently been subject to withering public criticism of its performance. In 1987 the National Consumer Council published a MORI report which revealed that 52% of consumers consider BT prices unreasonable, compared with only 40% in 1980. Likewise, a survey conducted by Oftel, BT's own regulatory body, revealed that 23% of all call boxes were out of order in 1987, compared to only 17% in the year before. This would seem to suggest that the consumer has not benefited from privatization; rather it illustrates the dangers of transferring a public monopoly to the private sector, as the company now has even more licence to ignore the consumer than it had before. To Nigel Lawson, however, the criticisms of BT are precisely the kind of market pressures to which the Government wanted to expose these industries. Writing in *The Observer* in October 1987, he argued:

> Privatisation has transformed the efficiency and performance of several of the biggest businesses in this country ... What BT is experiencing is, in fact, the healthy pressures that come with being in the enterprise sector. Customers who were resigned to putting up with a mediocre service from a nationalized industry expect more from the new BT – not least if they are shareholders themselves. I welcome that.

Furthermore, the breaking up of BT's monopoly, letting Mercury and Cable & Wireless compete on a large scale within the communications industry, has doubtless also focused minds on the BT board on the necessity of improving services.

The further claim for privatization that Mrs Thatcher makes is for its role in transforming attitudes within industry for creating an 'enterprise culture' which gets away from the archaic and debilitating 'us-and-them' structure of strike-prone British industry. To this end, employee share ownership has always been strongly encouraged to the extent that 94% of BT employees bought shares in their own industry. To Mrs Thatcher, this is an integral part of creating the classless, enterprise culture that is at the heart of her vision of Thatcherite society. As the 1987 election manifesto could point out in the wake of the huge asset sales of the 1983–7 Government: 'This is the first stage of a profound and progressive social transformation – popular capitalism. Owning a direct stake in industry not only enhances personal independence; it also gives a heightened sense of involvement and pride in British business.'

Whether this is true of the economy as a whole is difficult to assess, but it certainly seems to be true of the recently privatized industries. The institution that has profited most out of this surge of share buying has been the City, which is now the busiest stock market in the world. After the deregulation of the City in 1986 (the 'Big Bang'), there has been an unprecedented spate of mergers and takeovers amongst the financial institutions to cope with the expanding international trade in free market capitalist activity. If the City and financial services sector is the area that has seen the biggest expansion during the last five years (during which the total number of people working in finance, insurance and banking has risen to 330,000), it is the living embodiment of that new capitalist ethos, the 'Yuppie', who has come to symbolize the new wealth.

The Yuppie has been spawned by this extraordinary growth in the financial service sector of the last five years. In the best Thatcherite mould, he is just as likely to be a barrow boy from the East End as he is to be an Old Etonian. He is enterprising, careerist, ambitious and 'smart' – not 'intellectual', but 'smart'. The Yuppie is a new creation, outside the old social alignments of class, education and, ultimately, politics. There would be no Yuppies without Thatcherism. Bernard Levin, on the subject of Mrs Thatcher's critics, and their accusations of 'obstinacy', 'lack of compassion', of her vulgar manner, essentially the same qualities attributed to the Yuppies by their detractors, has written:

They lie, they hate her because they are afraid she might succeed, and transform Britain into a country where endeavour thrives, where merit advances, where the invaluable uniqueness of each individual is promoted and made much of, where success, not failure, is commended. To sum up in terms as offensive as I can find words for, Margaret Thatcher wants Britain to be a country in which nobody has power and influence *either* because he went to bed at Eton with a future Cabinet Minister, or because he commands at the Labour Party Conference hundreds of thousands of votes half of which were rigged and the other half bought.

The creation of a share-owning democracy as well as a property-owning democracy has served Mrs Thatcher handsomely in electoral terms and will continue to do so. Just as the old unionized public service sector used to provide a bedrock of the old Labour Party's vote, so the new petty capitalist is forming the bedrock of the Thatcherite vote. Since 1979, when the nationalized industries accounted for 10% of Gross Domestic Product (GDP), nearly one third of the State sector and over 600,000 jobs have been transferred to the private sector. As a result, and partly as a natural result of high unemployment, trade union membership has declined from 30% of the electorate in 1979 to only 22% in 1987. At the same time, the proportion of the electorate owning shares has risen from 7% to 20%. What was inconceivable only a decade ago is now on the verge of happening; with the sale of the CEGB and the Water Boards, there will soon be *more* private shareholders than there will be trade unionists.

This will be Mrs Thatcher's lasting social transformation, with all that that entails in terms of economic and social attitudes, to say nothing of voting patterns: a MORI poll in 1987 estimated that share-holders were $1\frac{1}{2}$ times more likely to vote Conservative. Just as Mrs Thatcher's novel appeal in 1979 was to those working-class voters who looked to her to save them from their union leaders, so the privatization programme struck most successfully at those voters who had always been the electoral fodder of the former Labour Party triumphs. Of the electorally important socio-economic group C2, which comprises the skilled manual workers, about 16% are now shareholders. Altogether, about 40% of the shareholders in privatized companies are in the lower socio-economic groups C2, D and E. It is in its creation of a loyal political constituency for Mrs Thatcher that privatization is likely to have its most important impact. In her own analogy, if she envisages privatization as restoring the 'family silver back to the family', she has successfully ensured that the family will remember who gave them the chance to buy it back.

There is no conclusive evidence that the British economy *as a whole* benefits from privatization, aside from the immediate income to the Treasury. It is arguable that Germany and Japan manage quite adequately with a very small stock market. What is not in doubt is that millions of first-time shareholders are going to vote for Mrs Thatcher as the safest way of guaranteeing their newly acquired investments, and as the programme continues under the present Government, so millions more will swell their numbers.

On a macro-economic level, in her second term of office Mrs Thatcher could afford to relax the tight control of the Government's economic policies which she had maintained throughout her first. This was partly due to the health of the reviving economy after the depths of the 1980–81 recession and partly due to the bullish financial expertise of her new Chancellor of the Exchequer, Nigel Lawson. Lawson, who as First Secretary to the Treasury under Sir Geoffrey Howe had been largely responsible for framing the controversial monetarist Medium Term Financial Strategy of 1980, was, after 1983, as Chancellor himself, able to preside over an economic policy which was able to dispense with most of the monetarist shibboleths the monetarists propagated during her first Government. The adherence to monetary targets has discreetly been dropped – M3 is no longer a celestial autoroute to sound money, but is once again merely a motorway into London.

This relaxation of the tight monetary and, to a certain extent, fiscal policies of the 1979 to 1983 period have been interpreted by some critics as constituting a U-turn on Lawson's part. In fact, it is a natural consequence of the harsh medicine administered during those first years, of changing circumstances, and of lessons learned. Since then, as predicted, the situation has improved dramatically and so the harsh medicine no longer came to be necessary. Monetarism was specifically designed to defeat inflation, which is what it had done by the 1983 election. During the second Thatcher Government, inflation stayed consistently low (between 3% and 5% per annum) and so Lawson has been able to relax his monetary controls. The economic policies pursued by Lawson have thus been more flexible and pragmatic, simply because due to the success of the early monetary policies he has had more money to play with. 'There have been no U-turns,' says the Chancellor, 'but there has been fine tuning.'

By the time of the 1987 election, the Conservatives were able to point to a very creditable economic performance on the criteria which they had set themselves in 1979, whilst at the same time Lawson was able to sweeten the pre-election budget with taxation cuts and higher levels of Government spending on sensitive areas such as the health service. Although statistics are never an absolutely reliable guide, and analysts rightly point out that economic performance figures will differ as long as political parties use different time spans of comparison, it is fair to say that the Conservatives did manage to make the seemingly elusive trick of maintaining high growth and low inflation over a sustained period of time during the 1983–7 Government. The average yearly economic growth in Britain over that period was 3% (though a rather less impressive 1.4% if one takes the average from 1979), whilst at the same time inflation remained at its lowest levels for twenty years and below the EEC average. Norman Tebbit frequently pointed out during the 1987 election that during the economic year 1986–7 Britain was expanding at a faster rate than Germany, France, Japan and the US. This healthy economic expansion also set new records for taxation revenue to the Treasury and, together with the continuing expenditure cuts of the 1983–7 Government, it meant that the PSBR was reduced to a mere £4 billion by 1987, or just 1% of GDP. It was all set fair for Nigel Lawson to announce in his March 1988 budget that for the first time since the 1960s, the Treasury did not have a deficit on its spending plans; indeed, with the Public Sector Borrowing Rate in surplus to the tune of £3 billion, the fortunate Chancellor proposed that the PSBR be rechristened the PSDR, the Public Sector Deficit Repayment!

This economic expansion has also made inroads on what remains as the most severe indictment of monetarist policies, namely the continuing high levels of unemployment. By the time of the 1987 general election, the unemployment figures had been on a downward trend for ten months, and the figure finally dipped below the psychologically important three million mark during the summer of 1987. The trend in employment has been towards newly created jobs: the old manufacturing industries which contributed most to the growing number of unemployed workers during the 1979–81 industrial meltdown have not revived, but the slack in employment has been taken up by the new service industries of what has been called the Third Industrial Revolution, or the Technological Revolution.

The decline in the old 'smoke-stack' industries has been dramatic and inevitable, indeed necessary to the economic revival of the country. As Michael Osborne, chief economist of Kleinwort Grievson, succinctly put it, from an investor's point of view, 'there is no mileage in Britain remaining an industrial antique show'. The new jobs have been created in the new industries, which are guaranteed a longer life expectancy than the core industries of the hammer and steel era – industries in which Britain was long ago comprehensively undercut by the Japanese, Taiwanese, Malayans *et al*.

Mrs Thatcher is an extremely shrewd politician, and if she exploited the potential of privatization as demonstrated by the British Telecom sale with her customary clever opportunistic alacrity, so the pre-election mini-budget of November 1986 showed the room that she and Lawson had to play with after seven years of tight finance, the White Paper of that month announcing plans for expanding expenditure over the next three years. The following March, Lawson's 'give-away budget', as his many critics called it, contained all the right ingredients to endear it to the electorate. An extra £1,700 million was earmarked for spending on social security; spending on the NHS was allowed to rise from £18.7 billion to nearly £20 billion. The Labour critics were bemused, and many of Mrs Thatcher's most ardent supporters dumbfounded. The *Daily Telegraph* was almost breathless: 'all semblance of fiscal control has been abandoned'. The chief economist of stockbrokers Phillips and Drew was quoted as saying that he found this autumn statement to be 'incredible, just incredible'.

What these commentators might have failed to remember is that behind the rhetoric Mrs Thatcher is a politician's politician, and after the years of financial restraint that had continually threatened to handicap her chances of re-election, she and Lawson were hardly going to let an opportunity like this slip by. Her grocery-store economics had always maintained that you spend the money *only* if you have it; now that the Treasury had, finally, after years of harsh struggle, *got* it, she was far too much of a pragmatic politician not to spend it. The autumn mini-budget was followed by the formal budget of March 1987 which, whilst otherwise retaining a steady grip on the economy, predictably took 2p off the standard rate of income tax, a tax-cut which filtered through to the payee just in time for the election on 11 June.

Despite Opposition claims of a looming balance of payments crisis, Mrs Thatcher thus entered the 1987 election with a better economic record than any Prime Minister in office since Harold Macmillan in 1959 and the days of 'You've never had it so good.' Together with the more relaxed Treasury policies, the strong popular enthusiasm for privatization (which many of the electorate had personally profited from) and the underlying economic expansion and falling unemployment, she was able to present the British people with an enticing economic record and the promise of more to come. Indeed, all the opinion polls in the weeks before the election predicted that she would win her cherished third term of office handsomely on this economic record, as indeed she did. A MORI poll in May 1987 predicted a majority of 120 seats, which was slightly over-optimistic but not far off the actual result. And yet although it was all right on the night, even now it seems incredible that only little more than a year before she had embarked upon what was to be the worst political year of her Government, in which there was one political crisis after another. Just as no one would have put any money on a Thatcher landslide in the next election during the darkest days of summer of 1981, so it would have been a brave punter who would have put any money on a majority of over 100 seats at the next election in the spring of 1986. In 1983, she was rescued by the Falklands, in 1987 she was rescued by her own economic record.

But the political events of 1986 that cast such a shadow on her qualities both as a political leader and as a human being rocked her Government to the core and left an after-taste in the mouth of the electorate. The qualities that she brought to transferring the economy – persistence, courage, conviction, political guile – were less evident during the many political crises that embarrassed the Government during 1986: the Westland crisis, the bombing of Libya, the issue of sanctions against South Africa and the *Spycatcher* affair. At times, the same persistence, courage, conviction and political guile might look like obtuseness, foolishness, narrow-mindedness and political ineptitude, and were certainly plausibly represented as such by her critics and opponents.

The first crisis to erupt in 1986 was that of Westland. How the fortunes of a small Somerset helicopter company came to occupy such a central position in the corridors of power does not matter for this book; what does matter is Mrs Thatcher's role in the affair, and the light that it might shed on how she manages her Cabinet. For when all the shouting was over, what occupied, indeed fascinated, the chattering classes for such an undue amount of time was not the plight of the Westlands Helicopter Company, but what was read from the affair into Mrs Thatcher's style of Government.

The strength of the cases for and against the two proposed rescue packages for Westland Helicopters – the American-orientated Sikorsky deal, and the European-orientated one inspired by Michael Heseltine – is arguable: what was agreed by everyone concerned was the fact that Westland was a badly managed company, that the old management had badly overreached itself and that unless a rescue bid was attempted the company would go under. The man whom Westland chose to rejuvenate the company was Sir John Cuckney, an ex-MI5 officer with excellent contacts in Whitehall and Westminster. His conclusion after looking at the options was that a merger should be effected with the US helicopter giant Sikorsky, who were known to be interested in bidding. The other option was for a European Consortium of helicopter manufacturers to bid for the company; this option, which only materialized much later and only after Westland had decided to merge with Sikorsky, was initially favoured by Leon Brittan, the Minister for Trade and Industry, but he soon came to prefer the Sikorsky bid, thus clashing with Defence Minister Michael Heseltine.

Throughout the autumn and winter of 1985 the financial plight of Westland worsened, so the two factions, Cuckney on the one hand and Heseltine on the other, began to lobby in Whitehall on behalf of their favoured schemes. Heseltine saw the European Consortium as a means of taking further steps towards his cherished vision of an integral European defence policy, a policy that he had done much to further with his creation of the European Fighter Aircraft (EFA) project in 1984/85. Heseltine's approach stemmed from a belief that Government *should* intervene in industry; he is an interventionist. Cuckney saw Sikorsky as a long term solution to Westland's manifold problems.

The Prime Minister claimed throughout the Westland affair that the future of Westland was a matter for the Westland Board and the shareholders, entirely consistent with her well-known and long established view that companies should make their own decisions on commercial grounds without any input from the Government. The Prime Minister's particular concern was that the company should not turn to the Government to bail it out. It was Heseltine's contention, however, that Mrs Thatcher favoured the American rescue bid all along, and that she manipulated the Government and the Cabinet system in particular *against* Heseltine in order to thwart his attempts to put the case for the European consortium to the Cabinet, where its claims might well have received a favourable verdict on the grounds of national security. It was the argument between Mrs Thatcher and Heseltine that sparked off the Westland crisis and it was Heseltine's resignation from the Cabinet on 9 January, in what he claimed was a protest against constitutional impropriety, that catapulted the crisis into the public arena.

There are two instances in which, it has been alleged by her critics, Mrs Thatcher behaved improperly and/or deceitfully. The first was the meeting of the Economic Committee on Monday 9 December, at which the two rescue bids were to be discussed, with Mrs Thatcher in the chair. The E Committee, as we have seen, was used from the 1979 election onwards as a means of economic decisions being arrived at without them having to be discussed by the Cabinet as a whole. The E Committee was not a tiny cabal; when it met, there were often fifteen or so Ministers present, all of them with responsibilities affecting the economy. The meeting opened at 4.30 pm with Mrs Thatcher stating her view that the deal which Heseltine had concluded with the 'National Armaments Directors' of the other European countries to create an exclusively European helicopter business (known as the NADS agreement) should be withdrawn at once. The NADS agreement would have committed the Government *not* to buy Westland-Sikorsky helicopters. Heseltine was trying to close the option; Government policy was to keep it open. For Heseltine to proceed with this deal, she said, would be for the Government to intervene, and be seen to intervene, in plans for the future of Westland. This would be a reversal of Government policy, which was to leave the future of Westland, as of all companies, to settle its affairs for itself.

Sir John Cuckney was then invited to address the E Committee. This was unprecedented; department officials do not attend Cabinet committee meetings, let alone non-governmental industrialists with an interest in the outcome. Heseltine's supporters therefore claimed that, while saying that the Government must not intervene in the Westland affair, Mrs Thatcher, by asking Sir John to speak to the Committee, was intervening in the affair herself. Sir John listed the merits of the Sikorsky deal and described the European deal as unrealistic: it would in any case have to be 'fully underwritten' by the Government. For the Government to agree to this would be to go back on Mrs Thatcher's most valued principle, one which she had asserted throughout the Westland affair. Moreover, it risked dangerous delay at the very time the company's financial situation was becoming desperate. After Sir John had left the meeting, Heseltine pointed out that so far he had not been able to put a European proposal to the Westland board, so he should be allowed until the end of the week to produce a firm European alternative.

Accounts differ about what happened next. Heseltine has claimed that a majority of those present expressed support for his European proposal. Since most of them were hearing about it for the first time, their support might not have proved substantial. Mrs Thatcher and Leon Brittan were strongly against support for the European deal being allowed to conflict with the principle of non-intervention in the affairs of Westland. After an hour of argument, in which Heseltine and Brittan clashed repeatedly, Mrs Thatcher made a remark which was to be fateful, said to be, 'Very well. We'll have to meet again on Friday at four o'clock after the Stock Exchange has closed.' According to some of those present the remark was made appreciably before the end of the meeting and before she began her summing up, and its significance was superseded by what subsequently transpired.

Mrs Thatcher's remark about another meeting, whether or not it was rendered void by other statements made later, had far-reaching consequences. Heseltine assumed it to mean that he was going to have another meeting on Friday, but other witnesses, such as John Wakeham, have said that his own understanding of the Prime Minister's words was that the meeting would only take place if there was a necessity for it. Mrs Thatcher would later claim that, 'The conclusions of the Cabinet Economic Committee on 9 December laid down a clear policy, and that made a further meeting unnecessary. No decision to hold a further meeting was taken or recorded. No meeting had been agreed, so there was no meeting to cancel.'

What is certain is that there was *not* another meeting on the following Friday. What is equally certain is that the Cabinet Office civil servants present duly noted the possibility of a meeting on Friday, which they would be responsible for setting up; at ten o'clock on Tuesday morning calls were made from the Cabinet Office warning Ministers to stand by for the meeting on Friday afternoon. Both Nicholas Ridley and Lord Young noted the fact in their diaries. Then a call went out from Downing Street which cancelled the Friday meeting. There are now two theories as to why this occurred. The Downing Street version was that the civil servants had made an unfortunate error in assuming that there was going to be a Friday meeting. The other theory is that the DTI (or Mrs Thatcher?) realized the implications of such a second meeting and that, fearing there would be a majority for Heseltine, prudently had it cancelled. The net result was that Heseltine was, in his own words, 'absolutely shattered' and from then on would claim that Mrs Thatcher was consistently subverting democratic Cabinet government to prevent him from gaining a fair hearing for his European consortium.

The second episode, which raised doubts in some quarters about Mrs Thatcher's integrity as a politician, was the leaking to the Press of the highly confidential letter to Michael Heseltine from the acting Attorney-General, in which he had advised Heseltine to correct 'material inaccuracies' in a letter to the European governments about the Westland deal with Sikorsky, which had been published in *The Times*.

Over Christmas and the New Year Heseltine had pursued a vigorous campaign to obtain support for his proposal for the European consortium. The media were kept well informed. Mrs Thatcher, some of her senior Ministers and some senior civil servants became very disturbed. For them the Westland affair was over; Heseltine was behaving as though it had only just begun. As they saw it, by continuing to push the European deal the Minister of Defence was violating the Cabinet's political principle of non-intervention in company affairs and the Cabinet's constitutional principle of collective responsibility. His behaviour, as the Westland board frequently reminded them, was also creating an extremely grave problem for the company: Sikorsky were becoming dubious about the deal. Sir John Cuckney was getting very worried. Heseltine's conduct, therefore, might result in Westland losing a good deal with Sikorsky and being stuck with a bad deal with the Europeans or with no deal at all.

Heseltine was pressing on. On Friday 3 January *The Times* printed a letter which Heseltine had sent to David Horne, managing director of Lloyds Merchant Bank, which was the financial adviser to the European consortium. The letter included a paragraph which purported to give the 'Government' view that, in the event of the Sikorsky deal going through, the British Government would not buy the helicopters which Sikorsky–Westland proposed to make and that the European governments would probably refuse to collaborate with Westland. If what Heseltine said in the letter was allowed to stand unchallenged, the Sikorsky deal would be sunk.

Later in the day Mrs Thatcher held a meeting with her advisers. At this time Sir John Cuckney was in the middle of meetings with Sikorsky and the bankers to finalize his deal. Documents were about to go out to Westland shareholders, and he had announced a press conference for 4 pm the following Monday at which he would announce his recommendation of the Sikorsky proposal. Westland's financial position was becoming critical. If Heseltine's letter giving Westland's shareholders and Sikorsky such a discouraging picture of the company's prospects was not discredited by 4 pm on Monday, Westland's plans might founder and the Government, publicly pledged to keep out of Westland's affairs, would, 'represented' by the Minister of Defence, be held to blame.

The situation was urgent. Action was required. Speed was vital. As a result of the meeting, Mrs Thatcher decided that statements made by Heseltine in his letter to David Thorne must be authoritatively refuted at once. To this end the Prime Minister, as she told the House of Commons when the Westlands affair was debated three weeks later, 'asked that a message be sent to [Mr Brittan] ... to suggest that he should ask the Solicitor-General to consider [Mr Heseltine's] letter and give his opinion on whether it was accurate and consistent with [the Government's position]'. Brittan did so. Sir Patrick Mayhew, the Solicitor-General – he was acting Attorney-General since Sir Michael Havers was away ill – would be asked to write to Heseltine pointing out that *The Times* letter contained 'inaccuracies' and that he should publicly correct them. It was not possible to contact Mayhew until very late the following day. Having cautiously agreed that Heseltine's letter did indeed contain 'inaccuracies' – he would have to study the documents – he undertook to write and tell him so. Mayhew checked his documents on Monday morning and the letter went off, with copies to the DTI and Downing Street. The letter ended with a piece of advice that was to become highly publicized:

> It is foreseeable that your letter will be relied upon by the Westland Board and its shareholders. Consistently with the advice I gave the PM on 31 December, the Government in such circumstances is under a duty not to give information which is incomplete or inaccurate in any material particular ... the sentence in your letter to Mr Horne does in my opinion contain material inaccuracies in the respects I have mentioned, and I therefore must advise that you should write again to Mr Horne correcting the inaccuracies.

Copies of this letter to the Minister of Defence were received the same morning at the Department of Trade and Industry and at Downing Street. The gist of it, its context and the phrase 'material inaccuracies' were reported in the early evening newspapers. The newspapers had got the story from the Press Association, to whom the all-important phrase 'material inaccuracies' had been leaked by the DTI. This leaking of parts of a confidential letter from the Government's senior law officer to a member of the Cabinet on such a highly sensitive and controversial national issue immediately caused intense argument and bitter criticism. Sir Patrick Mayhew and Mr Heseltine were outraged.

Mrs Thatcher said later that it was wrong for the letter to have been leaked. Several members of the Cabinet expressed the same view; so too did the Secretary to the Cabinet, many top civil servants and many others. In what circumstances then was such a letter leaked and by whom? What was Mrs Thatcher's part in the leak? These questions were asked immediately. There is no doubt about who actually telephoned the Press Association, told them about the general content of the letter and quoted the crucial words 'material inaccuracies'; it was the Chief Press Officer at the DTI. The Chief Press Officer did so because Mr Brittan wanted it leaked. Mr Brittan wished it to be leaked, though preferably not from the DTI, but from Downing Street. Before leaking it, therefore, his Press Officer talked to the Chief Press Officer at Downing Street, who made it clear that the letter would not be leaked from Downing Street.

Was the leak due to the wishes of politicians, to the initiative of civil servants or to misguidance, misunderstanding or muddle? To make a true assessment – and a fair judgement – about what happened that morning it is essential to bear in mind that, if the Westland-Sikorsky deal was to remain viable, Mayhew's views would have to be public knowledge before Sir John Cuckney's press conference at four o'clock that afternoon. There was not a moment to lose. The atmosphere in which those concerned had to make up their minds what to do was one of haste, tension and extreme irritation at finding themselves in this situation in the first place, driven into it, as they saw it, by the wilful Heseltine. What most likely happened, in the words of a senior civil servant who was well placed to know, was that 'the DTI seized the chance of shutting up Heseltine for good, but wanted Downing Street to take responsibility for it'.

What, the Opposition and many of her own party wanted to know, was Mrs Thatcher's role in the affair? In the aftermath the Commons Select Committee on Defence, charged with enquiring into the leak, asked to interview the officials involved. The Secretary to the Cabinet, in his capacity as the head of the Civil Service, Sir Robert Armstrong, told them that he could not comply with this request. He admitted that aspects of the affair had to be deplored and that the leak was 'very regrettable', but he could not permit the interrogation of civil servants, since to do so would not only be unfair to the individuals concerned but would also undermine the principles of confidentiality and anonymity on which the Civil Service worked. It would undermine the Civil Service. Once Sir Robert had taken this position, the Committee realized there could be no effective inquiry into the role of the politicians in the affair. Sir Robert told the Committee that the Prime Minister had authorized him to hold his own internal enquiry into the circumstances of the leak and he would report his conclusions to her. He made it clear that he was rejecting the Defence Committee's request to interview the key civil servants not to protect the politicians but to protect the civil servants and, indeed, the Civil Service.

An already fierce controversy was raised to the level of a political crisis when, on 9 January, Mr Heseltine walked out of a Cabinet meeting, telling the Prime Minister that he could no longer remain a member of her Government. Later that day he made a statement which amounted to an indictment of the Prime Minister. He made a number of charges against her. She had cancelled the E Committee meeting which he claimed had been agreed for 13 December and had refused to let him raise the European consortium bid in the Cabinet of 12 December. On the subject of the leak of 'damaging selective passages' of the Mayhew letter, he said, 'No one can doubt their purpose.' He claimed that, in spite of what the Government claimed in public, in practice it had 'throughout' favoured the Sikorsky deal 'even to the extent of changing Government policy'. He complained that Mrs Thatcher had tried to gag him by demanding that no member of the Cabinet make statements about Westland unless they had been cleared in advance by the Cabinet Office. In the next few days he tried to broaden this charge into one of unconstitutional behaviour on her part. He did not succeed, but many people, including Conservatives, saw further evidence of Mrs Thatcher's highhanded autocratic style of government. Heseltine's dramatic resignation roused high feeling.

The results of Sir Robert's enquiry were made known to the House by the Prime Minister on 23 January. Sir Robert's main conclusion was that the leak was the result of a 'misunderstanding' between the Press Office at Downing Street and the DTI. Mrs Thatcher said that, having made up his mind, correctly, that 'it was a matter of duty' for the Government to make it known publicly that there were 'material inaccuracies' in the Heseltine letter, Mr Brittan asked his officials to discuss with her own office whether the disclosure should be made and, if so, from where. He made it clear through them that, if Downing Street did not put out the letter, the DTI would do it. Speaking of her own role, she said:

> They [her officials in Downing Street] did not seek my agreement. They considered – and they were right – that I should agree with my Rt Hon. friend the Secretary of State for Trade and Industry that [Mayhew's view] should be made public knowledge as soon as possible, and before Sir John Cuckney's press conference. . . .
>
> It was accepted that the Department of Trade and Industry should disclose that fact and that, in view of the urgency of the matter, the disclosure should be made by means of a telephone communication to the Press Association.
>
> . . . had I been consulted, I should have said that a different way must be found of making the relevant facts known. . . . [Mr Brittan] was in my judgement right in thinking that it was important that the possible existence of material inaccuracies in [the Heseltine letter] of January 3rd should become a matter of public knowledge if possible before Sir John Cuckney's press conference that day. In so far as what my office said to the DTI was based on the belief that I should have taken that view, had I been consulted, it was right.

Having made her statement, the Prime Minister was subjected to vigorous questioning, many of her answers being received with derision by the Opposition and with scepticism from some of her own supporters. There were jeers when she said that 'an enormous number of facts were not known to me yesterday ... when I received the results of the inquiry'. Labour spokesmen refused to believe that she had allowed sixteen days to elapse before she learned crucial facts about a situation which meant so much to her Government. There was an immediate demand for an emergency debate. The 1922 Committee met later that day and it was soon clear that they wanted Mr Brittan's resignation. He submitted it to the Prime Minister the following afternoon. Mrs Thatcher did not want him to go, but it was clear that the majority of the Conservative back benchers did, possibly less because of what he did in the Westland affair than because he had made himself unpopular when he had been Home Secretary. Many of them were critical of the image of the Party he created when he appeared on television. So a second senior Cabinet Minister had been lost to the Government within a month.

The emergency debate demanded by the Opposition took place the following Monday 27 January. It did not add much to what was by then well known and, Mr Brittan's head having fallen, the Prime Minister recovered some ground. Dealing with the question of whether she had agreed to the leak, she said:

> My officials made it clear to the [Armstrong] inquiry that they did not seek my agreement. They told the inquiry that they did not believe that they were being asked to give my authority, and they did not do so. If they had believed that my authority was being sought, they would certainly have consulted me. Officials of the DTI told the inquiry that they regarded the purpose of their approach to my officials as being to seek agreement to the disclosure as well as to the method. They believed that they had the agreement of my office, and acted in good faith, in the knowledge that they had authority from their Secretary of State and cover from my office. Although clearly neither side realized it at the time, there was a genuine difference in understanding between officials as to exactly what was being sought and what was given.

The Prime Minister went on to say that she did not know about the leak 'until some hours after it occurred.... I discussed the matter with my office the following day, when I also learned of the law officers' concern. I was told that the Solicitor-General's advice had not been disclosed by my office.... I did not know about [Mr Brittan's] own role in the matter of the disclosure until the inquiry had reported. The difference of understanding between officials in my office and those in the DTI only emerged after the inquiry started.'

It had been a terrible January for Mrs Thatcher. At the end of the month her stock was very low. Some people could not believe that she had known so little about the leak for so long or that she had had so little hand in it. Some thought she had treated Heseltine badly, indeed, as he averred, unconstitutionally. Others thought she had treated Brittan badly and had let him take the rap. Others, including members of her own Party, said that she should have put her foot down and brought both Ministers to order several weeks before the final débâcle, in which case she could have averted it. Her reputation for bold, honest, straightforward dealing was dented. So was her image as a tough, shrewd, surefooted manager. The ship of State was rocking and two of the mates were already overboard. The storm was pounding. How far ahead were the reefs and shoals? Could she turn round and head for open sea? Whatever the rights and wrongs of the opinions held about her – and those closest to what had happened swore that she had behaved most honourably throughout – at the end of the Westland crisis the popularity rating of the Party slumped to below that of the Labour Party and the Alliance.

Bad as all this was, the nadir of her fortunes was still to come. As if ordained to compound her tribulations, at the beginning of March she was once again placed in an unflattering position as a result of President Reagan deciding to retaliate against Colonel Gadaffi for a series of Libyan-sponsored terrorist outrages around the world directed against Western civilian and military targets, culminating in a bomb explosion on 5 April at a discothèque in Berlin which had killed an American GI. In response to this latest outrage President Reagan determined to try and silence Gadaffi once and for all by bombing his base in Tripoli itself. The Americans, on the grounds that the dead GI was defending Europe, appealed to their European allies to support this initiative, by giving either material assistance or moral support. Mrs Thatcher alone saw the issue as the Americans saw it, with the added inducement of paying off some of the debt Britain owed for American logistical support during the Falklands War. The American intention to use USAF F-III fighter-bombers based in Britain at Upper Heyford was clearly dictated by diplomatic reasons – it was an attempt to spread around as many countries as possible the inevitable worldwide condemnation that would accompany the raid. Whatever the wisdom of using an air strike against Tripoli to teach Gadaffi a lesson, with its accompanying risks of civilian casualties caused by inaccurate bombing, it was a raid that Mrs That-

cher instinctively felt she had to support. When the request came
through from Washington on the morning of the raid for permission to
use the aircraft in Britain, she granted it. There was no military reason
for using the F-111s at Upper Heyford. The Americans were counting
on Mrs Thatcher seeing the issue as a test of the Western Alliance's
resolve to combat terrorism, and this was exactly how she saw it.

As expected, in the wake of the sudden and dramatic raid on 15 April,
the perpetrators of and accessories to the bombing faced a torrent of
abuse. Mrs Thatcher could not count on majority support within her
own Cabinet, and in Parliament her initial defence of the raid provoked
anger and derision. Once again she was seen as excessively authoritarian
and high handed, as having made a seemingly snap judgement against
the wishes of her own Cabinet and Parliament. For Mrs Thatcher, just
as the Falklands crisis was a test of Britain's readiness to counter
unprovoked aggression, so the bombing of Libya was a test of Britain's
will to strike back at international terrorism. Although the decision to
allow the Americans to use their British-based fighter-bombers was
roundly condemned at the time, she may well have taken a decision
that was right in practice as well as in principle. If the aim of the raid
was to silence Gadaffi, who can say now, in 1988, that it was wrong?
The anguish of the victims in Tripoli was vividly portrayed by the
television cameras in the immediate aftermath of the raid; it may be
that Gadaffi will not inflict such anguish on anyone else again.

The raid on Libya had been preceded by a less spectacular, a more
domestically orientated problem over Mrs Thatcher's relationship with
the United States, causing another near revolt within the ranks of her
own supporters, and further denting the morale of her administration.
Only a few days after the Westland saga had appeared to run its course
with the resignation of Leon Brittan on 24 January, his successor as
Trade and Industry Secretary, Paul Channon, learned that the last
remaining wholly British-owned car company, Austin Rover, had been
involved in secret talks with the American car multinational, the Ford
Motor Company, with a view to Ford buying Austin Rover. Negotiations had also been proceeding with the American company General
Motors to buy the ailing British Leyland truck division. There was an
outburst of patriotic indignation in Parliament and in the press,
although the dictates of the free market seemed to suggest that sooner
or later such a shrinking medium-capacity car company as British
Leyland would have to amalgamate with one of the American car giants
to survive. Mrs Thatcher was now portrayed as presiding over the
ultimate surrender of British industry. The situation exemplifies how

the values of Thatcherism could sometimes clash with each other, in this instance, the rationalities of market forces being in conflict with the emotive powers of 'Land Rover' as the symbol of national industrial virility. A MORI poll showed that only 19% of the public supported the Government's plan to sell British Leyland to the Americans.

The geographical location of British Leyland and the implications of such a sale for jobs may have determined the outcome in this case. Most of the company's production was concentrated in the West Midlands, an area of key marginal constituencies in which election results were decided. The expected shedding of jobs if the American deal went through would cause consternation in the local constituencies and might effectively wipe out the Conservative Party in the area. When nervous Midlands Tory MPs like Anthony Beaumont-Dark declared that he was 'not prepared to be the pall-bearer at the British motor industry's funeral', he might have also declared that he was not prepared to hand over his cherished Midlands seat to his Labour opponent on a plate. Faced by this collective protest, the Government withdrew the proposals, thus further denting its diminishing credibility. Further evidence of the Government's declining stock was provided by the refusal of Parliament to pass its Sunday Trading Bill to repeal the laws restricting trading on Sundays. The bill was effectively sunk by the machinations of Mrs Thatcher's own Conservative supporters, sixty-eight of whom voted against it. Not only was her stock sinking in the country as a whole, but she seemed to have lost her authority in the Houses of Parliament as well. Then on 8 May the Conservatives not only fared badly in the local council elections, but in a particularly dispiriting result the Government also lost the previously safe parliamentary seat of Ryedale to the Liberal-SDP Alliance.

The summer allowed no let-up for the beleaguered Premier as once again she felt obliged to take a singular, some would say stubborn, stance on an international issue which only served to attract the odium of the rest of the world. In June the situation in South Africa had deteriorated to such an extent between the minority white Government and the unenfranchized black majority population that a state of emergency was declared. The Western media began to expose their audiences and readers to a daily diet of police brutality, shootings, arbitrary Government justice and political suppression. South Africa had always been an emotive issue and now the situation, explosive for so long, looked as though it was finally about to blow up. The majority of the Commonwealth countries felt that the best way to help the blacks was to impose comprehensive and punitive sanctions upon South Africa, thus forcing the dismantlement of the apartheid system. As public perceptions formed, it was those politicians advocating sanctions who came to be seen as the moral crusaders fighting to overturn apartheid.

Mrs Thatcher took a different view, arguing that the history of sanctions showed that, as in the case of Rhodesia in the 1960s, they were ineffective and counterproductive because they tended to provoke a more stubborn siege mentality in the people one was trying to reason with. Furthermore, the imposition of sanctions would retard the cause of black freedom in Africa by making millions of them unemployed as soon as sanctions damaged the South African economy – thus making black workers even more dependent on their white employers. Mrs Thatcher frequently stated her detestation of apartheid, but equally stood by her conviction that the imposition of sanctions would not help the blacks. She could also point to the official estimates of December 1985 that 120,000 British jobs could be jeopardized by a British ban on trade with South Africa. This was a powerful argument to deploy against her domestic political opponents who expressed so much concern about the levels of unemployment in Britain.

Having taken her stance, she stuck to it in her usual forthright and undeviating way. Britain rapidly became isolated in the Commonwealth and the majority of MPs from all parties favoured some degree of sanctions against South Africa. What made her stand against sanctions so prominent was Britain's peculiarly sensitive relationship with South Africa; Britain was still one of that country's major trading partners and also had strong historical and emotional links as the original colonial ruler of Southern Africa. The Commonwealth leaders knew that a programme of sanctions without Britain would be meaningless; the lobbying of Mrs Thatcher and the Government to change her mind was therefore all the more vigorous.

Her stand on South Africa incurred its most damaging publicity when it was reported in the *Sunday Times* that the Queen and her Prime Minister had had sharp differences over the question. Whether this is true or not, it did highlight the increasingly divergent views on world affairs held by the two most important women in the country. Mrs Thatcher took a rigorously realistic view of the Commonwealth as an archaic institution which benefited the member states as a convenient platform for raising their voices far more than it benefited Britain – which invested infinitely more in its relations with the EEC and the USA than it did in its relations with the Commonwealth countries. There was, she believed, only one British institution that gained from the romantic and sentimental prestige attached to the Commonwealth, and that was the monarchy. The Royal Family had a vested interest in cosseting and promoting the Commonwealth; a diminished Commonwealth would only mean a diminished monarchy, not necessarily a diminished Britain. This was why Mrs Thatcher was prepared to take risks with the unity of the Commonwealth, which the Queen must have found distasteful. And risks there were, for as Britain found itself in diplomatic isolation within the Commonwealth, so there was always the danger that the other nations would split away or secede individually in protest. So far, Mrs Thatcher's act of political brinkmanship seems to have worked, and the Commonwealth leaders meet annually to agree to disagree on the issue. But the possibility of a split seemed very real in the summer of 1986. Mrs Thatcher stuck to her guns. She told the author just before the 1987 general election: 'Look, I don't like apartheid any more than you do, but I am not prepared merely to hit out. I want to try to get rid of it. I think we have held the day because what we were proposing to do was right.'

To clash 'publicly', or to seem to clash, with an institution as popular as the monarchy was obviously further going to damage Mrs Thatcher's domestic standing, and this was exactly what happened. Her poll ratings fell, she was even booed when she attended the wedding of Prince Andrew and Sarah Ferguson, whilst guests such as entertainers Elton John and Pamela Stephenson were greeted with delirious cheering. And yet again, Mrs Thatcher's stand on the sanctions issue, right or wrong, was seen by many as gratuitously obstinate and rigid. It was, they said, as if she were adopting the 'resolute approach' merely for the sake of being resolute whether the situation merited it or not: even some of her admirers murmured that she was in danger of becoming a parody of herself.

The autumn of 1986 saw her engaged in a principled stand that at times seemed to occupy the Government to an almost obsessive degree. A retired and disillusioned former Assistant Director of MI5, Peter Wright, now resident in Tasmania, was seeking to publish a book called *Spycatcher*, which amounted to his autobiography, ghosted by a television producer to give it something of a John le Carré flavour. The reasons why Peter Wright elected to write what was to amount to the most detailed description of the workings of Britain's security service remain known only to himself, but by doing so he was clearly in breach of his duties of confidentiality, to say nothing of the Official Secrets Act. The Government took the view that it had to enforce the principle of confidentiality by preventing publication of the book – thereby indicating that other civil servants who contemplated writing such candid autobiographies would also incur the full legal wrath of the British Government.

Since Peter Wright now lived there, the case against publication was to be heard in Australia. After his saving testimony for the Government during the Westland crisis, it was perhaps inevitable that Sir Robert Armstrong was sent out to put the Government's case in court. Laudable as the principle of confidentiality may be, it soon became obvious that the Government's attitudes towards the publication of espionage matters had never been consistent, and the skilled Australian advocate Malcolm Turnbull, acting on behalf of Peter Wright, soon began to pick large holes in the Government's case. If the object of the exercise was to prevent Peter Wright's book from gaining wide readership, the trial quickly turned into a prolonged nightmare for the Government as the court case only provided undreamt of publicity for *Spycatcher*, and as soon as the court allowed publication of the book to proceed in February 1987 it rapidly shot to the top of hardback bestseller lists around the world.

In the short term Mrs Thatcher seemed to have lost on every account. The Government had to enter into a string of unprecedented legal actions against British newspapers and television to prevent them from publishing extracts from *Spycatcher*, thus incurring the resentment of the quality press and the broadcasters. Once again, a principled stand that Mrs Thatcher chose to identify herself with closely seemed to have cost her a lot of political prestige in the House of Commons. It is too early to tell what the long-term benefits of the Government's action might be, although on the Prime Minister's current track record of principled stand the action might have been unerringly right in discouraging further emissions from disgruntled maulers of the security services. Whether this is worth the cost in civil liberties is yet too early to tell.

All these political episodes were damaging to her domestic standing; but it is hard to discern whether these issues held much interest for the world beyond Parliament and the political activist. If the 1983-7 Government suffered from a disturbing series of political gaffes on the surface, at the level that mattered – the economic level – everything was going well. Modern British Governments are judged, in the end, mainly on their economic record, and by any standard Mrs Thatcher's economic record since 1983 was extremely good. It was on this record that she would stand and fall in the eyes of the voters.

Indeed, once the worst of the political controversies was over in the early autumn, it was noticeable that the Conservatives were once again edging ahead of Labour and the Alliance in the opinion polls, and that Mrs Thatcher's own personal rating was beginning to recover from a very low point. Even despite the fact that she had been on the political defensive over the previous ten months, the basic popularity of the Government had remained unimpaired as all the economic indicators began to point in a markedly encouraging direction – to say nothing of the attractions of popular capitalism. The key years to date in Mrs Thatcher's career as Prime Minister have been 1981 (the year of the tight economic squeeze), 1982 (the Falklands) and 1986. If she could come out of a year which was as politically fraught as 1986 and within six months still romp home to a 104 seat majority, this was truly an ample testimony to her transforming effect on the country.

With such a firm economic base from which to campaign, it was no surprise that most political commentators made Mrs Thatcher the odds-on favourite for any election that she cared to call during 1987. The pundits were divided between an autumn and an early summer date. Mrs Thatcher, overcoming her habitual caution in these matters, plumped for the latter and named 11 June as polling day. Ever since the strong Conservative recovery in the polls of the previous autumn it was always unlikely that anything could rob her of a historic third victory, and indeed the record of the campaign itself shows that, despite all the shouting and anxiety at the time, the 1987 general election was over before it began. In fact, the campaign made virtually no difference to the standing of the parties. On 11 May, a month before voting, a 'poll of polls' put the standing of the parties at: Conservatives 43%, Labour 30%, Liberal-SDP Alliance 25%. The actual result on polling day was: Conservatives 43%, Labour 32%, Liberal-SDP Alliance 23%. As the political commentator Peter Jenkins has laconically observed, 'Labour had made marginal progress at the expense of the Alliance. That was all that happened.'

Before the election took place there were two events which much enhanced the Prime Minister's reputation as a leader of the free world: a visit to Moscow at the end of March to meet Mr Gorbachov, and the Western economic summit in Venice during the first week of actual campaigning. The meeting in Moscow was the most spectacular and successful foreign visit of her political career. It was also a success that the Kremlin consciously helped build for her by granting her unprecedented freedom and respect for a visiting Western statesperson. Why the Kremlin was so eager to make her visit such a success is harder to discern. After all it was *Pravda* which had originally bestowed on her what was meant to be the mocking sobriquet of the 'Iron Lady', and it was Mrs Thatcher who had first made her mark on the international stage as a fierce anti-Communist in an age of *détente*. Indeed, she was highly suspicious of Mr Gorbachov's ambitious programme of internal and international reforms before going to Moscow, and her feeling at a high-level briefing on Soviet affairs at Chequers before the visit, attended by academic experts as well as officials, was that laudable though Mr Gorbachov's plans were, we had seen and heard it all before and there was no reason to suppose that this time would be any different.

However, what transformed her perception of *glasnost* and *perestroika* was meeting the architect of these reforms himself in the Kremlin. There is no doubt that the Prime Minister and Mr Gorbachov quickly grew to respect each other, not because they managed to influence each other on matters of policy, but because they recognized in each other the same qualities – they were both conviction politicians with visions for their respective countries.

They had thirteen hours of talks alone together in Moscow, a privilege not previously accorded to any other visiting leader, and in a further break with precedent Mrs Thatcher was permitted fifty minutes of uncensored television time to answer questions from Soviet journalists. Neither leader gave an inch on international questions, and it was one of her clear intentions to tell the Soviet leader that she was determined to keep the British nuclear deterrent as well as NATO nuclear weapons in Europe. But it was Mr Gorbachov's ideas of domestic modernization that interested her most, for she too had thought of herself, in the 1970s, as a much-needed, long overdue modernizer.

The Russian visit gave her the opportunity to engage with Mr Gorbachov and official Russia, *and* to encounter dissident Russia through meeting Andrei Sakharov and Iosif Begun. In a remarkable *tour de force*, she could both light 'candles of freedom' in the monastery at Zayarsk and publicly praise the Soviet leader's policies. The enthusiasm with which she was publicly received in Russia was perhaps only equalled by the attention given to the visit in Britain, the news coverage dominating the front pages for the better part of the week. It was invaluable publicity for a Prime Minister about to embark on a third meeting with the electorate. And, crucially, it also confirmed her as a politician of world standing, as the senior political figure of the West, at a time when Ronald Reagan was floundering in the quagmire of the Iran-Contra hearings. The Russian visit yielded few practical, tangible results, a fact that Opposition politicians at home were quick to seize on when she returned. But the intangible results of another important

bridge built between East and West were perhaps all the more important.

The visit was favourably contrasted with that of Mr Kinnock and Mr
Healey to Washington the week before. The Labour leader and Labour's
former Defence Secretary had been granted an audience by Reagan
which, to judge by the press, resulted in nothing more than an alter-
cation about how many minutes they should have been allowed by
protocol and the news that Reagan had confused Healey with the former
British Ambassador to Washington, Sir Oliver Wright.

Earlier in the year the author had interviewed Mrs Thatcher at length
about a number of topics, including her views about the problems that
lay ahead of her in Britain, and how she viewed her relationships with
the United States and the Soviet Union. About the future in Britain,
she said:

> There is a great deal to be done, but we do not have the problems we had in
> 1979–81. We do not have to make the very big turn-around we had to make
> between 1979 and 1981, not knowing when we began that it would have to be
> done in the middle of such a big world recession. But, by making our
> decisions in 1981 to get the country on a sound financial basis, we were able
> to go on and deal with our problems. We had to have slightly higher taxation
> than we would have wished. We had to take firm decisions about trade union
> law. We had to fight inflation. We had to be tough. My opponents said, 'Oh,
> they'll be rid of her within three years, because what she's doing is *too* tough.'
> But we did not run away from the difficult decisions. And I think people
> realized that, and that's why we won the election of 1983 and why we shall
> win again. I think people appreciate our fundamental attitude, which is that
> elections are not about promises of what the Government can do for people;
> they are about promises to run the country in a way which enables people
> to do more for themselves, to protect those who are unfortunate, and to
> defend what we believe in.

At the time, Mrs Thatcher was looking forward to her next visit to
Mr Gorbachov. As a result of her first meeting with him in Mr Brezhnev's
time, they had struck up 'a very good understanding', she declared.
'Look,' she had said to him, 'let us try to talk to some of the next
generation!' And they had gone forward from there. She did not underestimate the difficulties of making further progress. Asked if she thought
she had made a contribution to Anglo-Soviet relations she replied:

> Yes, I think so. And it is on the basis of mutual respect. . . . I understand his
> viewpoint, and that he will put it fearlessly. He understands mine. I know I
> will not convert *him*. He knows he will not convert *me*. We know that the

peoples whom I represent democratically and whom he represents through Communism have an interest in getting along together, that there are certain things we can do together and that, if you want to influence people, you do not *stop* talking to them. You *start* talking to them. Both sides recognize that we have a viewpoint founded on fundamental belief, founded on being reliable allies, founded on being loyal not only to our allies but also to our beliefs; and understanding that those beliefs have something to give, some contribution to make to the development of the wider world.

Had Mrs Thatcher made a special contribution to Britain's relations with the United States?

Yes, I think so. I knew President Reagan in the seventies when he was a campaigner and I was still a campaigner. We were both trying to persuade our peoples to give us the opportunity to bring about fundamental change to clear the road to political and economic freedom. We have done some straight talking about the things we believe in.

America is our ally. It did not need any formal alliance for America and us to be fighting on the same side in two world wars. It needed the fundamental beliefs which our two countries shared. These beliefs are important to our European friends as well, but we and the Americans are the English-speaking people, and the English-speaking people have a particular responsibility to the world because of their particular kind of experience.

Look where we have got to now with the United States. We are close to each other not because we always accept what they may say, but because we can influence each other by frank discussion. The Americans know that what we say to them will be based on reason and good sense. So we are trusted there.

And what about Britain's place in the world eight years after she had come to power? 'I think we count for far more now in the world than we used to do ... And we are not afraid. We are not afraid.'

It was with the exhilaration of the Moscow visit behind her, and a successful result for the Conservatives in the council elections of May, that Mrs Thatcher chose 11 June as the day on which she would make her historic bid for a third term of office. However, if the Conservatives had expected Labour to continue in the pattern of Mr Kinnock's unproductive visit to Washington, they were quickly disabused. From the start the Labour campaign was impressive, slick, professional and politically attractive. By focusing on the manifestly warm character of Neil Kinnock, rather than on the intellectually dubious Labour policies on defence and taxation, the Labour Party managed to wrong foot their opponents from the word go. The Conservative campaign began in a

211

relaxed mood with Mrs Thatcher taking advantage of the economic summit in Venice to proclaim not only her own achievements but also to demonstrate how the rest of the Western world were now following her economic policies. Meanwhile the Labour vote was rapidly improving, so that after the first week not only did the Alliance appear beaten, but the Conservative vote seemed to be on the slide as well.

In retrospect, with Mrs Thatcher's eventual majority of 104 in the House of Commons, it is hard to put the campaign in its proper perspective. What everyone agreed on was that Labour undoubtedly had the best campaign and the most alluring videos, thus out-Saatchiing the Saatchis' advertising organization at Conservative Central Office. If this is so, then the Conservative performance on 11 June was all the more remarkable to win a majority of 104 seats even after a poor campaign. During the last week there was alarm at Conservative Party headquarters as one rogue opinion poll reduced their lead to a mere 4%. There was certainly a great deal of acrimony within Central Office about how the campaign was conducted, which led to the official Party chairman Norman Tebbit and his team being virtually supplanted as campaign managers by the trusted Cecil Parkinson, Lord Young and the original Saatchi & Saatchi linkman whom Mrs Thatcher had always leaned heavily on during elections, Tim Bell.

The Conservatives were particularly vulnerable to Opposition claims that their Government and particularly Mrs Thatcher herself did not care about the victims of the previous eight years of Thatcherism – just as they presided over the decline of the NHS and Welfare State. Whilst this seems to have made an impact on the electorate at the time, with Mrs Thatcher emerging as a plutocrat rather than a populist, in retrospect it does not seem to have made much difference to the general election.

The victory of 11 June 1987 confirmed the hegemony of Mrs Thatcher over the political scene that all the opinion polls had predicted a month before. For all their advertising gimmicks and red roses, the Labour Party gained only twenty more seats than they had done in 1983, the year of their electoral nadir. Labour more than ever were forced back into their traditional strongholds of the declining council estates and manufacturing cities of the North, Scotland and South Wales. By some estimates, the Conservatives won 36% of the working-class votes, demonstrating the electoral hold amongst the electorate that the Conservatives had now attained. Outside London, where Labour lost three seats anyway, Labour won only two seats in the whole of the South of England. Not since Lord Liverpool had won three elections in a row between 1812 and 1827 had a British Prime Minister equalled that shining record.

As the results came in, one in particular – not significant to many, perhaps, but noteworthy for nostalgic post-war Labour enthusiasts – caught the eye: Walthamstow, a suburban constituency in North-East London, had fallen to the Conservatives. Walthamstow had once been the impregnable seat of Clement Attlee. Now, it may have seemed to his faithful veterans, not only were the bastions of his post-war Welfare State being threatened but his loyal bailiwick had been taken by storm.

# 13

# MRS THATCHER AND THE FUTURE
# OF BRITAIN

J udged by the criteria she set herself in 1979, Mrs Thatcher's achievements deserve to become historic. Her economic targets have all been reached and in many cases surpassed. Inflation, identified as the main economic problem of the 1970s, rising to 25% in 1975, has been reduced to an annual average of little over 4%, and this figure has been coupled during the past six years with a steady growth rate of 3% in the British economy as a whole – a performance equalled in recent years only by Japan. This combination of high growth and low inflation is a task that *every* post-war government has set itself since the 1950s and only Mrs Thatcher's Governments have consistently managed it. The public finances are now in better shape than at any time since the war. The bane of post-war governments, the Public Sector Borrowing Requirement, has been entirely eliminated; Nigel Lawson announced in his 1988 budget that it is now in surplus to the tune of £3 billion.

Manufacturing output is now rising at a higher level than at any time since 1973 and industrial productivity for the year 1987–8 is the highest in Europe. Mrs Thatcher has fulfilled her pledge to reduce direct taxation; the buoyant state of the economy allowed Nigel Lawson to take the most radical step so far in this direction, in his 1988 budget, by reducing the standard rate once 33% to 25% and the top (and now the only other) rate from 83% in 1979 to 40%. 'The 1988 budget', Mrs Thatcher said, '[was] a humdinger.... It represented the defeat of everything Labour thought was permanent in political life. It was the epitaph of Socialism.' The trade union problem, the 'British Disease' that seemed to plague industry in the 1960s and 1970s, has been eradicated from the body politic, and the annual rate of industrial stoppages in the late 1980s is running at its lowest level since the late 1930s. It is a remarkable economic transformation when seen against the seemingly irreversible economic decline to which the British people appeared to be resigned in the 1970s.

If Mrs Thatcher said she was going to do all this at the outset, why should anybody be impressed by the fact that she has done it? It is her manifest ability to *do* what she said she would that makes her unique. All governments and political parties since the early 1950s have sought high growth, low inflation and increased productivity. These goals were just as implicit in Harold Macmillan's 'never had it so good' economic policies as they were in Harold Wilson's appeal to the 'white heat of technology', Edward Heath's 'quiet revolution' of 1970 and the 'social contracts' of the late 1970s. But none of these governments and politicians succeeded in delivering the goods; they all diagnosed roughly the same sickness, but failed to cure it. The problem of Britain's seemingly perpetual and miserable economic decline preoccupied all post-war governments to one degree or another. The analysis was not lacking, but the political will was. Britain's economic decline had reached such a low in the 1970s that the ability of governments to govern effectively was itself open to question, bogged down as they were in archaic, arcane, corporatist red-tape that stifled any reactive policy-making in either Whitehall or in industry. Governments lurched from one economic crisis to another without displaying either the competence or the will to grapple with the underlying problems.

The sharper, more radical political minds knew only too well that, if this process was to be reversed, a new ruthlessness and a new energy were needed. Tony Benn, a member of Harold Wilson's first Cabinet, was just such a politician and he recorded his despair at the inability of his Government to do anything in his diary as early as 1966:

> I realize that I am getting precious close to saying that parliamentary democracy is not working in this country.... The answer is, of course, a really dynamic political party that is elected knowing the difficulties that will face it and determined to get control of the Whitehall machine and really use it to carry through fundamental changes. I just don't believe that this impetus exists in the Labour Party or within the Labour Cabinet, and it may well be that it does not exist anywhere, that we are going to go on floating, governed by Civil Servants with Ministers from the two parties coming in and out by a curious quirk known as the electoral cycle.

The missing 'impetus', the missing dynamism, turned out to be Mrs Thatcher. She brought to the arena of government the virtues of courage and simplicity. Successive governments had argued that the Byzantine complexities of Britain's economic decline needed equally complex solutions; endless new layers of government administration were applied to solve problems that never went away. Conviction politics, to use her own phrase, consisted of a clear and simple vision applied with indomitable and dynamic political will. This is perhaps the only way to govern a late twentieth-century body politic like that of Britain.

It is a testament to that political will that she survived the initial crises of her administrations during the embattled days of 1980 and 1981. At that time the Prime Minister was virtually isolated within her own Cabinet, let alone in the country at large. To a degree which is without precedent in the history of British politics Mrs Thatcher can lay claim to an overwhelming share of personal credit for the economic successes of three successive governments. Only Gladstone, perhaps, has had such a profound personal effect on government and politics, on shaping society according to a vision. The Ministers in Attlee's celebrated Labour Government of 1945–51, which created the Welfare State, could all easily have swapped jobs and the results would have been exactly the same; not so with Mrs Thatcher's Governments – without her everything would have ground to a halt by the end of 1980. She thus deserves her high profile throughout the world and her political standing. Sir Nicholas Henderson, the composer of the elegant but pessimistic valedictory despatch of 1979, is in no doubt as to the transformation that Mrs Thatcher has wrought in Britain and how she is thus regarded abroad. He told the author in 1988 that though 'there are many features of life in this country that remain disturbing . . . nevertheless it is impossible for any unbiased witness not to be struck by the profound changes, whether measured by objective statistics or subjective scrutiny. To cite two indicators: since 1981 GDP and productivity have achieved stronger growth in the UK than in either France or the FRG . . . 'Mrs Thatcher herself is probably better known to the public from Lima to Beijing than any British political figure since Winston Churchill. What she stands for is unblurred. Her determination is seen as positively de Gaullean. Without seeking to quantify this in terms of specific benefits to immediate British interests, I am in no doubt of the clear ring it gives to Britain's voice in the world.'

The question of whether Mrs Thatcher's neo-Liberalism is ideologically adequate for the problems of Britain in the late twentieth century continues to be debated. The Prime Minister's aim is to spread freedom of choice and personal responsibility throughout all areas of human endeavour, to prise away the dead hand of the State and encourage people 'to stand on their own two feet'. This she has visibly achieved in the economic sphere, but it is paradoxical that elsewhere Mrs Thatcher's Government has had to take more power into its own hands than governments have had before. Samuel Brittan, one of the earlier converts to monetarism, anticipated this trend when he wrote in *Encounter* in 1980 that 'It has always been an intellectual paradox that the non-Muscovite left favours freedom in everything but economics, while the right is sympathetic to freedom only in the economic sphere.'

The Conservative Governments of the 1980s, supposedly so mistrustful of government in any form, have found themselves legislating in a wide spectrum of areas on an unparalleled scale – whether it be gun control, secrecy laws, football hooliganism, criminal law, broadcasting guidelines, homosexual rights or capital punishment. In late twentieth-century society, neo-Liberalism cannot help but be paradoxical, since legislation will always be necessary to curb some of the social and ethical consequences of a laissez-faire economic doctrine. The paradox of Thatcherism has been the contrast between the increased economic freedom of the individual and the centralizing, statist tendency that has entered so many other areas of human activity.

The moral criteria of Thatcherism, the emphasis on Victorian values, has also proved difficult to reconcile with the economic condition of Britain, let alone the world, in the late twentieth century. The virtues of hard work, thrift and personal responsibility which underpin Mrs Thatcher's own ideology and her vision for Britain are indeed Victorian, but many people ask whether those values are archaic rather than relevant in the late twentieth century. Victorian values were the ideological or moral dynamism of the first Industrial Revolution; the essential value of work could indeed be preached as a doctrine of personal salvation because work was always in plentiful supply. The Industrial Revolution was labour intensive, and thus the value of 'work' was both economically and morally important. But the same is certainly not true of the present technological revolution; industry is no longer labour intensive, but technologically intensive. Mrs Thatcher has rightly accelerated and encouraged the switch from the smoke-stack industries of the first Industrial Revolution to the new service industries of the present technological revolution – without, her critics say, and they

217

include some Tories, asking herself whether her morality might have become outdated. Human activity no longer has the same necessary connection with economic growth, but is a rapidly declining appendage to that growth. To build a national morality in such circumstances on the moral value of work is not only, perhaps, economically shortsighted in the long term but also offends those who, by virtue of the fact that they cannot get a job, are excluded from the moral and social fabric of the time.

There is no doubt that Britain's economic growth in the 1980s has been brought about at a cost. A cost of three million unemployed, a further five million living in poverty, and a widening difference between the rich and the poor, the North and the South.

As in America, neo-Liberalism risks creating a permanent underclass who are excluded from enjoying the freedoms that the rest of society can afford. The old class system that Mrs Thatcher rightly resented and identified as a rigid obstacle to economic growth could be replaced by another, increasingly rigid class system which is the consequence of neo-Liberal economic growth in the 1980s – those in well-remunerated employment, and those without a job in the poverty trap. The cohesion conferred on Britain by the Welfare State may be forfeited. Lord Salisbury, the great nineteenth-century Conservative Prime Minister, surveyed the social wreckage of Britain at the height of her economic powers in 1883 when he described the 'bundle of unfriendly and distrustful fragments' which had replaced 'that spirit of the old constitution which held the nation together as a whole'. Precisely what preoccupied Lord Salisbury in 1883 is what concerns the majority of the British electorate who voted against Mrs Thatcher in 1979, 1983 and 1987. Are Mrs Thatcher's economic criteria enough? The fact that Britain is now tangibly, statistically richer than it was in 1979 does not necessarily lead to an increase in the quality of life for the population as a whole, either rich or poor.

Mrs Thatcher and those Conservative Party leaders who have been closest to her in bringing about the great Thatcherite change in British politics are aware of this and of the need to deal with it. The Tory Party's concern for those who have least benefited from Thatcherism was plain to see when thirty-eight MPs voted against the Government on the Poll Tax issue on 18 April 1988, bringing down Mrs Thatcher's majority to an embarrassingly low twenty-five. In October 1987, four months after the election victory of June, Leon Brittan said in a speech in Bolton in the North-East, a part of the country which has not shared in the economic fortunes of the South:

But if we are to win over the country to support the changes implied in [our] thinking, we must also make it clear that our purpose is not just to save money and cut taxes, important though those aims are. It is also to free resources in order to give more help for those genuinely in need, and to tackle with renewed vigour our outstanding social problems. This is only one example of the twin-track approach which we should now be taking....

If we are to broaden our appeal, as well as extend our present policies, we must also show that entrepreneurial values and the enterprise culture form part of our political philosophy but do not constitute its entirety. Indeed, one of the purposes of promoting the free market is to enable us to look after those who are not able to succeed in it. A society in which individual talent is liberated should also aim to be one which is tolerant, self-confident and united.

This means a new focus on what binds society together, an increased concern for policies that will make society more cohesive and not just richer.... The common thread should be a determination to show that alongside opportunity for the individual, we recognize the need for enhancing the feeling of membership of a single community which has always been the hallmark of Conservatism at its best.

And, talking to the author on the eve of the general election in 1983, in response to his final question, 'Have you a vision of how you would like Britain to be?', Mrs Thatcher replied: 'My vision of society? The *Responsible* Society.' She told the 1986 Conservative Women's conference: 'A responsible society is one in which people do not leave it to the person next door to do the job. It is one in which people help each other, where parents put their children first, friends look out for the neighbours, families for their elderly members, that is the starting point for care and support – the unsung efforts of millions of individuals, the selfless work of thousands upon thousands of volunteers ... Caring isn't measured by what you say; it's expressed by what you do.'

# SOME BIOGRAPHICAL
# NOTES

*Sir Robert Armstrong (1927–     )*

Educated at Eton and Christ Church, Oxford. From a classic establishment background, Sir Robert rose swiftly through the ranks of the Civil Service to become a loyal and distinguished Principal Private Secretary to both Edward Heath and Harold Wilson during their respective tenures of 10 Downing Street between 1970 and 1975. Sir Robert was Permanent Under-Secretary at the Home Office 1977–9, then became Secretary to the Cabinet until 1987, when he retired. He combined this post with being Head of the Home Civil Service 1983–7.

*Sir William Armstrong (1915–1980)*

Equipped with a First in Greats from Oxford, Sir William joined the Treasury and thereafter became the epitome of a Civil Service mandarin. In 1962 he became the joint Permanent Secretary of the Treasury and in 1968 he was made the head of the Home Civil Service, also occupying the new post of Permanent Secretary of the Civil Service Department.

He was particularly prominent during the premiership of Edward Heath, 1970–4, becoming Heath's confidant. He, and no member of the Cabinet, accompanied Heath in the latter's ill-fated negotiations with Joe Gormley, the miners' leader, which led to the miners' strike of 1974 and the subsequent fall of the Heath Government. Some regarded his influence as excessive, and he thus picked up the unwelcome sobriquet of 'Deputy Prime Minister'.

In 1975 he became chairman of the Midland Bank.

# SOME BIOGRAPHICAL NOTES

## Tony Benn (*1925–* )

The son of a Labour peer, Viscount Stansgate, Tony Benn joined the Labour Party in 1943 and was president of the Oxford Union in 1947. A persuasive orator, Benn entered the House of Commons in 1963 after a successful and celebrated campaign to disclaim his hereditary peerage. He served in several ministerial posts under Harold Wilson from 1964 to 1970, as Minister for Trade and Industry 1974–5 and finally as Minister for Energy 1975–9. Unlike virtually all his Ministerial colleagues of his generation in the Labour Party, he has moved further and further to the left in politics. By 1980 he had firmly established himself as the leader of the left within the Labour movement, a position he has retained. The nearest that the left has ever come to capturing the Labour Party from the centre and right was in 1981 when Tony Benn challenged for the deputy leadership of the Party and was only beaten by a whisker by the incumbent Denis Healey.

## John Biffen (*1930–* )

One of the most lucid and original thinkers in the Conservative Party. Biffen entered the House of Commons in 1961. As one of the earliest advocates of what was to become known as monetarism, he served as Chief Secretary to the Treasury 1979–81, Secretary of State for Trade 1981–2, Lord President of the Council 1982–3 and lastly as a popular and successful Leader of the House of Commons 1983–7. He lost this post and his place in the Cabinet after the 1987 election having been publicly critical of Mrs Thatcher's style of Government during the two years leading up to the election.

## David Blunkett (*1947–* )

Elected to the Sheffield City Council at the age of 22, Blunkett's whole working life has been devoted to local politics, and in 1980 he became the Labour leader of the City Council. An accomplished and popular leader, he managed to implement socialist policies in South Yorkshire without indulging in any of the ideological excesses that disfigured similar Labour controlled councils in London and Liverpool. With the abolition of the Municipal councils in 1986, Blunkett inevitably looked to the wider field of national politics, and at the 1987 general election was elected Labour MP for Sheffield Brightside.

## Leon Brittan (*1939–* )

Practised as a barrister before entering Parliament as a Conservative MP in 1974. Under Mrs Thatcher he has been Minister of State at the Home Office (1979–81), Chief Secretary to the Treasury (1981–3), Home Secretary (1983–5) and Minister for Trade and Industry (1983–6). He resigned from the Government over the Westland crisis in January 1986 and has since remained on the back benches.

### Samuel Brittan (1933– )

One of Britain's most influential commentators on economic and financial affairs. Author of *How to End the Monetarist Controversy, The Role and Limits of Government, A Restatement of Economic Liberalism* and other important works. Elder brother of Leon Brittan. Assistant Editor of the *Financial Times*.

### James Callaghan (1912– )

Labour Party leader defeated by Mrs Thatcher in the 1979 general election. He worked as a civil servant for the Inland Revenue from 1929–39 and served with the Royal Navy during the war. He entered the House of Commons in 1945 and subsequently held every senior office in Government: Chancellor of the Exchequer (1964–7), Home Secretary (1967–70), Foreign Secretary (1974–6) and Prime Minister (1976–9). He retired from the House of Commons and went to the House of Lords in 1987.

### Lord Carrington (1919– )

He served in North-West Europe during the war and ended as a Major in the Grenadier Guards. His numerous posts in successive Conservative administrations during the 1950s and 1960s were mainly concerned with Defence and Foreign Affairs and he served as First Lord of the Admiralty 1959–63. Under Heath, he served as Secretary of State for Defence 1970–74 and briefly as Secretary of State for Energy. In 1979 Mrs Thatcher appointed him her Secretary of State for Foreign and Commonwealth Affairs, a position for which he was by then uniquely qualified. His tenure of that office counted as one of the few obvious success stories during the first three years of Mrs Thatcher's Government. In 1982 he resigned, together with his ministerial team at the Foreign Office, in the immediate aftermath of the Argentinian invasion of the Falkland Islands. From 1984–8 Lord Carrington was Secretary-General of NATO.

### Sir Frank Cooper (1922– )

A career civil servant after service as an RAF pilot in the Second World War, Sir Frank was Permanent Under-Secretary at the Northern Ireland Office from 1973–6 and Permanent Secretary at the Ministry of Defence from 1976–82.

### Anthony Crosland (1918–1977)

Educated at Highgate School and Trinity College, Oxford, of which he later became a lecturer and a fellow. Having been President of the Oxford Union in 1946 he entered Parliament as the Labour MP for South Gloucestershire in 1950. Very much an intellectual in politics, he became the guru of post-war social democracy with the publication of *The Future of Socialism* in 1956, described by Roy Jenkins as 'the most important theoretical treatise to be written from the moderate left in British politics in the twenty-five post-war years'. Crosland was Secretary of State for Education and Science 1965–7 and President of the Board of Trade 1967–70. He was Foreign Secretary 1976–7, dying in office.

## Bernard Donoughue (1934–   )

Educated at Secondary Modern School and Grammar School, Northampton, and Lincoln College and Nuffield College, Oxford. In his own words 'the son of a factory worker from the poorest working class', Bernard Donoghue has excelled in many careers. He was a lecturer at the London School of Economics from 1964–74 whence he was plucked by Harold Wilson to head the new Downing Street Policy Unit after Labour's election victory in March of that year. He remained at this post until 1979 after which he took up a career in the City as head of research and investment policy with Grievson Grant.

## Sir Edward Du Cann (1924–   )

Educated at Woodbridge School and St John's College, Oxford. He entered Parliament as MP for Taunton in 1956. Founder, Unicorn Group of Unit Trusts 1957; Minister of State, Board of Trade, 1963–4; chairman of the Conservative Party 1965–7. Chairman Keyser Allman Holdings, 1970–75. Influential within the Conservative Party through his Chairmanship of the all-important 1922 Committee of Tory back bench MPs from 1972–84. Chairman of Lonrho PLC since 1984.

## Michael Foot (1913–   )

Educated at Leighton Park School, Reading, and Wadham College, Oxford. Scion of a famous political family, Michael Foot was president of the Oxford Union in 1933 and worked thereafter as a journalist, mainly for the Beaverbrook press (he was editor of the London *Evening Standard* from 1942 to 1946). Although initially a Liberal he was converted to Socialism in the 1930s and entered the House of Commons as Labour MP for the Davenport Division of Plymouth in 1945. As a strident spokesman of the Bevanite left within the Labour Party he did not achieve Cabinet rank until the 1970s; he served as Secretary of State for Employment from 1974–6 and then as Leader of the House of Commons from 1976–9. From 1976–80 he was deputy leader of the Labour Party and from 1980–83 he was leader. A prodigous writer and pamphleteer, he still sits as MP for Blaenau Gwent.

## Sir Ian Gilmour (1926–   )

Educated at Eton and Balliol College, Oxford. Sir Ian practised as a barrister, and was editor of *The Spectator* from 1954–9, before entering Parliament. He served as Secretary of State for Defence in 1974 under Edward Heath and as Lord Privy Seal in Mrs Thatcher's first Cabinet from 1979–81. One of the most articulate of the wets and the author of one of the most lucid expositions of classical Conservatism (*Inside Right*), he was sacked from the Cabinet in 1981 and has remained an unrepentant and often scathing critic of Mrs Thatcher's Governments.

## General Alexander Haig (*1924–* )

Educated at schools in Pennsylvania, University of Notre Dame and West Point Military Academy.

A career soldier who fought in Korea and Vietnam, he served under President Nixon as Chief of the White House Staff from 1973–4 before becoming Supreme Allied Commander in Europe from 1974–9. In 1981 he became President Reagan's Secretary of State, and acted as a mediator between Britain and Argentina during the Falklands crisis. He resigned his post in the autumn of 1982 as a result of policy differences with the President.

## Denis Healey (*1917–* )

Educated at Bradford Grammar School and Balliol College, Oxford. He graduated from Oxford with a First in Greats in 1940 and when the war ended was a Major in the Army. He entered Parliament as a Labour MP in 1952, served as Secretary of State for Defence 1964–70 and as Chancellor of the Exchequer 1974–9. He was twice passed over as leader of the Labour Party in 1976 in favour of Jim Callaghan and in 1979 in favour of Michael Foot. Widely regarded as the best leader the Labour Party never had. From 1979–87 he shadowed Sir Geoffrey Howe as Opposition spokesman first on economic affairs and then on foreign affairs. He retired from the Labour front bench after the 1987 election but still plays an active part in politics. Nicknamed 'The old bruiser' for his combative political style, but his gregarious and generous nature is widely acknowledged throughout Westminster and Whitehall.

## Edward Heath (*1916–* )

Educated at Chatham House School, Ramsgate, and Balliol College, Oxford. After a distinguished war career, Major Heath entered Parliament in 1950 as MP for Bexley. He made his mark with the Conservative Party hierarchy as the Chief Whip from 1955–9 and was particularly influential during the Suez crisis of 1956. He was appointed Lord Privy Seal in Harold Macmillan's Government with special responsibility for negotiating Britain's entry into the European Economic Community, a cause with which he came to be closely identified. He was elected leader of the Conservative Party in succession to Alec Douglas-Home in August 1965. He served as Prime Minister from 1970–74 and was then defeated by Mrs Thatcher in the Conservative Party leadership election of 1975.

An admirable musician (Organ Scholar at Balliol College) and an accomplished yachtsman, in many respects a most gifted politician but has long been in the wilderness. For the last thirteen years he has expressed uncompromising criticism of the policies of the woman who replaced him as Party leader.

### Sir Nicholas Henderson (1919–   )

Educated at Stowe School and Hertford College, Oxford. A career diplomat who served as Assistant Private Secretary to Anthony Eden and Ernest Bevin from 1944–7. He was Private Secretary to successive Secretaries of State at the Foreign Office in the 1960s. Sir Nicholas was Ambassador to Poland 1967–72, to West Germany 1972–5, to France 1975–9 and to the USA 1979–82 being there throughout the Falklands crisis. He has been chairman of the Channel Tunnel Group and is a noted enthusiast for the cause of closer links between Britain and her partners in the European Economic Community.

### Michael Heseltine (1933–   )

Educated at Shrewsbury School and Pembroke College, Oxford. President of the Union at Oxford in 1954, Michael Heseltine first established himself in business, founding the Haymarket Press, before entering Parliament as a Conservative MP in 1966. For years the darling of the annual Conservative Party Conference, he was Minister for Aerospace and Shipping 1972–4 in Heath's Government. Under Mrs Thatcher he was Secretary of State for the Environment 1979–83, and Secretary of State for Defence 1983–6. He resigned from the Government over the Westland crisis in January 1986.

He has since campaigned for various issues from the back benches and remains an avowed enthusiast for the EEC. Although not openly critical of Mrs Thatcher, he remains the most likely moderate candidate to succeed her as leader of the Party. He reputedly managed an extensive personal speaking tour for the Conservative Party during the 1987 election campaign without once mentioning Mrs Thatcher.

### Sir John Hoskyns (1927–   )

Educated at Winchester College. The archetypal entrepreneurial businessman who worked for IBM UK Ltd from 1957 to 1964 before founding his own computer company, John Hoskyns Co. Ltd. He was head of Mrs Thatcher's personal Policy Unit in Downing Street from 1979–82. He has been Director-General of the Institute of Directors since 1984.

### Sir Geoffrey Howe (1926–   )

Educated at Winchester College and Trinity Hall, Cambridge. Sir Geoffrey practised as a barrister before entering Parliament in 1964. As Solicitor General in Edward Heath's Government 1972–4 he was closely involved in the drafting of the ill-fated trade union legislation of 1971, the Industrial Relations Act. He was Minister for Trade and Consumer Affairs from 1972–4. He was Chancellor of the Exchequer from 1979–83 and has been Secretary of State for Foreign Affairs since 1983. Currently ranks second only to Mrs Thatcher in her Cabinet.

## Peter Jay (1937– )

Educated at Winchester College and Christ Church, Oxford.

The son of the economist and Labour peer, Lord (Douglas) Jay, he had a distinguished academic career at Oxford and was president of the Oxford Union in 1960. Since then he has had a varied career at the heart of the British establishment, starting in the Treasury from 1961–7. From 1967 to 1977 he was economics editor of *The Times* and presenter of the prestigous *Weekend World* TV programme 1972–7. The son-in-law of the then Prime Minister, Jim Callaghan, he was a surprise appointment as Britain's Ambassador to the United States from 1977–9. On his return he was involved in the ill-fated debut of the breakfast television station TV-am, and since 1986 he has been 'Chief of Staff' to the publishing tycoon and proprietor of the Mirror group of newspapers, Robert Maxwell.

## Roy Jenkins (1920– )

Educated at Abersychan Grammar School, South Wales, and Balliol College, Oxford. Son of a former South Wales miner who later became Parliamentary Private Secretary to Clement Attlee, Jenkins entered the House as Labour MP for Central Southwark in 1948, rising within the Labour Party to become Chancellor of the Exchequer 1967–70, and deputy leader of the Party 1970–2. After being Home Secretary 1974–6, left the British political scene to become President of the European Commission 1977–81. Subsequently he broke with the Labour Party and became co-founder of the Social Democratic Party. For a time he was its leader and also of the SDP/Liberal Party Alliance. Now in the House of Lords.

## Sir Keith Joseph (1918– )

Educated at Harrow and Magdalen College, Oxford. A hereditary baronet and fellow of All Souls College Oxford, Sir Keith was instrumental in changing fundamentally Conservative Party thinking between 1974 and 1979. He trained as a barrister and entered Parliament in 1956. He was a junior minister in the Conservative Governments 1961–4 and Secretary of State for Social Services 1970–4. He was the co-founder (with Sir Alfred Sherman) and chairman of the Centre for Policy Studies. He was Secretary of State for Industry (1979–81) and Secretary of State for Education and Science 1981–6. He left the House of Commons for the House of Lords in 1987. He is the politician to whom, Mrs Thatcher has said, she owes most.

# SOME BIOGRAPHICAL NOTES

*Neil Kinnock (1942–   )*

Educated at Lewis School, Pengam and University College, Cardiff.

The son of a South Wales 'labourer', Neil Kinnock entered Parliament in 1970 as Labour MP for Bedwellty in 1970. Schooled in the Nye Bevan style of radical politics, Kinnock has gradually shifted to the centreground of Labour Party politics in his swift rise up the party hierarchy. As the protégé of Michael Foot, he succeeded Foot as leader of the Party and as leader of the Opposition in 1983. A telegenic personality and a powerful platform orator, Kinnock has done much to restore morale within the Party since the disastrous election campaign of 1983.

*(Mrs) Jeane Kirkpatrick (1926–   )*

United States Permanent Representative to the United Nations, 1981–5. Distinguished diplomat and academic. Expert on Latin America, and wrote *The Peronist Movement in Argentina*, published in 1972. Former member of the Democratic Party, she joined the Republicans in 1985. Thought highly of by President Reagan, she was prominent among his advisers at the time of the Falklands crisis.

*Nigel Lawson (1932–   )*

Educated at Westminster and Christ Church, Oxford. He graduated with a First in Philosophy, Politics and Economics in 1954 and his subsequent career in economic journalism has made him perhaps one of the best qualified politicians ever to hold his present job as Chancellor of the Exchequer. He was a financial journalist on the *Financial Times* and *Sunday Telegraph* before becoming editor of the *Spectator* from 1966–70. He was special adviser to Sir Alec Douglas-Home when Prime Minister, 1963–4, and became MP for Blaby in 1974. He was Financial Secretary to the Treasury 1979–81, Secretary of State for Energy 1981–3, and has been Chancellor of the Exchequer since 1983.

*Admiral of the Fleet Sir Henry Leach (1923–   )*

Educated at St Peters Court, Broadstairs, and the Royal Naval College, Dartmouth. After seeing action on destroyers during the Second World War, Sir Henry rose to be the Chief of the Naval Staff and First Sea Lord from 1979–82. He was thus the service head of the Navy during the Falklands War.

*Admiral of the Fleet Sir Terence Lewin (1920–   )*

Educated at The Judd School, Tonbridge. Lewin joined the Royal Navy in 1939, and after distinguished war service ascended the post-war naval hierarchy to become Chief of the Naval Staff and First Sea Lord 1977–9 and Chief of the Defence Staff 1979–82. At the time of the Falklands crisis he was thus Mrs Thatcher's chief professional service adviser. He retired in 1982 and was created a Life Peer.

## Ken Livingstone (1945– )

Educated at Tulse Hill Comprehensive School and the Philippa Fawcett College of Education.

A product of radical politics of the late 1960s, Livingstone joined the Labour Party in 1969 and subsequently devoted his energies to local politics in London, serving as a Councillor in Lambeth and Camden. In 1981 he was given great national publicity as the new leader of the Greater London Council. After the GLC was abolished in 1986, he graduated to national Labour Party politics and became MP for Brent East in the 1987 general election.

## Sir Patrick Mayhew (1929– )

Educated at Tonbridge and Balliol College, Oxford. President of the Oxford Union 1952. Barrister. Entered Parliament as a Conservative in 1974. Minister of State, Home Office, 1981–3. Solicitor-General 1983; Attorney-General 1987.

## John Moore (1937– )

Educated at the London School of Economics. He worked in the financial services sector in the City of London before entering Parliament as MP for Croydon Central in 1974. From 1983 to 1987 he was Financial Secretary to the Treasury in which post he is largely credited with having overseen the Government's privatization programme. He was appointed Minister for Health and Social Services in the wake of the 1987 election victory and is tipped in some quarters as a successor to Mrs Thatcher.

## Robert Mugabe (1924– )

Prime Minister of Zimbabwe since creation of the State (formerly Rhodesia, a British colony) in April 1980. Joint leader with Joshua Nkomo of the Rhodesian Patriotic Front 1976–80, Mugabe heading the Marxist wing of the Front, Zimbabwe African National Union (ZANU), and Nkomo the other wing, Zimbabwe African People's Union (ZAPU). Mugabe defeated Nkomo in election of February 1980.

## Airey Neave (1916–1979)

Educated at Eton and Merton College, Oxford. Neave will always be remembered for his brave and resourceful record in the war, the highlight being his escape in 1942 from the notorious Colditz Castle prison and return to Britain. Amongst his numerous decorations were the Military Cross and the Croix de Guerre. He entered Parliament as a Conservative in 1953. His subsequent political career never matched the heights of his war career until he ran Mrs Thatcher's campaign for the leadership of the Conservative Party in 1975. He was immediately appointed head of her Private Office and later was made Shadow Secretary of State for Northern Ireland. At the beginning of the election campaign in 1979 he was killed by the IRA, a bomb exploding under his car as he drove out of the House of Commons car park.

## Joshua Nkomo (June 1917– )

Joint leader with Robert Mugabe of Patriotic Front in Rhodesia, 1976–80, and prominent at the Lancaster House Conference on future of Rhodesia, 1979. Defeated by Mugabe in the election of February 1980, Mugabe representing the Marxist wing of the Patriotic Front, the Zimbabwe African National Union (ZANU), and Nkomo the other wing, the Zimbabwe African People's Union (ZAPU). Mugabe became Prime Minister, and led Rhodesia into independence as the new state of Zimbabwe. Nkomo accepted the post of Minister for Home Affairs.

## Sir John Nott (1932– )

Educated at Bradfield College and Trinity College, Cambridge. He was President of the Cambridge Union in 1959 and practised as a barrister before entering Parliament as a Conservative in 1966. A monetarist, under Mrs Thatcher he served as Secretary of State for Trade 1979–81, and as Secretary of State for Defence 1981–3. He retired from politics in 1983 to pursue a career in the City where he is now chairman and chief executive of Lazard Brothers & Co. Ltd.

## Dr David Owen (1938– )

Educated at Bradfield College and Sidney Sussex College, Cambridge. On graduation he trained as a medical student at St Thomas's Hospital, London and worked as a doctor there before entering Parliament as a Labour MP in 1966. His rise was spectacular, becoming Under-Secretary of State for the Royal Navy in 1968, and Minister for Health from 1974–7. On the death of Anthony Crosland in 1977, he was promoted above numerous senior Party colleagues to become Foreign Secretary, the youngest since Anthony Eden.

His increasingly tenuous relationship with the Labour Party was severed in 1981 when Dr Owen, with Roy Jenkins, Shirley Williams and Bill Rodgers, formed the Social Democratic Party in protest at what was perceived as the leftward drift of the Labour Party. The SDP's disappointing showing at the 1987 general election was followed by a fission within the Party. Dr Owen refused to consider a merger of the Party with the Liberals and resigned the leadership of the merging SDP later in the year, to remain leader of the non-merging section of the Party. Widely regarded as the only Opposition politician who looks like an alternative Prime Minister to Mrs Thatcher.

## Cecil Parkinson (1931– )

Educated at Royal Lancaster Grammar School and Emmanuel College, Cambridge. A self-made businessman, he founded Parkinson Hart Securities Ltd in 1967. He entered Parliament as a Conservative in 1970 and enjoyed a rapid series of promotions under Mrs Thatcher, beginning as Minister for Trade at the Department of Trade 1979–81 and rising to the chairmanship of the Conservative Party and Chancellor of the Duchy of Lancaster 1981–3. He was made Secretary of State for Trade and Industry in 1983 after the election victory. An affair with his former secretary became public during that year's Party Conference, and he resigned. After the 1987 election he returned to the Cabinet as Secretary of State for Energy. The kind of political leader Mrs Thatcher admires most.

## Sir Anthony Parsons (1922–   )

Educated at King's School, Canterbury, and Balliol College, Oxford. A career diplomat, Sir Anthony was Ambassador to Iran 1974–9 and was Britain's Permanent Representative to the United Nations 1979–82. He so impressed Mrs Thatcher with his handling of Britain's diplomatic case in New York during the Falklands crisis that she made him her Special Adviser on Foreign Affairs in Downing Street 1982–3.

## Enoch Powell (1912–   )

Educated at King Edward's School, Birmingham, and Trinity College, Cambridge. A maverick Conservative politician, now widely seen as the monetarist precursor of Mrs Thatcher within the Party. He has combined an erudite, scholastic manner with advocacy of populist causes. He was born a product of the Empire in India and has retained a lifelong interest in and devotion to its ideals. He entered Parliament in 1950 and served as Financial Secretary to the Treasury 1957–8, before resigning with the other two Treasury Ministers in protest at Harold Macmillan's refusal to make cuts in Government expenditure. He served as Minister for Health 1960–63, and then refused to serve under the new Prime Minister, Sir Alec Douglas-Home.

Although widely tipped as a future leader of the Conservative Party, he burned his bridges in 1968 by making his 'rivers of blood' speech on the dangers of coloured immigration to Britain. He thereafter sat as an Ulster Unionist in the House of Commons, but lost his seat in the 1987 general election.

## James Prior (1927–   )

Educated at Charterhouse and Pembroke College, Cambridge. A farmer and land agent in East Anglia, Jim Prior entered Parliament as Conservative MP for Lowestoft in 1959. In the Heath Government, Prior was Minister of Agriculture, Fisheries and Food 1970–72 and Lord President of the Council and Leader of the House of Commons 1972–4. Under Mrs Thatcher he served as Secretary of State for Employment 1979–81 and as Secretary of State for Northern Ireland 1981–4. One of the most prominent wets within the Government, he resigned in 1984 and retired from the House of Commons in 1987. He was created a Life Peer in the same year and since 1984 has been chairman of the General Electric Company.

# SOME BIOGRAPHICAL NOTES

## Francis Pym (1922– )

Educated at Eton and Magdalene College, Cambridge. The quintessential Tory 'knight of the shires'. After a successful war career he became an MP in 1961. He rose to prominence within the Conservative Party as the Government's Chief Whip 1970–3, and then served as Secretary of State for Northern Ireland 1973–4. Under Mrs Thatcher he was Secretary of State for Defence (1979–81), Lord President of the Council (1981–2) and finally Foreign Secretary 1982–3. He has the peculiar distinction of being the first Foreign Secretary ever to be sacked; Mrs Thatcher decided to terminate his career at the Foreign Office after he had made some remarks about the desirable size of her hoped-for House of Commons majority during the 1983 election campaign. A reluctant wet, he has since written a widely acclaimed book, *The Politics of Consent*, in which, according to his own preface, he attempts to describe how 'a loyal Conservative in the centre of the Party has increasingly been branded as a rebel of the left'.

## Lord Rayner (1926– )

Educated at the City College, Norwich, and Selwyn College, Cambridge. When a director of the highly successful retail chain Marks & Spencer – he is now chairman – Lord Rayner was asked by Mrs Thatcher to run an 'efficiency unit' within Whitehall from 1979–83.

## Arthur Scargill (1938– )

Educated at Worsbrough Dale School, White Cross Secondary School and Leeds University. A member of the Young Communist League from 1955 to 1962, Scargill made his name as a militant member of the National Union of Mineworkers in 1972 when he effectively led the miners to victory against Edward Heath's Government. In 1981 he was elected President of the NUM, a post to which he was re-elected, but with a decreased majority, in 1988.

## Sir Alfred Sherman (1919– )

Educated at the Hackney Downs County Secondary School and the London School of Economics. From being the president of the student Communist Party at the LSE and fighting for the International Brigade during the Spanish Civil War, Alfred Sherman has traversed the full political spectrum to be today more Thatcherite than Mrs Thatcher. His outstanding contribution to politics was his influence over Sir Keith Joseph with whom he founded the Centre for Policy Studies in 1974, which propagated the neo-Liberal cause within the Conservative Party.

## Lord Soames (1920–1987)

Educated at Eton College and the Royal Military College, Sandhurst. After a military career in the Coldstream Guards, Christopher Soames entered the House of Commons in 1950 as Conservative MP for the Bedford Division of

Bedfordshire. He married Winston Churchill's daughter Mary in 1947 and subsequently served as an indispensable Parliamentary Private Secretary to Churchill when he was Prime Minister from 1952 to 1955. His later political career did not achieve as much as it had once promised and he was eventually to leave his most permanent mark as a diplomat; as Ambassador to France 1968–72, as a Vice-President of the Commission of the European Communities 1973–7 and lastly and most famously as Governor of Rhodesia 1979–81, presiding over the transference of power in that country from white minority rule to democracy. From 1980–81 he was Lord President of the Council and Leader of the House of Lords in Mrs Thatcher's Cabinet, but was sacked in 1981.

## Norman St John-Stevas (1929– )

Educated at Ratcliffe and Fitzwilliam College, Cambridge, where he was the president of the Cambridge Union in 1950. He trained as a barrister and lectured in Law at Oxford University and is the editor of the collected works of Walter Bagehot. He was the Chancellor of the Duchy of Lancaster, Leader of the House of Commons and Minister for the Arts, 1979–81. One of the most prominent wets of Mrs Thatcher's first Cabinet. Some of his epithets for Mrs Thatcher, such as 'the Leaderene' and 'the immaculate misconception' have become historical and may have contributed to him being sacked in 1981. He left the House of Commons for the House of Lords in 1987, taking the title Lord St John of Fawsley. Since 1985 he has been chairman of the Royal Fine Arts Commission.

## David Steel (1938– )

Educated at Prince of Wales School, Nairobi, Kenya, George Watson's College and Edinburgh University. Became the youngest member of the House of Commons in 1965 when he was elected as Liberal MP for Roxburgh, Selkirk and Peebles. He made his parliamentary reputation as the sponsor of a Private Member's Bill to reform the law on abortion in 1967, a bill that relied upon the enthusiastic endorsement of the then Labour Home Secretary and later key member of the Liberal–SDP Alliance Roy Jenkins to see it through the House of Commons. In 1976 David Steel became leader of the Liberal Party in succession to Jeremy Thorpe, and was responsible for the Liberal/Labour electoral pact that kept the minority Callaghan administration in power until 1979. From 1983–7 he was joint leader of the Liberal–SDP Alliance together with David Owen, but after the 1987 election he initiated a process of fully merging the two separate parties into one, thus irrevocably alienating Dr Owen.

## Norman Tebbit (1931– )

Educated at Edmonton County Grammar School. A politician more closely identified with Thatcherism than most. Entered Parliament in 1970 after a career as a civil aviation pilot from 1953 to 1970. He was made Secretary of State for Employment in 1981 and moved to the Department of Trade and

Industry in 1983. In 1984 he was badly hurt and his wife crippled when the IRA bombed the headquarters hotel at the Conservative Party Conference in Brighton. In 1985 he was made Chancellor of the Duchy of Lancaster and became Conservative Party chairman. He resigned both posts after the 1987 election, and returned to the back benches.

## John Wakeham (1932– )

Lord Privy Seal and Leader of the House. Government Chief Whip, 1983–7. Under-Secretary of State for Industry, 1981–2. One of the inner circle of the Cabinet. The first Mrs Wakeham was killed in the bombing of the headquarters hotel at the Conservative Party Conference in Brighton, 1984. The present Mrs Wakeham was at one time private secretary to Mrs Thatcher.

## Peter Walker (1932– )

Educated at Latymer Upper School. He has been MP for Worcester since 1961 and is the only wet who has remained a Cabinet Minister throughout Mrs Thatcher's three terms of office. His success may be attributed to his tough political style and modest background, both remarkably similar to Mrs Thatcher's, and to his skills as a communicator, which she admires. He was Secretary of State for the Environment, 1970–72 and Minister for Trade and Industry (1972–4) under Edward Heath; under Mrs Thatcher he has been successively Minister of Agriculture, Fisheries and Food, 1979–83, Secretary of State for Energy, 1983–7 and from 1987 Secretary of State for Wales.

## Sir Alan Walters (1926– )

Educated at Alderman Newton's School, Leicester, University College, Leicester, and Nuffield College, Oxford. An economist and articulate exponent of monetarist economic theories, he has been Professor of Political Economy at Johns Hopkins University, Maryland, since 1976. From 1981–3 he was full-time personal economic adviser to Mrs Thatcher, and from 1983 has played a part-time role.

## Sir Douglas Wass (1923– )

Educated at Nottingham High School and St John's College, Cambridge. A career civil servant, Sir Douglas occupied the post of Permanent Secretary to the Treasury from 1974–83, the most turbulent decade in modern British economic history. He was joint head of the Home Civil Service from 1981 until 1983 when he retired.

## Caspar Weinberger (1917–   )

Educated at Harvard Law School. He trained as a lawyer and practised in California before entering State politics as a Republican. It was in Californian politics that he met Ronald Reagan, with whom he moved to Washington in 1981 to become Reagan's Secretary of Defence until 1987, thus becoming the longest serving member of the two Reagan administrations. As Secretary of Defense Weinberger presided over the biggest arms build up in post-war American history and was also a staunch proponent of the President's Strategic Defence Initiative or 'Star Wars' programme. A renowned Anglophile, Weinberger was particularly helpful to Mrs Thatcher during the Falklands crisis; a fact acknowledged in 1988 when he became an 'honorary knight' after an investiture at Buckingham Palace – a very rare and singular honour for a foreign citizen.

## Lord Whitelaw (1918–   )

Educated at Wincester College and Trinity College, Cambridge. After serving in the Scots Guards during the war, he served as a Member of Parliament from 1955–83. He was the only member of Edward Heath's Cabinet to serve with apparent equanimity in Mrs Thatcher's Cabinet and thus provided an essential thread of continuity between the Heath and the Thatcher eras in Conservative Party politics. He was Chief Opposition Whip from 1964–70 and Secretary of State for Northern Ireland 1972–4. He was Home Secretary from 1979–83, and Deputy Prime Minister (a titular rather than substantive post) and leader of the House of Lords as Viscount Whitelaw from 1983–7. He then retired from politics because of ill health.

## Shirley Williams (1930–   )

Educated in schools in UK and USA and Somerville College, Oxford. Entered House as MP for Hitchin, 1964. Wide variety of Governmental jobs, becoming Secretary of State for Prices and Consumer Protection 1974–6, then Secretary of State for Education and Science 1976–9. Left Labour Party and became co-founder of the SDP in 1981. Now its President.

## Lord Young of Graffham (1932–   )

Educated at Christ's College, Finchley and University College, London. Created a Life Peer by Mrs Thatcher in 1984, Lord Young trained as a solicitor before going into business. He gained the admiration of Mrs Thatcher as a director of the Centre for Policy Studies from 1979–82. From 1982–4 he served as chairman of the Manpower Services Commission and also as a special adviser to the Department of Trade and Industry. He was promoted to the Cabinet in 1984 as Minister without Portfolio, and from 1985–7 was Minister for Employment.

Lord Young became one of a small group of Ministers on whom Mrs Thatcher relied for advice – advice that by all accounts became crucial during the 1987 general election campaign. After the election Lord Young became Secretary of State for Trade and Industry.

# SOURCE NOTES

CHAPTER 5: ALFRED ROBERTS'S DAUGHTER

1 Quoted by Geoffrey Parkhouse, *Sunday Express*, 20 July 1975.
2 *Ibid.*
3 *Ibid.*
4 *Ibid.*
5 *Ibid.*

CHAPTER 7: UPHILL STRUGGLE

1 Quoted by Martin Holmes, *The Labour Government, 1974–1979* (Macmillan, 1985), p. 96.
2 Quoted by Martin Holmes, *op. cit.*, p. 98.
3 *Thatcherism: Personality and Politics*, Edited by Kenneth Minogue and Michael Biddiss (Macmillan, 1987), p. 5.

CHAPTER 8: PRIME MINISTER

1 Quoted by Martin Holmes, *The First Thatcher Government, 1979–1983* (Wheatsheaf Books, 1985), p. 25.
2 Minogue and Biddiss, *op. cit.*, p. 57.
3 Alan Walters, *Britain's Economic Renaissance: Margaret Thatcher's Reforms 1979–1984* (Oxford University Press, 1986), p. 81.

CHAPTER 9: THE FALKLANDS WAR

1 Alexander Haig, *Caveat* (Weidenfeld & Nicholson, 1984), p. 280.
2 Max Hastings and Simon Jenkins, *The Battle for the Falklands* (Michael Joseph, 1986), pp. 325–6.
3 Hastings and Jenkins, *op. cit.*, p. 40.

4 Martin Middlebrook, *The Falklands War* (Penguin Books, 1987), p. 67.
5 Hastings and Jenkins, *op. cit.*, p. 68.
6 Alexander Haig, *op. cit.*, p. 272.
7 Alexander Haig, *ibid.*, p. 266.
8 Quoted by Hugo Young and Anne Sloman, *The Thatcher Phenomenon* (BBC Books, 1986), p. 119.
9 *Ibid.*, p. 118.
10 Alexander Haig, *op. cit.*, p. 272.
11 Nicholas Henderson, *Channels and Tunnels* (Weidenfeld & Nicolson, 1987), p. 108.

### CHAPTER 11: SHOWDOWN WITH THE MINERS

1 Peter Walker, *Trust the People* (Collins, 1987), pp. 92–3.
2 Ian MacGregor, *The Enemies Within* (Collins, 1986), p. 233.
3 John Lloyd and Martin Adeney, *Loss without Limit* (Routledge & Kegan Paul, 1986), p. 291.
4 Peter Jenkins, *Mrs Thatcher's Revolution* (Jonathan Cape, 1987), p. 241.

### CHAPTER 12: THE USE OF POWER

1 Melvyn Marckus, *Observer*, 25 October 1987.

### CHAPTER 13: MRS THATCHER AND THE FUTURE OF BRITAIN

1 Tony Benn, *Out of the Wilderness: Diaries 1963–1967* (Hutchinson, 1987).

# BIBLIOGRAPHY

Adeney, Martin, and Lloyd, John, *The Miners' Strike, 1984–5* (Routledge & Kegan Paul, 1986)

Arnold, Bruce, *A Study in Power* (Hamish Hamilton, 1984)

Bogdanov, Vernon, and Skidelsky, Robert, *The Age of Affluence, 1951–1964* (Macmillan, 1970)

Blake, Robert, *The Conservative Party from Peel to Thatcher* (Methuen, 1985)

Brittan, Samuel, *How to End the 'Monetarist' Controversy* (Institute of Economic Affairs, 1981)

Bruce-Gardyne, Jock, *Ministers and Mandarins* (Sidgwick & Jackson, 1986)

Bruce-Gardyne, Jock, *Mrs Thatcher's First Administration* (Macmillan, 1984)

Burridge, Trevor, *Clement Attlee: A Political Biography* (Cape, 1985)

Butler, David, and Kavanagh, Dennis, *The British General Election of 1979* (Macmillan, 1979)

Butler, David, and Kavanagh, Dennis, *The British General Election of 1983* (Macmillan, 1983)

Callaghan, James, *Time and Chance* (Collins, 1987)

Cole, John, *The Thatcher Years* (BBC Books, 1987)

Cosgrave, Patrick, *The First Term* (Bodley Head, 1985)

Donoughue, Bernard, *Prime Minister* (Cape, 1987)

Gamble, A, *Britain in Decline* (Macmillan, 1981)

Gardiner, George, *Margaret Thatcher* (Kimber, 1975)

Gilmour, Ian, *Inside Right* (Quartet Books, 1977)

Haig, Alexander, *Caveat: Realism, Reagan and Foreign Policy* (Weidenfeld & Nicolson, 1984)

Hall, Stuart, and Jacques, Martin, *The Politics of Thatcherism* (Lawrence & Wishart, 1983)

Harris, Kenneth, *Attlee* (Weidenfeld & Nicolson, 1982)

Henderson, Nicholas, *Channels and Tunnels* (Weidenfeld & Nicolson, 1987)

Hennessy, Peter, *Cabinet* (Basil Blackwell, 1986)

Hennessy, Peter, and Seldon, Anthony, *Ruling Performance* (Basil Blackwell, 1987)

Holmes, Martin, *Political Pressure and Economic Policy: British Government 1970–4* (Butterworth, 1982)

Holmes, Martin, *The Labour Government 1974–9: Political Aims and Economic Reality* (Macmillan, 1985)

Holmes, Martin, *The First Thatcher Government, 1979–1983* (Wheatsheaf Books, 1985)

Hurd, Douglas, *An End to Promises* (Collins, 1977)

Jenkins, Peter, *Mrs Thatcher's Revolution* (Cape, 1987)

Junor, Penny, *Margaret Thatcher* (Sidgwick & Jackson, 1983)

Kavanagh, Dennis, *Thatcherism and British Politics* (Oxford University Press, 1987)

Keegan, William, *Mrs Thatcher's Economic Experiment* (Penguin, 1984)

Lewis, Russell, *Margaret Thatcher* (Routledge & Kegan Paul, 1975)

Linklater, Magnus, and Leigh, David, *Not Without Honour* (Sphere Books, 1986)

Loney, Martin, *The New Right and the Welfare State* (Pluto Press, 1986)

MacGregor, Ian, *The Enemies Within* (Collins, 1986)

Middlebrook, Martin, *Task Force: the Falklands War 1982* (Penguin, 1987)

Minogue, Kenneth, and Biddiss, Michael, *Thatcherism: Personality and Politics* (Macmillan, 1987)

Morgan, Kenneth O., *Labour in Power, 1945–51* (Oxford University Press, 1984)

Owen, David, *Personally Speaking to Kenneth Harris* (Weidenfeld & Nicolson, 1987)

Prior, Jim, *A Balance of Power* (Hamish Hamilton, 1986)

Pym, Francis, *The Politics of Consent* (Sphere Books, 1985)

Riddell, Peter, *The Thatcher Government* (Robertson, 1983)

Thatcher, Margaret, *In Defence of Freedom*, introd. by Ronald Butt, foreword by Lord Home (Aurum Press, 1986)

Waldegrave, William, *The Building of Leviathan* (Hamish Hamilton, 1978)

Walker, Peter, *Trust the People* (Collins, 1987)

Walters, Alan, *Britain's Economic Renaissance* (Oxford University Press, 1986)

Wapshott, Nicholas, and Brock, George, *Thatcher* (Macdonald, 1983)

Young, Hugo, and Sloman, Anne, *The Thatcher Phenomenon* (BBC Books, 1986)

# INDEX

Page references in *italic* type indicate headings in the Biographies. MT stands for Margaret Thatcher.